LAST WORDS

*A Memoir of World War II
and the
Yugoslav Tragedy*

LAST WORDS

A Memoir of World War II and the Yugoslav Tragedy

Boris J. Todorovich
Edited by J. Stryder and Andrew Karp

Walker and Company
New York

Biog
Tod
t

First published in the United States of America in 1989 by the Walker Publishing Company, Inc.

Published simultaneously in Canada by Thomas Allen & Son Canada, Limited, Markham, Ontario.

Library of Congress Cataloguing-in-Publication Data

Todorvich, Boris J.
    Last words / Boris J. Todorovich; edited by J. Stryder and Andrew Karp.
        p.   cm.
    Includes index.
    ISBN 0-8027-1067-0
    1. Todorovich, Boris.   2. World War, 1939–1945—Personal narratives, Serbian.   3. World War, 1939–1945—Underground movements—Yugoslavia.   4. World War, 1939–1945—Prisoners and prisons, German.   5. Prisoners of war—Germany—Biography.
    6. Prisoners of war—Yugoslavia—Biography.   7. Escapes—Germany.
    I. Stryder, J.   II. Karp, Andrew.   III. Title.
    D811.T583   1989
    940.54′82′4971—dc19   88-26112
                                                                                                        CIP

Printed in the United States of America

10   9   8   7   6   5   4   3   2   1

*For my children,
and the children of those
who have good cause to remember
General Draza Mihailovich*

Contents

Introduction

IN THIS MEMOIR, Boris J. Todorovich tells primarily of the years from 1941 to 1944.

Taken as a whole, the book is a report of one soldier's life at war. It is direct, vigorous, and bluntly characterizes the men he came in contact with and their activities. It is not an intimate story in the autobiographical sense, nor is it particularly self-reflective. Boris was in essence a self-confident man who did not brood about the past, yet remembered it well.

Others have written of the notable events and issues touched on in these pages. Who lost Yugoslavia? Who was to blame? Popular and scholarly works with a broad range of opinions are readily available, and the debate persists. The emphasis here, however, is on what Boris observed, personally verified, and himself believed to be true.

As a professional soldier, Captain Todorovich went into battle in defense of his country against the Germans. During an eighteen-month period, he led the life of a war prisoner and of an escapee on the run.

He saw Frankfurt at the height of Nazi Germany's success, London after the deadly Blitz, the idyll of faraway Capetown, and Cairo when it was the nerve center of the Mediterranean theater of war. He learned to outwit police agents in French Vichy, to elude Spanish border guards, to improve his English on the South Atlantic, to parachute in Palestine, and to survive in the mountains of occupied Serbia with guerrilla forces.

In those Serbian mountains, he met a man he had come to consider a great patriot—General Draza Mihailovich, the leader of the Chetnik resistance group. Opposed to both the Communist Partisans and the foreign occupiers, General Mihailovich was admired and beloved by many persons. His fate, perhaps more than anyone's, personifies the tragic course of Yugoslavia's recent history.

The present book covers in his own words two-thirds of Boris's wartime adventures. Regrettably, he did not live to write the last third. It would have dealt with the period from 1944 to 1945 and Boris's efforts on behalf of General Mihailovich in Washington, D.C. Promoted to major, Boris was an assistant military attaché in the Yugoslav embassy. He later left voluntarily on a mission with American approval to Yugoslavia, but was held en route at British request in Bari, Italy. The complete Communist takeover by Tito meant his permanent exile.

Lacking this final part, the story ends suspended in midair in manuscript. The reader would doubtless wonder what happened and would be justifiably disappointed were nothing more revealed. Therefore, a concise explanation has been added, based on additional sources and prepared by his editors, to conclude Boris's account.

George Bernard Shaw's quip that the Americans and the British are one people divided by a common tongue could be stood on its head for the Serbs and Croats of Yugoslavia. They are, it often seems, one people of a common tongue—and very little else.

The Serbs are Orthodox, write the language in Cyrillic letters, and at the beginning of World War II supported a centralized government. They thought the Croats divisive. The Croats, on the other hand, are Roman Catholic, use the Latin alphabet, and strive for a more autonomous position, contemplating the "rustic" Serbs with a certain civilized air of disdain.

"Croat or Serb," then, was historically an effective national way of choosing up sides—though nothing is ever quite that simple in Yugoslav ethnography. Those of the Muslim faith (predominantly in Bosnia), the Slovenes, the Macedonians, and a dozen other minorities all had their own concerns. However, it is generally safe to assume that these groups would bargain support to the Croats if placating the Serbs were the alternative.

The German annexation of Austria on March 11, 1938, suddenly made the Third Reich a neighbor. The Yugoslav government hastened to cement warmer relations and closer economic ties.

Within another year, full scale war had erupted in Europe. Italy invaded Albania on April 7, 1939, and Germany rolled into Poland on September 1. France and Great Britain declared war against the Axis powers.

While Yugoslavia watched from the sidelines, one nation after another fell to the Nazis, culminating with the German triumph over France. The U.S.S.R. had its share of Poland and a pact with Hitler; Britain stood alone and in mortal peril. Hungary, Rumania, and Bulgaria were hastening toward the Axis fold.

Except for Greece, the Yugoslavs were surrounded by countries with old scores to settle and lands they wished to repossess. There were also plenty of "fifth columnists" to reckon with inside Yugoslavia, members of the various minority groups whose ancestral ties now pulled more strongly than those to Belgrade. The German Yugoslavs in particular were becoming openly defiant, displaying the swastika and holding Fascist rallies.

Then, on October 28, 1940, Mussolini invaded Greece, a move that even Hitler was not previously informed of. When the Greeks stoutly resisted and began to press the Italians back into Albania, Yugoslav apprehensions only increased. Someone would likely have to come to the rescue of Il Duce's army, namely the Germans.

When Britain dispatched troops to support Greece, a countermove appeared inevitable. Would the Germans respect the territorial integrity of Yugoslavia? As 1940 drew to a close, the Yugoslav Army began active preparations for war.

*   *   *

Although he certainly did not spring full-blown in the tailored uniform of the Royal Yugoslav Army, Boris scanted on the details of his personal life in his manuscript, considering them irrelevant to much of what he wanted to discuss.

In this regard some initial accommodation of the reader's curiosity is in order, if only to better establish Boris in his time and milieu. Moreover, even a thumbnail sketch of his early years reveals formative aspects of his lifelong character.

Boris was born in Belgrade on February 2, 1913, and was raised there. (Named Borislav in Serbo-Croatian, he was called Bora by his friends and intimates.) His father, a successful banker, died from typhoid fever ten days after his birth.

One of three brothers, Jovan Todorovich was a man who had risen above humble peasant origins, spoke six languages, and was actively involved in the building of the first private airplane in Yugoslavia. He had been a widower with a young son when he met and married Divna, Boris's mother. Another son and daughter were born prior to Boris—his older brother, Branaslav, and sister, Natalija.

Jovan's death left the family with a home in Belgrade but little else. Despite the deprivations of World War I and the extensive fighting in the Balkans, his widow was somehow able to keep the family intact. To supplement her meager earnings, she rented out the inherited house and lived with the children in the crude servants' cottage.

There is this assessment by Boris of his mother's influence:

Perhaps it was my mother's desire to make up for my being born in adversity and weaned in sorrow which made me feel since early childhood that I ought to strive to be recognized. She would tell others, 'He never saw his father, never enjoyed the life of plenty as my other children did.' Thus she would rationalize special small favors bestowed on me, even when criticized by her friends for it. But while planting the seed of ambition in my heart, she never missed a chance to tell me I had to work hard for success.

Without resources, Boris's mother coped as best she could. She sent her youngest son to military school, which he at first disliked. But as he began to excel, Boris found the military life more congenial.

As a young army officer, he was selected for advanced training at the Higher Yugoslav Military Academy and War College in Belgrade. He was graduated in 1939, ranking second in his class; the valedictorian was a general's son with political clout. He was then posted to a battalion garrisoned in Kraljevo, a small city considerably south of Belgrade and nestled in the mountains of Serbia.

Having always lived in the capital, he had to adjust to less sophisticated ways. His commanding officer, Major Mikota, was "a very tall, slightly bent man with dark brown eyes, a receding hairline, and an engaging smile." Instead of an immediate assignment to one of the artillery batteries, Boris was asked to complete a training manual for the new 88-mm antiaircraft guns. Mikota was pleased with the result, and they struck up a fast friendship over a few glasses of slivovitz at the battalion's canteen.

Settled into the life of a peacetime soldier, Boris stayed abreast of national and European developments. He was not anxious for war, but the Yugoslav Army, especially its Serbian troops, had a proud military tradition. Memories of World War I were often invoked, and patriotic spirit ran high. Only a call to battle seemed needed.

That test of duty and national honor was imminent.

J. Stryder
December 4, 1987
New York City

WESTERN EUROPE

Map Key

1941

1. BJT captured in Kraljevo and sent to BELGRADE
2. Sent to Offlag 5-D, near Offenburg, Germany
3. Sent to Offlag 13-B, near NUREMBURG

1942

4. Escape outside Wurzbur: on the run, via train to NUREMBURG then to FRANKFURT.
5. Via train to Metz (annexed by Germany) and across border to France. On to NANCY.
6. By train and foot to LYONS.
7. Move to MARSEILLE.
8. Across the Pyrenees to BARCELONA, Spain.
9. Sent to MADRID by car.
10. Sent to GIBRALTAR by train.
11. By ship to Greenock, UK.
12. Sent by train to LONDON, England.

1943

13. Sent by LONDON to Cairo (via ship around Africa). (Sent to Palestine for training as paratrooper, then returned to Cairo.)
14. By plane from Cairo and parachuted into SERBIA (YUGOSLA-VIA).

1944

15. From Serbia to coast and evacuation from Cavtat (near Dubrovnik) to BARI, Italy.
16. By plane to Cairo, then on to U.S.A.

NOTE: *Shaded area in Yugoslavia = area of Chetnik operations*

YUGOSLAVIA—1945

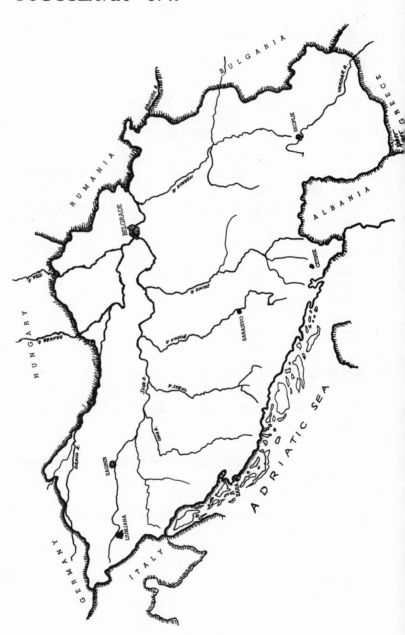

1941

As WORLD WAR II entered its third year in Europe, the conflict steadily widened. At the beginning of the year, neither America nor Russia was directly involved; by its end, both were. The British-Axis matchup escalated into confrontation on a global scale. Every ocean had naval battles. Fighting raged on three continents. The death toll was mounting toward an estimated total of forty-five million people killed.

The lightning speed of the German war machine was astonishing. Whole countries were overwhelmed in weeks, their armies helpless to react quickly enough. This was made possible by a new blend of military technology and tactics. It was the wave of the future. The Germans were winning not because they had more or better equipment, or because they outfought the foe—their stalemated attempt to batter England into submission from the air in 1940 proved that—but because they were ruthless, determined, and temporarily superior in the art of war.

Nazi Germany had overrun or cowed all the nations of Europe on the continent. On February 14, 1941, when Hitler met with Yugoslav Premier Cvetkovich and the foreign minister near Salzburg, Austria, he was arguably the most powerful man in the world. After Prince Paul visited Hitler on the following March 4, he and his government were prepared to do everything they could to prevent annoyance to the Third Reich.

Boris was twenty-eight in 1941, a captain second class in the Royal Yugoslav Army Artillery. He was in command of the

Second Battery of the 662nd Antiaircraft Division, which was attached to the Fifth Artillery Battalion and located in Kraljevo.

(Unlike the Americans or British, the Yugoslavs had two grades of captain. Boris's friend Captain Leonid Pachany, who held the senior grade at the time, outranked him. This technical distinction has been ignored otherwise throughout the memoir, though it should be noted that Boris was promoted in early 1943 to the first class rank.)

Kraljevo is close to the geographic center of Serbia. It lies below the Shumadija, the woodlands area to the south of Belgrade, and the Danube River. Two tributary rivers that eventually empty into the Danube join here. The area is well suited for guerrilla warfare, with mountains ranging from four thousand to forty-five hundred feet high, with plenty of forest cover.

Kraljevo's air defenses consisted of the Fifth Battalion of heavy antiaircraft guns, two squadrons of fighter planes based at the Kraljevo airfield, and two companies of light antiaircraft guns. Dug in at villages on the surrounding hillsides, the battalion's units held commanding positions above the town and its two key bridges.

A young officer stationed in a small Serbian city thus found himself poised before the whirlwind about to descend on his country. Yugoslavia's neutrality had lasted some sixteen months, but at the start of the new year, Boris sensed that a fateful moment was at hand. Either they would completely bow to the Germans, or they would go to war.

Most Serbs agreed that bowing was not part of the national character.

1

The Advent of War

IN THE DEAD of night, I lay fully dressed on my cot trying to sleep. Although exhausted, sleep never came. I heard Corporal Lukich in the anteroom, repeating a message over the telephone: "Several hundred enemy bombers. Spotted crossing the Rumanian border. Heading southwest." Before he could enter my room, I was out the door.

"Sound the alarm. Call all the officers," I ordered.

"Yes, sir, Captain!" The corporal took off on the double.

The battery position was less than two hundred feet away. By the time I got outside, the alerted troops were manning the machine guns and our heavy weapons, two M-28 antiaircraft guns. My junior officers—First Lieutenant Velkovich, Second Lieutenants Todorovich (no relation) and Milenkovich—joined me. In total darkness, we waited. And waited.

By daybreak, nothing had happened. I ordered the men to stand down. It was evidently another false alarm, just like one four days ago and others before that. Wearily, I trudged back to my room.

Preparing the daily provisions request, a mandatory chore, I turned on the radio. It was 5:30 A.M., on Sunday. The Belgrade station wasn't yet broadcasting, but I managed to tune in a weak foreign station. Was that Von Ribbentrop? What was he doing on the radio so early? It had to be exceptionally important.

The Nazi foreign minister's words reverberated through the

3

static: ". . . from this moment, the Reich considers itself at war with Yugoslavia and Greece. Our troops have already crossed the borders of these countries. . . ."

So this is it, I thought. We're through with useless alerts. The war's begun after all.

April 6, 1941, dawned bright and sunny. I summoned my officers and gave them the unofficial news. The enlisted men were not to be told until we received division orders. Gas masks would be distributed. I feared a heavy bombing of Kraljevo within the hour.

Instead, everything stayed quiet. Yet the war had to be raging at our borders. Frustrated, I paced about the house we used as our command post and officers' quarters. What exactly was going on? By phone, my superiors offered vague information and steady optimism.

Seven o'clock passed without a sign of German planes. To distract myself, I did some paper work, despite my sense of its probable irrelevance. Again I listened to the radio. National music was playing on the Belgrade station.

"Enemy planes are bombing Belgrade," a voice suddenly broke in. "Bombs are dropping along Knez Mihailo Street . . ." The station went dead. I looked at my watch—7:12 A.M. I didn't know it then, but I had heard Radio Belgrade's final transmission as the voice of a free capital.

The unit remained on alert. When the next air raid warning came in, I threw down my pen. We rushed to our posts at the battery.

"Planes over Krushevac!" one of the spotters cried out excitedly. That was thirty-five miles to the southeast. As I watched through my field glasses, a group of about thirty planes made a bombing run in the distance. Division headquarters was informed and a general alarm wailed across the river in Kraljevo.

Inexplicably, the planes then turned back. For some reason, the city was being spared Hitler's opening trademark bang. But we knew the blow must come. It had to. Located 120 miles south of Belgrade, Kraljevo was an important industrial, railway, and communications center. At the juncture of the Ibar and the West Morava rivers, it controlled the main routes into western Serbia. The Germans couldn't ignore us.

All that first day, I expected higher headquarters to issue detailed briefings. Instead, it was midafternoon before a sketchy report filtered through to us. Our forces were marching toward Albania and Bulgaria in a counteroffensive! Forty-seven enemy planes purportedly had been shot down over Belgrade. The official outlook was encouraging. We would hold off the invaders and turn the tables on them.

The next day, April 7, went by placidly as well for us. The one dramatic difference was in the bulletins heard on my shortwave radio. From London, the British continued to hail our staunch resistance; the Bulgarians in Sofia spoke of Yugoslav setbacks and certain defeat. All the news was of war—while my unit hadn't smudged a single gun barrel.

I swore my guns would not stay clean. Our orders called for strictest readiness, and we obeyed. The men had great enthusiasm and a spirit of self-sacrifice. They spent day and night near the battery. No one removed his uniform. Boxes of ammunition were kept open at the ready.

Near twilight of April 8, I was working in my office when I heard a commotion outside. "A German plane, a German plane!" somebody shouted. I smiled. A German plane could not have penetrated this far without detection.

When I heard a growling engine noise, though, I ran outside. To my shock, I saw a Messerschmitt fly over my head and descend peaceably to the Kraljevo airfield. Nobody, including my unit, had fired a shot.

I never learned why the plane landed. It was small consolation that the crew was taken prisoner and the plane itself repainted with Royal Yugoslav markings and added to the air corps. The incident was a disgrace for us and for every air defense watchpost from the border on. Mitigating circumstances didn't matter. The battalion was rightly held accountable, and stung by the humiliation, I had to order stricter watches.

We'd soon have the chance to redeem ourselves, I believed. A secret dispatch reported that a sortie of German planes was flying from Rumania that night. It was an opportunity to even the score.

Once again, we were prepared. No one slept. No planes came.

Nothing exhausts men more than futile anticipation. I was half convinced that these intelligence reports were somehow a product of the Germans and their collaborators. We had become increasingly fatigued, precisely the result the enemy would have desired.

Working in my room in the morning, I was interrupted by Corporal Lukich. "Enemy aircraft patrol spotted, sir, headed up from Krushevac." I picked up my field glasses and revolver and sprinted outside to the guns.

Everyone was set. The spotters began reading off the coordinates of the oncoming planes. They were closing in fast, very fast. It wasn't anything like practice. With my field glasses, I recognized the Italian make (a type flown by the Germans *and* our own air force) but I couldn't distinguish the markings on either the wings or bodies.

A terrible struggle raged inside me. If I waited until the markings were absolutely clear, the bombers would be on top of us. It would be too late to fire. Lieutenant Velkovich, in charge of the platoon on the big antiaircraft guns, was at my side.

I checked off facts in my mind. The approaching planes didn't give the current signal for "friendlies." They weren't flying at the prescribed altitude. None of our aircraft were officially scheduled to arrive.

"Shall we shoot at them, Captain? They're in the best position now," Lieutenant Velkovich whispered.

This was it. "Ready!" The lieutenant signaled to the gunners. "Fire!" I shouted. Bullets went instantly tearing through the air. The battery rang with deafening noise.

One of the bombers faltered. "It's a hit! It's a hit!" the men yelled happily. The crippled plane dropped steadily, almost out of control. The rest veered away sharply.

Our elation was brief. In a half hour I had the official story. The planes were indeed ours.

The crew of the downed bomber had fortunately escaped unhurt. I felt regret and disappointment but refused to second-guess my decision. My action was correct. If it had been the enemy attacking, delay might have proved fatal, the consequences disastrous.

Consistently bad as our luck had been, the change in our fortunes was as sudden. Without warning, German bombers and reconnaissance planes repeatedly flew over Kraljevo. My unit and the battalion turned them aside. After four days of war, we were in action at last. We fought the enemy, and our guns showed it.

During the few moments of rest I snatched on April 9, disturbing questions filled my mind. I was proud of my Serbian heritage and our military traditions. Surely, the fight went well for us, and not just in Kraljevo.

Yet I couldn't stop thinking how different the war was from what we were taught it would be. We had prepared for this conflict by the book and to the letter. Then, from the day it broke out, confusion was the rule.

What was happening to our armies? Hadn't we been ready for months? Weren't the plans of the General Staff being carried out? With each day that passed, I was less sure of the answers.

The situation was getting worse. There were no regular briefings from headquarters. The few orders I received by courier often countermanded one another. Why? My first amazement turned to deepening concern. What had broken the elaborate military procedures drilled into us in the hypothetical wars of the classroom?

In my student exercises, I was expected to master concepts of coordinated action, to know what to do and why. Now I was adrift. I was being forced to operate on my own. With only the foggiest notion of our strategy, battlefield position, and objectives, I felt as if we had been left to face a rising storm whose direction and intensity no one cared to judge.

But I was certain of one thing. I was as determined to defend Kraljevo as any native son. Assigned to the city in October 1939, after my graduation from the Military Academy and War College, it was a new experience for me. I had lived in Belgrade my whole life. Yet despite some initial wariness, my adjustment proved relatively easy. I found the simple and unassuming socializing with my fellow battalion officers a refreshing change from the empty formalities of the capital.

While the war in Europe spread elsewhere, Kraljevo remained a place of spirit and beauty. The town was surrounded by rugged, picturesque hills. Its high terrain was as much a challenge to mountain climbers as the rolling meadows of the lowlands were a delight to cross-country skiers. The town itself was filled with laughter and smiling faces. Songs and music played in the outdoor cafés, and like the townspeople, I thought it should go on forever.

Besides a well known aircraft factory, many visitors came to see Zica, an ancient Serbian monastery that was the home of Bishop Nikolaj, a renowned and respected philosopher of the Serbian Eastern Orthodox Church. To the delight of the younger officers, young women flocked to the mineral spa, Mataruga. The waters were reputed to improve fertility.

On summer weekends, I'd ride the narrow-gauge railroad up Mount Goch. Powered by logs the passengers gathered and split themselves and operated by a single engineer, the train would puff and groan its way uphill, stopping often to gather steam. When the tiny horse could go no farther, we would continue on foot to the mountaintop. There the magnificent view, fresh mountain air, and cold spring water to drink always filled me with contentment.

But as the war intensified in 1940, such pleasures became mere memories. The Germans were terrifying in their strength, and the weak Yugoslav government seemed desperate to appease them. Meanwhile, our military command took precautionary steps. As the year ended, we regulars were fully preparing to leave our peacetime garrisons.

In March of 1941, my unit deployed to the village of Kovan-luk, a few miles to the east of Kraljevo, and set up the guns in a meadow by a cemetery. The entire battalion's mission was to defend the Kraljevo aircraft factory, the bridges over the rivers, and an ammunition dump in the village of Mrsac. We were joined at the field battery by our reserves after the national mobilization of March 12.

Though it occurred at an inconvenient time (work in the fields was just beginning) the response was excellent. It took but a short while to fortify our battery position and retrain the reserves. Within a week, all the men were performing like old artillery hands. My division commander, Captain Stojkovich, the battalion commander, Major Mikota, and the head of the air defense zone, Lieutenant Colonel Trampuz, inspected the unit and expressed their satisfaction.

It was still very cold for living in tents, so I had selected a few of the nearer houses to serve as billets. The owners enthusiastically complied. My host, as he insisted I consider him, was Bogdan Lazarevich, a likable farmer who also worked in a railroad car factory. In his house, I put my office and telephone switchboard. From a window I could conveniently view the entire battery.

Every day when Bogdan returned from work, he would timidly knock at my room. When invited in, he'd bring forth a bottle of brandy to offer me a drink and to chat a little. "We will not join Germany like the other nations of Europe, will we, Captain?" he'd ask.

There was talk that our government would sign the accursed Tripartite Pact of the Axis powers, following in the footsteps of Bulgaria. This would in effect declare our allegiance to their cause.

"Have faith, Bogdan. The army will not stand by quietly and watch German columns enter our country." This was what he wished to hear, and as if I were somehow omniscient, he believed me. Actually, I had no great faith in the Yugoslav government or its intentions.

By March 24, the political situation had deteriorated. None of my superiors told me anything. The army high command seemed to be retreating into a shell. To keep up my own unit's zeal, I increased the drill and workloads. I spent all my time with the men, eating with them, even playing soccer—anything to keep their minds off what might happen.

"Well, this is not like the mobilizations of last year and the year before," one of my men said. "This smells of action. We won't just give ourselves to Hitler, will we?"

"Of course not. Don't even think of it. Just obey and follow me," I answered. There was nothing else to say.

Another soldier did ask, "Why are we training all the time, Captain, when we'll only return home after the Jerries arrive?" We knew that Prime Minister Cvetkovich and the Yugoslav foreign minister, Cincar-Markovich, were presently conferring in Vienna with the Nazis. I loathed the idea of us signing a pact with them. It went against the very grain of the Yugoslav people.

On March 25, I returned to Kraljevo and tried to convince other officers to pledge armed resistance in the event of a pact. Most of them wouldn't commit themselves. They didn't know what to think. Only Captain Leonid Pachany agreed with me wholeheartedly.

It did not surprise me. Since meeting in Kraljevo, Pachany and I had gotten along splendidly. We shared a common interest in outdoor sports. He excelled in swimming and diving; I in fencing, skiing, and horseback riding. We both loved the classics, theater, and good music. In contrast to most of our colleagues, we were both keenly interested in politics and social movements.

Pacha, as his friends called him, was not the kind of man to attract your attention at first sight. He was a year my senior, with a slightly curved nose and a curl of blond hair over his high forehead. His tight lips and greenish eyes behind his glasses did not radiate immediate warmth, but those cool features belied an inner man of deep feelings. A man ready and willing to support a cause, to sacrifice unselfishly for a friend.

He prided himself on being like the proverbial English gentleman—calm, self-composed, upright, honest, and brave. Small wonder, then, that he studied the language, one totally strange to me. He was a frequent visitor to the various English clubs in prewar Yugoslavia.

Pachany and I both hoped that the ministers and Prince Paul, the ruling regent, would manage to avoid the Germans' fatal embrace. But after luncheon in Kraljevo on the afternoon of March 25, I heard the news on the radio. The government had signed.

I felt as if something had snapped in me. I couldn't stand this betrayal. I couldn't live in a country that wasn't free. My first thought was how to best fight the Germans. I decided I must get out of Yugoslavia and into Greece, to head for the British troops recently stationed there.

As I passed in uniform through a crowd demonstrating against the pact, I heard whispering behind my back: "Will *they* at least protect us from the Germans?" My heart sank. The people had been quite confident in the military until now.

Everybody in my unit was silent when I returned. Not a word was spoken. I went directly to my room to avoid unpleasant questions, but I couldn't avoid Bogdan. I had to comfort him as best I could.

At seven the next morning, my men lined up in front of the guns to bid me farewell. They greeted me without their usual enthusiasm. It was even more difficult than I had imagined to say good-bye to these familiar comrades in arms. But I had no choice.

Just as I began to address them, my telephone operator, Corporal Lukich, came running up. While still several feet away, he began to shout: "Captain, the government has been over-thrown! Army and air force officers have toppled the government of Prince Paul! The young king has assumed the throne! General Simovich has formed a new government!"

"My God!" I couldn't believe my ears. "Who told you?"

"The division commander, personally," he replied as he tried to catch his breath.

The pact was renounced. My wish had been granted. I could defend my country's freedom on our native soil. As if by magic, the faces of the men changed. How easy it was for me to continue.

"God has helped us to step forward and find our way," I declared to them. "Difficult times lie ahead, but I have utmost confidence in each and every one of you. We must remain alert, since the humiliated 'ally' of yesterday may seek immediate satisfaction. Now we must all rally 'round the young king and bravely defend our independence!"

"Long live the king! Long live the king! Long live the king!" the men cheered.

When I hurriedly returned to Kraljevo to confirm the news, the streets were bubbling with life. People embraced one another exuberantly. Strangers greeted me with bright smiles and cries of "Long life to you!"

I ran into my division commander, Captain Stojkovich, and we embraced and congratulated each other. For the moment, we could not imagine how short-lived our joy would prove—and we did not want to.

Exactly two weeks later, the military circumstances in Yugoslavia were an open question. The euphoria of the coup had given way to foreboding by April 10. With five days of war under our belts, the enemy had not yet succeeded in bombing Kraljevo. That was what I stressed to my men.

My struggle to be upbeat was threatened by a sudden change in the weather. The temperature dropped. It began to drizzle off and on. As the rain mixed with the snow on the ground, the roads turned into pools of mud.

The overcast skies did bring us temporary relief from air attacks, but the persistent rumors of German panzers behind every hill had an insidious effect. Radio Sofia reported that Skoplje had fallen and boasted that German units were approaching Kragujevac, less than twenty-five miles to our north. I laughed at these lies. Our forces had been advancing. Were we not smashing our way into Bulgaria and Albania? So how could German tanks be deep within our borders?

Then I received new orders relayed by Captain Stojkovich from Major Mikota. I couldn't believe my own eyes: "Prepare for quick evacuation. Cross over Ibar River tonight." The message continued that enemy motorized units were in Trstenik, only twenty miles away.

Radio Sofia had been telling the truth.

I boiled with anger, pain, and disappointment. We hadn't been attacking at all. We'd been retreating. I had been thoroughly misled. On top of that terrible realization, what I'd most feared had also come to pass. In a pelting rain, I was under orders to change position.

Dangerously, I had never been allocated any means of transport. Months ago, when I'd asked for trucks, I'd been told laconically to use livestock. In the little village there weren't many animals, and a single antiaircraft gun weighed five tons.

I pleaded with the captain by phone. "Sir, the order is impossible to carry out. We have only eight oxen and four horses. Better we should remain at the present position and fight until the last shell, then destroy the guns and withdraw into the mountains."

"I can't help you in the least," he told me. "Do your best, but by all means you must be in a new position on the other side of the river by five o'clock this morning."

The word had already spread that our unit alone stood south of the Morava River, and morale plummeted. No one wanted to be a sitting duck for German tanks. I realized we simply had to evacuate, whether I liked it or not.

After destroying our fortifications, we conscripted the village oxen and set out toward Kraljevo. In the process, we abandoned all our spare parts and nearly eight hundred grenades. Down the muddy path, I rode at the head of the column with a carbine in my hand, ready to fire. But there was no hint of the enemy.

We worked the entire night in terrible weather. The men were wet and exhausted, yet it seemed not to weaken their dogged determination. The heavy guns sank deep in the mire and moved slowly and grudgingly. It took six hours to cover a distance of two and a half miles.

In the predawn light, we hit the paved road leading to the Ibar River. At the bridge, some of the men wanted to blow it up behind us. I had to use threats to prevent this premature destruction. It was, I knew, the unreasoning fear of men driven to the limits of endurance.

Without further incident, the unit crossed over and entered Kraljevo. It had faint resemblance to the town of a fortnight ago. The shops were closed, with wooden shutters nailed across the windows. In the streets, furtive people carried away undistributed army supplies, while disorganized soldiers straggled about. They seemed lost. Where were their commanders?

With bowed head, I led the unit to its new position on another small plateau. It was near the local agricultural college. We dug in, cleaned our guns and equipment, and prepared for battle. I kept the essential men and sent the other support personnel on to Chachak, twenty miles to the west.

During the day, I met colleagues from various military groups, officers who'd been assigned to Kraljevo and others who were passing through. Major Raunig, my excellent friend and commander of the 61st Antiaircraft Division, was there. He had been at the Bulgarian border a hundred miles to the east.

Just like myself, he'd never been given any true idea of strategic developments. After the enemy broke through a weak point on the border, the major was left absolutely on his own with his division. No one told him anything. He was forced to withdraw before the incredible speed of the German offensive.

Everyone's story was the same: Contact, retreat . . . contact, retreat.

To my great surprise, Captain Stojkovich came to see me. It was clear he was in same boat. He agreed that eventually I might have to spike the big guns and retreat toward Chachak. But for the moment, I was to hold my position and await orders.

Despite the desperate conditions, my troops were spirited and confident. In a great stroke of good luck, Sergeant Zivko found a fleet of seventeen new Chevrolet trucks in a canyon behind the college. Earmarked for a base that had never been mobilized, they were standing idle. I quickly appropriated them. Now we'd be able to move swiftly if we had to. We could change position and stay in action to the last possible minute.

I felt ready for the enemy, but once again the enemy wasn't quite ready for us. By the end of the day, it was obvious that reports of advancing enemy panzers were exaggerated. The air zone commander received increasingly favorable dispatches from southern Serbia.

The new position was, I finally decided, tactically inferior to the old one. I requested advice from my superiors. With their apparent blessings, they duly ordered the unit back to Kovanluk.

Our return was far more impressive than our exit. As we entered the village at dawn, looking like a parade in the shiny new trucks, the villagers greeted us with cheers. The women waved their kerchiefs and cried, thankful that we had not abandoned them. Bogdan embraced me and took out his best liquor for a toast.

Oh God, how much I wanted to please these good people. In our presence, they felt secure and unafraid of Hitler's vast armies. We savored our moment of glory.

For the next three days running, we fought regularly against enemy planes. By chance I learned from my quartermaster (who had a knack for gathering news as well as provisions) that the air defense zone was ordering the evacuation of towns as far west as Uzice, some forty-five miles away. When I queried headquarters, I was told not to get excited. I would receive additional orders shortly. It was the usual evasive reply.

Late on April 15, we heard the sound of artillery fire from the direction of Kragujevac. As night fell, the firing continued without letup. Finally, at two in the morning, I got a specific order. It did not come as much of a surprise: "Return immediately to your position across river. Trstenik has fallen. German panzers are advancing."

Thanks to our trucks, in two hours we were back in position near the college. The battery of Captain Miljevich was entrenched nearby. Below us on the mountainside was a howitzer unit sent in from Chachak. Kraljevo was deserted. The bridges over the Ibar and Morava were still intact, as was the airplane factory and the airfield. Their demolition was to occur at the enemy's first appearance.

How long was my unit to stay at this position? What, if any, were my subsequent orders? I didn't know. Nonetheless, I resolved to face the oncoming Germans.

2

Defeat

BY NOON, THE enemy had not reached Kraljevo. We had been on full alert since the early hours of April 16, ready at our position near the agricultural college. As I had angrily come to expect, my orders had never been updated.

I felt it was worth risking a short run over to the college. Its telephone was reportedly working, and I might get through to headquarters. On the way over, I happened upon the commander of the local army infantry unit. He and several junior officers were standing by a disabled staff car.

What was going on? Typically enough, his answer revealed his confusion. He ordered me to keep my unit in place until the bridges were destroyed. Then, while our ammunition lasted, we were to cover the withdrawal of forces. With this "clarification," he dismissed me and returned to his chief concern, the car.

It made no sense. Who was there to cover? As far as I knew, few other units remained. And if everyone was to withdraw when the bridges went—and they were to be blown precisely on first sight of the Germans—then a direct engagement had indeed been ruled out. So why let the panzers close in on us?

Logically, military tactics would dictate that we slip away immediately. The timing of the movement was critical. We had to abandon our position in an orderly fashion. Above all, I did not want to be captured, for the one notion that never left my

17

mind was to eventually join reorganized resistance in the mountains.

I had been at the college only a minute or two when artillery
fire let loose. A machine gun burst raked the building and glass
broke everywhere around me. The thought flashed through my
mind: *They're here.*

Dropping the phone in mid-sentence, I ran outside. The stray
attack plane had flown on. I rushed back to my unit as fast as I
could go in the momentary lull.

Once more in command at the battery, I scanned the Ibar
River bridge through my field glasses. For several minutes, we
heard shots but saw nothing. Then, like a pair of lumbering
monsters, two German tanks appeared. They moved deftly, firing
at will into the thin ranks of the defenders.

Neither bridge was blown up.

From our dominant position on the small plateau, and with
the antiaircraft gun barrels lowered to the horizontal, we could
control the approaches to the Ibar bridge. The tanks must have
known this, for they now backed off, evidently to await air cover.
As they retreated, two spotter planes appeared in the sky. Our
machine gunners went after them, without success, and the
"storks" left as leisurely as they had arrived.

They were followed by the thunderous appearance of a squadron of Stuka dive bombers. Instantly, I ordered the barrels raised.
Pandemonium broke loose. The antiaircraft guns fired continuously. The noise was deafening and the ground shook under our
feet. As the bombers attacked our position, explosions burst
around us, shrouding us in thick black smoke.

Miraculously, not a single bomb struck home. The men stayed
glued to their weapons, either from fear of the shrieking Stukas,
or from the deeply embedded habits of military drill. As we fired
away, I vainly tried to observe and order aiming corrections. My
voice couldn't be heard over the din. To my deafened ears, even
the machine gun bursts from the dreaded Stukas were soundless.

More German tanks appeared on the opposite slope. I ordered
half the battery to shoot at them. When the planes disappeared

from the sky, we redirected our entire firepower at the tanks. Not one was able to reach the bridge.

Finally, the last of the tanks retreated behind the ridge. As the firing ceased, the hills grew quiet again. Two and a half hours of fighting had seemed merely minutes. No one in the unit had been hurt, and the men beamed with pride. I heartily congratulated them. Yet I realized all was lost.

A count of the remaining shells made it clear. We were almost out of ammunition, while the nearest ammo dump was over fifteen miles away. Messengers quickly confirmed that the same was true of Captain Miljevich's battery and of the howitzer unit that had bravely stood beside us. There was no way we could withstand another German attack.

The orders I had last received forbid a useless last stand. The position had to be abandoned. Although nothing else had gone according to plan, I was at least determined that my retreat wouldn't turn into a rout. I ordered the loading of the trucks. We would take the two big guns and whatever other equipment we could manage.

As we left in the trucks headed west toward Chachak, several thunderous explosions rang out. Better late than never, the bridges, the airplane factory, and the airfield were being destroyed. My heart burst with sorrow. The German attack on Kraljevo had been repulsed, yet we were abandoning the town to its fate.

My unit did not stop at Chachak. We couldn't, for the Germans were poised to sweep onward. We had to push west and hope they wouldn't catch us.

At Uzice, nestled in the mountains, our forces might have held a defensive line. We could join them there. The fight wasn't over.

The afternoon gave way to evening. By the time we reached the next place of any significance, Uzicka Pozhega, it was 10:00 P.M. We were all dead tired. The men hadn't eaten since the previous night.

The town was full of retreating units. The coffee houses were packed with officers and soldiers, and there was much drinking and disorder. Since there were no empty rooms, we had to spend the night on the streets, huddled next to our trucks and shivering from cold. My own fitful sleep was filled with dreams of renewed resistance in the Serbian mountains. Surrendering was out of the question.

At dawn of April 17, we went on toward Uzice. It was only some ten miles away, though the winding road increased the travel distance. Not long after we were underway, I heard the unnerving sound of artillery fire up ahead of us. A passing motorcyclist gave us the bad news: more enemy units had come sweeping south from Valjevo.

The Germans had already taken Uzice.

What now? There was little choice. Enemy forces were on two sides, to our east and west. The last road presumed open ran south to Ivanjica, and then deeper into the Sandzak region of Serbia.

With great effort, we backed the trucks around on the narrow highway and returned to the crossroads. There we made the turn. Two hours later, en route to Ivanjica, the unit pulled into the village of Arilje.

In the village we somehow miraculously ran into Captain Stojkovich. Here his superiors had planned a defensive position to cover the evacuation of higher staff as they came south. Yet of the entire 662nd Division, it seemed only my two guns were intact, along with about sixty grenades.

I was ordered to mount a defense. The mission was presumably suicidal in the event of German attack, but I accepted it calmly. Dividing the battery into two groups, I placed the smaller in the village near the church and the other about three miles outside. Commanding this advance group myself, I had the men take rocks from the road and build shelters. Then we surveyed gunnery distances and prepared what was left of the ammunition.

The trucks were placed thirty feet behind us, at a bend in the road where they couldn't be seen. My plan was to fight until the last shell and then destroy our weapons. We'd try to get back to the trucks under the protection of the machine guns, (which I had placed above us to our right) and with supporting fire from the reserve group by the church.

My scheme was never carried out. At three in the afternoon of April 17, I was handed new written orders by Captain Stojkovich. An armistice had been signed with the Germans. They were to enjoy the right of free movement.

I was stunned. I couldn't believe it. I had been ready to sacrifice my battery for the good of others, but this . . . this was capitulation. This was beyond endurance. I refused to budge.

Captain Stojkovich again ordered me to remove the guns from their positions. I was to park them at the village market grounds. Under penalty of death, I still refused. He reminded me that noncompliance would only aggravate the enemy, not defeat him, and that innocent people would suffer if we should fail to cooperate.

In this, he was right. After an hour's hesitation, I capitulated. Perhaps, as he claimed, the area would be declared a "free zone" by the Germans. That would be to my advantage.

Arilje was in utter chaos. Soldiers from broken units, state employees, and railroad men wandered about aimlessly, heeding no one. My unit remained the only intact force. Using the strictest measures, I set up strong patrols and guards and succeeded in bringing about some order. With little cash and few goods left in the shops, I was fortunate to obtain by threats and begging some meager rations for my men. They had not had food in nearly two days.

But I had to do something more. I decided to go to army divisional headquarters in Ivanjica to personally ask for instructions and to seek money for provisions. Borrowing a staff car, a small Opel, I set off late in the afternoon.

I left the senior platoon leader, First Lieutenant Velkovich, in charge. As long as I was in command, I had felt confident the men would follow orders. Now I promised that I would return immediately and asked them not to disperse.

When I arrived in Ivanjica, I found the army staff in complete disarray, readying to surrender. No one cared about me or the needs of my troops. It was an unconscionable attitude. Determined not to be tamely captured, I drove my Opel back north at high speed. I was troubled by the prospect of my men being taken prisoner or deserting.

About eight miles outside of Ivanjica, halfway back, I ran into a column of German armored vehicles speeding south. In the lead car I saw a pitiful sight. Surrounded by several German officers, a Yugoslav officer in uniform sat holding a white flag of surrender.

I put my foot down on the gas pedal and veered to the side to pass them. I had to get through. My men were counting on me. Suddenly, a German N.C.O. leaped from the front car, leveled his gun at me, and shouted, "Halt!" I slammed on the brakes and nearly swerved off into a gully. The entire column stopped.

Through the open car window, the German rammed the gun muzzle against my chest and in a gruff voice ordered me out. I was too preoccupied to be afraid. I got out. Then he reached in, grabbed the keys from the ignition, and backtracked to his own vehicle. At once, the motorized column resumed its headlong dash toward Ivanjica, leaving me there beside the Opel.

Delighted at still being free, I proceeded to hot-wire the car. I was so happy at my escape that I didn't think to hide and wait for the column's rear elements to pass. Less than a mile and a half further on, I drove right into more Germans. And I had no one to blame but myself.

This time I was ordered to surrender my pistol. The car was commandeered. Yet I wasn't detained or held under guard—I imagine because I was small potatoes compared to the generals and other high-ranking officers the Germans were about to corral at army headquarters.

As soon as they were gone, I continued on foot in the gathering night. After walking about a mile, a truck driving to Arilje stopped and picked me up. Luck was still with me.

Back at the unit, my worst fears were substantiated. The men had seen the German column sweep through on its way to Ivanjica. Some twenty of my troops had left, saying that I had betrayed them and surrendered to the Germans. The majority, however, knew me well enough to wait. I had to practically fend off their embraces when I returned, so glad were they to see me alive and well.

Time was short. I distributed what remained of the unit's money and all of the portable arms. We destroyed the remaining weapons and instruments. Then I told the men: "Whoever wishes may return home. I, for my part, plan to retreat to the woods to continue resistance. Who will follow me?"

"But, Captain, why shouldn't we go to Uzice?" one of the men asked. "The Germans say they will give us papers. We will all be able to return normally to our homes."

"The Germans are tricksters," I answered. "To return home is to surrender voluntarily to slavery. This I will never do." Seeing my conviction, my faithful soldiers readily agreed to follow me.

The next morning, we packed up what we could carry. Crossing a swift stream that paralleled the road, we began to climb the hills east of Arilje. A fine rain fell, the kind that penetrates to the marrow. The mud was knee-deep on the mountain paths and hiking was difficult. Still, it was better to be there in freedom than on highways patrolled by German tanks.

Since many of my men were from the vicinity of Kraljevo and Trstenik, I decided to circle back to that area. It was the geography they knew best, and the move would give me the best chance to regroup for guerrilla operations. On the way, we spent the first night in a little village school in Vica.

The rain didn't let up the following day. We pressed on anyway to Rocevice, getting there about noon. Here my unit clerk, the engineer Urosevich, had his home. I could get some rest and plan our next moves.

I was worn out after the hard march, thoroughly soaked to the skin, and my head pounded from a cold. My aches and pains mixed with anguish over Yugoslavia's surrender, and I thought that my misery would forever banish sound sleep. But after a good lunch at Urosevich's house, I promptly fell asleep like a felled tree.

In the morning, I sent off the men who lived in the neighboring villages, advising them to put on peasant clothes, observe the situation, and report back. I sent Corporal Lukich to nose around Kovanluk and Kraljevo. Meantime, Sergeant Kostovich and I headed for a nearby vineyard where we could watch all the mountain roads.

The weather improved. The earth steamed under the warm spring sun, and far below in the distance, I could actually glimpse Kraljevo. It was a strange feeling that I was prohibited from going there. A few days ago, the town had been my home—how much everything had changed!

Taking my freedom for granted, I had assumed it was essential for life. Today, I realized my freedom belonged to the enemy who had temporarily conquered us. I thought of my family, of my mother. Were they still alive? God, what had become of them? And what did the future hold in store?

I was convinced that the majority of my comrades were hiding in the woods like myself, awaiting the right moment to band together and continue the fight. In all their history, the Yugoslav people had never given in to an invader.

"Captain, there's a soldier looking for you." The sergeant's words snapped me out of my thoughts. He pointed to a man fast approaching us.

It was one of my troops reporting. German motorized units had been seen moving through the Ibar River valley toward Kraljevo. Apparently the victorious enemy saw no reason not to withdraw his forces rapidly. Our defeat had taken them all of two weeks.

The Germans assumed civilian life would return to normal—as henceforth they defined the term. I refused to accept this. The nation was defeated, yes, the result of political corruption, the Croatian betrayal, and the work of "fifth columnists." But had the Yugoslav military really been outfought?

No. There had been few battles. Instead, an army prepared for static warfare had been demoralized by the German onslaught. Insufficiently mobile units had been dispersed before they even got a chance to fight.

The fact was we had lost. And it was a great shame, especially for the Serbs, that there was no glory won in our defeat. But the people had not spoken their last word by any means. This war had just begun.

On Sunday, April 27, I assembled my remaining men to give them my next instructions. We would all meet again on the mountain of Stolovi in forty-eight hours. However, if someone couldn't make the rendezvous point, well then, he was free to return to his village. I wanted only the truly stalwart to join me.

Meanwhile, I had a private mission of my own. Dressed in peasant garb, I left alone and descended the hills toward Kraljevo. The skies were clear, the weather balmy, the fields and meadows slightly green. The roads were trafficless, except for the occasional German vehicle.

Whenever I did hear an engine, I ducked out of sight, overcome with apprehension. I could not stop remembering my encounters with the German column. Never before had I experienced such a terrifying, loathsome feeling—that of being a fugitive at large in my native land.

Steadying my nerves, I observed the overturned cars perched on embankments outside of town, the numerous craters in the slopes around the agricultural college. The bridges showed some crude repairs. There was little else to indicate that this peaceful-looking countryside had been a recent arena of war.

I got to Kraljevo at noon. Most of the stores were closed, the wooden shutters drawn over the windows. Here and there, a local inhabitant moved silently about his daily business.

German soldiers were coming in and out of the two modest hotels, and the avenue to the railroad station buzzed with their vehicles. Taking the side streets, which were practically deserted, I tried to stroll naturally. I did not want to attract the slightest attention.

The local butcher shop was up ahead. Old man Mrvos, the owner, stood at the door. Small, with hunched shoulders, he looked sadly withdrawn. He leaned passively on the heavy wooden cane which he used to shake so vigorously.

When I approached him, he raised his large head, a faint smile lit his craggy face, and his piercing eyes twinkled slightly. We shook hands. I asked for news of my colleagues, especially Pachany, but he knew nothing.

The butcher bemoaned his own situation, explaining how he was forced to supply meat to the Germans while the peasants stubbornly refused to part with their livestock. Sighing deeply, remembering the past, he looked to me for help or advice. Alas, I had none to give him. He sadly lowered his head, then wished me good luck.

My old neighborhood was only a few steps further. The sight of it stirred my emotions, but it was hard seeing the evidence of occupation. The high school had been turned into a barracks, the house opposite mine was an officers' club. I gazed at the garage where Captain Kostich, a close friend, had housed his dilapidated automobile. A glimpse of the old jalopy through a dusty window flooded me with memories.

Occasionally, for a lark, we had driven the 120 miles north to Belgrade. Almost every hour something would go wrong. If it wasn't the engine, it was the tires. Fortunately, Kostich was a gifted mechanic, despite his primitive tools and the odd assortment of fuels he used. His confidence in himself and his old jalopy was unshakable, and we always did manage to reach our destination, sooner or later.

Just as I was about to continue down the street, a voice stopped me cold. "Captain Todorovich! Is it really you? I'm so happy you're alive and well." The voice belonged to none other than Lieutenant Colonel Trampuz, commander of the air zone. My friend Captain Kostich had been his assistant.

Dressed in full uniform but minus his revolver, the colonel looked more like a schoolteacher than a professional soldier. He wore glasses, his eyes constantly blinked, and he spoke quickly with an occasional stammer. Seemingly, he was always chasing after his own thoughts.

Though I could admire his expertise in the tactics and technology of antiaircraft weaponry, I'd never had any confidence in the man's leadership or bravery. As far as I knew, Trampuz was mainly enamored with the image of being a leader. During the recent action, he had been nowhere in sight. I wasn't at all sure if I was glad to see him.

"But how is it you walk the streets openly?" I asked him wonderingly.

"The Germans are allowing the Croats to go free," he responded.

I was very surprised because I hadn't known he was a Croat. As we walked together toward my apartment, I gave him a full account of my encounters with the Germans, my men in the hills, and my concern over the future.

"I think I can help you, Captain," the colonel said, lowering his voice and putting his arm around my shoulder. He spoke quickly, not pausing for breath. "There is money at the airbase at Raska, nearly three million dinars." He pulled a sheet of paper from his pocket. "Simply register on this list, give your name and address in Kraljevo, and I will see to it that an appropriate amount of money is drawn for you."

I didn't really believe he could get any money, but what did I have to lose? I signed the paper and said farewell to him. Then I went across the street to my apartment house. A feeling of warmth and comfort overcame me when I passed through the door.

There were practical and sentimental reasons for my risky trip into Kraljevo. I needed to equip myself better for a soldier's life in the mountains, and there were personal documents I wished to retrieve. As for the sentimental reasons, those I care not to admit, but I simply wanted a last look before the occupiers changed everything.

By the next afternoon, I had done all I could and was preparing to leave. An unexpected loud rap on the door made my heart jump. Perhaps it was a friend. Swinging it open, I found myself facing a German sergeant with a Sten gun. Several more soldiers backed him up.

Speechless, I stared at them in disbelief. They had no way of knowing I was there.

"Are you Captain Todorovich?"

"I am." My voice was calm.

"Croat or Serb?"

"Serb," I answered proudly.

"Please gather your belongings and follow me."

My capture was not like anything I had anticipated beforehand. To my puzzled mind, an answer came in a flash. I had been betrayed. Under the guise of helping me, my superior officer, Lieutenant Colonel Trampuz, had turned me in. He had seen to it that I was neatly trapped in my own apartment.

Why? Was that the price of his own freedom? I felt anger, and a strange pity for him. And then a terrible sense of sorrow filled me as I thought of the men in the mountains who were awaiting my return. I had let them down.

Even though I heard the sergeant's orders in a daze, I wasted no time in obeying. I packed my satchel with clothes and food, then numbly changed into a spare uniform. One last time, I glanced around the familiar rooms. I felt a sudden premonition that I was leaving forever.

3

Imprisonment

THE SQUAD OF German soldiers led me through the streets of Kraljevo. I moved mechanically, ashamed of my situation and disgusted by the turn of events. There had been no time for fear, or for escape. Passers-by barely glanced at us.

I was brought to the barracks where my division had once been stationed. Passing through the gate, I saw that the yard was full of disheveled men, some in uniform, some in peasant attire. They were carrying heavy crates under the watchful eyes of German guards.

The clicking of heels signified our arrival at the office of the commanding officer. The procedure was painfully simple. My name, rank, and serial number were recorded. My uniform and satchel were searched. In the blink of an eye, I had become an official prisoner of war.

I was beginning another life, a life I knew nothing of save in stories told by old men. When the heavy gate of the compound slammed behind me, my freedom was gone, and I was cut off from the outside world. What irony that these barracks, which had been a symbol of our national liberty, should now serve to hold us in captivity.

After processing, they hauled me off to the empty artillery storehouse. Inside, Yugoslav officers were packed together. Still dressed in their uniforms, they had to lie on loosely strewn hay without blankets. The lights remained on at all times by order of the commandant.

Finding a place in a dark corner, I heaped up some dirty straw for myself. I tried to sleep, hoping to somehow dream away the terrible reality.

When I opened my eyes, awakened by low voices, it was morning. At first, I didn't know where I was. Then I looked around and saw the horrible squalor. In the dreary light of day, my miserable new existence revealed itself fully.

I got up. I tried to step my way to the door, over mud-splattered bodies, accidentally landing on a sleeping comrade's hand. He didn't stir. Finally, I made it outside.

The morning was dismal and rainy. As I walked about the compound, I observed my fellow prisoners. To a man, they looked downhearted and lost. Some paced aimlessly, while others sat on the ground and stared into space. At the entrance to the storehouse, a few washed their faces from flasks. Bread was being portioned out, but the usual large kettle of dirty, bitter tea hadn't yet arrived, I was told.

I took special note of several uniformed men who wore white arm bands. After coming closer, I saw the Nazi swastika on the bands and the word *Volksdeutscher*. These were Yugoslavs of German ethnic background. Many of them had been openly Fascist sympathizers before the war.

The guards were assembling a group of our enlisted men in peasant costumes. They were undoubtedly to be sent to a labor camp where they'd help the Germans gather and store ammunition and supplies around Kraljevo. They were the best and cheapest manpower available—modern slaves.

The sound of a sharp crack turned my head. I saw a pitiful sight. A crook-necked Volksdeutscher was whipping a poor peasant-soldier, forcing him into line for the labor camp. The German guards looked on, sneering with enjoyment.

My blood boiled. These Volksdeutschers were partly to blame for the collapse of my country. It was inconceivable to me that they'd turned against the land which had given them so much. How could they slough off their fraternal ties and obligations to become collaborators? Disgustingly, they often contended among themselves to see who could be more cruel toward their former countrymen.

Of all the Yugoslav nationalities, only the Croats were equally ruthless and subservient. Across the barracks, I could see the living quarters of the Croat officers who were scheduled to leave soon. They were now allies of the Germans, citizens of the newly organized "Independent State of Croatia."

The Croats had taken the bait dangled in front of them, a "free" Croatia carved out of Yugoslavia and separated from the Serbs. In reality, the Germans had created this weak vassal state to suit their own grandiose purposes, but the policy had already borne bitter fruit. Every Serb in camp was to remark on the Croatian betrayal.

My one consolation was the unexpected presence of Captain Pachany. He had been captured, too. In peacetime, when he had first come to our division, I had liked him for his fine character, modesty, and his willingness to work. We had often passed off-duty hours together. Yet I would not say that our association was closer than mine with many other men in the battalion. Imprisonment was to change that.

I would come to know and appreciate Pachany as a rare human being. We'd previously spent many hours in discussion and, although both stubborn, we usually managed to reach an agreeable decision. Neither of us could hide anything from the other, even the most intimate of thoughts.

It was here, locked up in the Kraljevo barracks in the last days of April, that Pachany and I first understood that we needed each other to survive. It was not a spoken commitment but something that transcended easy promises. It was a bond forged in the crucible of defeat, a shared determination to never surrender in our hearts.

I was painfully aware that I was without rights or the protection of the law, yet I began to think of escaping. Even though the compound was well guarded, I believed I could do it. The problem was, what would I do on the outside?

In Kraljevo many people knew me, and not everyone was likely to help. There were certainly collaborators and others too scared of German reprisals. If I were spotted by one of them, that would be it. I would be tracked down quickly.

Like everyone in camp, my chief concern was what the Germans were up to. All the guesses were an idle exercise until my sixth day in captivity, when Pachany and I learned we were to be transported the next morning. No one knew where.

That same night, I found a copy of the *Belgrade Municipal News*. The paper had, of course, been totally revamped by the occupiers. I skipped the articles written by the Germans and their hirelings, which nauseated me, and read the ads. One of them stopped my breath. It read: "I am looking for my son, Active Cpt. B. T., who was last known to be with his battery on the front near Kraljevo on April 15 . . ." It was signed by my mother.

Poor Mother. At least she was alive and well. I tried to let this news console me, or at least reduce my anxiety about my family. I imagined I would have more than enough to worry about wherever I was headed.

In the morning, it was cold and raining. The grounds were a sea of black mud as the prisoners plowed about in the mire, gathering up their meager belongings. The guards, armed with light machine guns, herded us from the compound to the train station in groups of twenty. There we were packed like sardines into freight cars.

As I stood in an open car door, I looked out over the sea of people milling about the station. They were trying to catch a final glimpse of their departing men. In the distance, off to one side, I saw a woman completely alone. Her forlorn look was more piercing than anyone's.

The doors were slammed shut and the train began to move. We traveled through the entire night with barely room to breathe.

There was no opportunity to use a bathroom. The atmosphere became unbearable.

Eventually, some of the soldiers couldn't hold out and were compelled to relieve themselves. Although there were shouts of protest, in the end each man had to make peace with his fate and turn to his own inner thoughts for solace. With such a situation, we were overjoyed when the ride ended and a guard opened the door. He ordered us out, and we found ourselves at the Belgrade railroad station.

The entire area had been severely bombed. Under heavy guard, in rows of five, we marched through the streets, headed for the barracks of the Royal Guard at Dedinye. Everywhere, as if ravaged by a great earthquake, there were piles of dirt and rubble. The deep scars of Hitler's savage air attacks marred the charming boulevards; and Belgrade, my native Belgrade, looked like a city in its death throes.

The dispirited capital had withdrawn into itself. I remembered a city whose streets always resounded with friendly laughter and the shouts of vendors. Now, sullen and impassive, the people ignored us. They neither soothed our disturbed hearts with any words of compassion nor cried out to encourage us. The only sound we heard was the lonely stamp of our own heels on the pavement.

Situated on a hill overlooking the city, the old Royal Guard barracks teemed with more than a thousand captive Yugoslav officers. The buildings, once the pride of the Yugoslav Army, had been badly damaged by the heavy air bombardment. Doors had been blown up. The yard was filled with craters and debris. To add to the desolation, the spacious grounds of the compound had been sectioned off with rows of barbed wire.

As I entered the yard, one of the older German guards looked at me pityingly. When I answered a few of his questions and he was convinced that I was not a barbarian, he said, "I feel sorry for you. Your lot will not be an easy one."

With several generals in the lead, our group of about 350 men was taken to the cavalry pavilion. Everything I'd seen before paled in comparison. All the windows had been blown out. The floors were covered with thin layers of straw crawling with lice and bugs. Shamefully, officers and enlisted men were mixed together in another contemptuous gesture of the Germans, done to strip us of our dignity, to destroy any vestiges of our morale or authority.

German soldiers with machine guns stood guard at the doorways, ready to fire. Volksdeutscher lackeys walked among us haughtily, promising release from captivity in return for large sums of money. The only way to respond to these pests was to ignore them.

After three days in this hellhole, we were transferred to the barracks' basement. The windows were boarded up, but the enemy was "kind" enough to give the officers separate quarters, bunked two to a bed. Pachany and I shared an iron frame, inset with three wooden planks instead of a mattress.

Our daily meal consisted of a piece of moldy corn bread and soup so rancid I couldn't eat it. A huge crater in front of the building became an open-air latrine. Otherwise, our captors paid us little mind as long as we stayed away from the fences and obeyed the fat commander's regulation to remain in our quarters after 7:00 P.M.

There was nothing lackadaisical about enforcing the latter order. Sadly, two soldiers caught outside the barracks in the first week were shot. Later, when everyone had gotten the message, the guards played "innocent" little games with us. They would shoot at prisoners who accidentally showed their faces at open windows or were spotted in the hallways after hours. Such was the German idea of fun.

Despite the occasional packages allowed into camp, hunger was constant. Everyone wanted to be assigned to cleanup duties in Belgrade and thus be in a position to secure food and necessities from civilians. When the Germans discovered this, they segregated the laboring prisoners with barbed wire. Several days later, a number of officers tried to crawl through the wire. I watched as a German N.C.O. nonchalantly pulled out his revolver and fired away. Four men were badly wounded.

By mid-May, almost a month after our defeat, the weather was getting warmer. There was little to do between the camp's frugal meals except talk. From the Dedinye hill, Pachany and I often looked longingly down at our beautiful Belgrade, barely able to believe it was beyond our reach. The Germans managed to increase our mental suffering by distributing copies of the new Belgrade paper *Novo Vreme* ("New Time"), which gave the impression that life had returned to normal. While we waited and languished behind barbed wire, the paper proclaimed a city alive with cafés, movies, theaters, and sporting events.

All indications were that our stay in Belgrade was only temporary. Soon we would be shipped elsewhere. An intensified weeding out of our numbers was a sure sign this transfer was approaching. Here, as in Kraljevo, the Germans promised to liberate anyone who did not consider himself a Serb.

Pachany and I bitterly resented the comrades who took this offer to disclaim their heritage and pledge allegiance to one or another of the new "nations" fashioned out of Yugoslavia. Some of these men, the less despicable, said they were regaining their freedom to continue resistance. But we condemned them all. Even if their motives were sound, their present action was decidedly helpful to the enemy.

The only honorable course was to resist at every opportunity. Had not the world seen what happened when you made compromises with the Nazis? Unsure of whom to trust, Pachany and I talked of these defectors only when alone together. Better to remove such men from the camp, we agreed, lest they contaminate the rest of us with their attitude.

Already, most of the officers seemed resigned to a life in prison. Though the physical hardships proved bearable, it was the inner self that suffered. Given our unexpected defeat, the petty humiliations, and the Germans' successful efforts to gain collaborators, few saw any hope in the future. Desperately, we clung to every rumor of Allied victories. Even if false, these were our only way to counter the enemy's propaganda. We had to have something to hold on to, something to give us the will to resist subjugation and to endure whatever was yet to come.

One day around May 16, we were awakened by a shrill whistle. The guttural shouts of a German officer ordered us out of the basement with our belongings. In the yard, we prepared to be searched.

The morning sunshine was like some parting gift from my native city. I basked in the glorious warmth, and for a moment I was oblivious to the stark scene around me. Then the feeling faded and reality returned. A body search was conducted.

The column of prisoners was formed up. Eight abreast, we stood for hours in hushed silence, waiting for the main gate to be opened. The longer I stood, the louder it seemed my heart beat.

Finally, the gate swung free. Armed guards surrounded us, and with our heads sadly bowed, the column marched down the hill into Belgrade. Every street, every nook we passed, almost each cobblestone was familiar. As we went through my old neighborhood, I was caught up in childhood memories.

In those days, every house was graced with a garden and a fruit tree. As a youngster I had played happily in the unpaved streets that were full of dust during the dry summer months and practically impassable with mud in early spring and late fall. I never ventured much farther until my grade school teacher, Mr. Rista, took us around Belgrade.

He taught me the city's history. With my class, I visited all the neighborhoods. We learned how each street and house bore witness to the great deeds and sufferings of our forefathers. My mind was so filled with such stories that I quickly grew to love and take pride in our great city.

The prisoner column turned a corner. Slowly we plodded along another street . . .

Here my grade school class used to parade on Palm Sunday eves to commemorate the triumphant entrance of our Lord and

Savior into Jerusalem. I would beam with pride, dressed in the new clothes my mother had taken weeks to sew. Carrying a branch of pussy willow and jingling a small, shiny bell, I'd sing religious hymns until hoarse, while my jubilant, smiling mother looked on. Such days seemed long ago now.

The column reached the pontoon bridge that spanned the Sava River, and we stopped briefly. A crowd of people suddenly flocked about us and rushed to shake our hands. Calls, sobs, words of hope and encouragement engulfed us.

"Where are you going, brothers?" someone shouted. "Please, don't leave us alone!"

"The Good Lord will protect you and bring you back!" another cried out.

The guards prodded us on. After crossing the bridge, we arrived at the Zemun railroad station. Looking back over the river, I could see the imposing silhouette of the old Belgrade fortress against the late afternoon sun.

As a child I had been awed by it. An air of mysticism pervaded the walls and massive ramparts, and if I was secretly frightened by the dungeons and subterranean passages, I was inspired by the heroic tales. I was told the souls of those who had died on the fortress ramparts lived permanently in the crevices below.

To the people of Belgrade the fortress was much more than a medieval relic. It was their very spirit, proud and disdainful when confronted with armed might. Standing since Roman times, it spoke a challenge to the Germans, declaring them simply another in a long line of occupiers who had come and gone through the centuries.

In a grotto under the lower bastion of the fortress was the Church of Saint Paraskeva. Every Friday, my widowed mother had walked our family there in strict formation. As the youngest child, I had to hold her hand while my older brothers and sister trotted ahead.

My mother was a striking woman. Her large, dark brown eyes shaded by long lashes stood out against her milky white skin. Those eyes dominated her personality, overshadowing her tiny stature and attractive figure. With a look, she could warm my heart or fill it with fear, make me want to sing joyfully or stop me cold in the midst of mischief.

Dressed in a black jumper with her beautiful brown hair tightly combed into a chignon, my mother walked proudly. Like most Serbian women, she believed in Saint Paraskeva, protector of all mothers, and prayed daily in the grotto. She drew strength from her faith. It had enabled her to endure the sufferings and privations of a life ripped asunder by World War I.

My father had died during the war. Left widowed in 1914 with four small children, myself barely ten days old, my mother had no wherewithal save her two able hands. Somehow she had managed to feed, shelter, and protect us—like a lioness guarding her cubs.

On those Friday devotions, I had always gripped her hand tightly when we entered the darkness of the grotto. The heavy scent of incense made my head spin. The candles flickered, and the piercing eyes of the saints looked down from the icons with dreadful menace. My mother's reassuring touch would gently calm me.

Now standing at the train station, one prisoner among many, I knew I had to face my fears alone. I wondered if I would ever see my mother again. I thought of her devotion. She might even then be praying to the Mother of God and to Saint Paraskeva to help me through my ordeal.

Packed into overcrowded and unventilated freight cars, the prisoner train lumbered north. At the Osijek station, our first stop after Belgrade, I witnessed yet another instance of the bestial behavior of some Croats. Still wearing Yugoslav military uniforms (but with newly attached insignia) our Croatian guards beat off a group of civilians who attempted to give us food and fresh water. Their faces full of hatred, they cursed us P.O.W.s as if we were the enemy.

Pachany and I could hardly believe our eyes. What possessed these men? A desire to show their loyalty to the Nazis? A deep feeling of resentment against our different religious and political beliefs? Or a reaction to what German propaganda called their years of exploitation by the Serbs? I had no answer. Unthinkable as it was, I was grateful for the presence of German guards to shield us from these extremists.

The long train ride quickly grew exhausting. For endless hours, the monontonous clatter of the wheels drummed in our ears. There were infrequent breaks at remote stations. I realized that if we didn't stop soon, the train would carry us into the very heartlands of the Third Reich.

The train did not stop. We crossed the border into Austria.

At a layover in Salzburg, Pachany and I were presented with a golden opportunity. After an entire night in the sealed car, we were unexpectedly allowed off the train to use the station washroom facilities. The guards had their hands full watching us and pushing away curious civilians.

What a chance for escape! On impulse, we hastily locked ourselves in adjoining toilet stalls. Slowly, the bathroom emptied. We heard the guards shouting as they ordered everyone back on board.

Then I began to think. There would be a prisoner count. Surely they would check every stall and we would be caught. Or, if by some miracle we weren't detected, then where could we go? Dressed in our Yugoslav uniforms, we would be doomed from our first step, easy to spot for even an untrained civilian eye. We weren't likely to get far without money, papers, or anything to eat.

After a whispered consultation between stalls, Pachany agreed. An escape attempt was imprudent. Sadly, and ever so reluctantly, we left the bathroom and returned to the train.

Back in the freight car, I mentally reviewed every detail of the Salzburg fiasco. The unexpected permission to leave the car had certainly seemed like an opportunity. Yet it had meant little because we weren't prepared. We lacked a plan of action and the means for successful flight afterward.

My eyes had been opened to the practical aspects of escaping.

Salzburg had taught a valuable lesson: preparation was essential. It had to be our primary task. Only then could we take full advantage of any chance moment. For Pachany and me, it became the guiding principle of our inner lives.

The train rolled on. When we entered Germany, I looked out a crack in the car door. Ironically, before the war I had once planned a long trip to this region.

I could glimpse what had to be the headwaters of the Danube. Did such a little stream really become our mighty river? I recalled a book I'd read. Here so insignificant, the Danube was a newborn babe; but at the gates of Belgrade, it was a mature man, powerful and wide.

As we traversed the famous curves of the Schwarzwald (the Black Forest) at high speed, I heard someone say this was the most scenic rail route in all Germany. The countryside was beautiful, but my mood was far from what it might have been in years past.

In pink twilight, the train wound from one tunnel to another. It sped above a well-cultivated valley where a white church tower stood out against the green meadows, then plunged amidst towering fir trees that blocked out everything. When night fell, the sense of isolation was complete.

The train jerked to a halt. It was dark and raining lightly. Ordered out for the last time, we prisoners murmured the station name among ourselves: Offenburg.

Everything was in turmoil. A fresh group of guards stood on the platform under pale blue lights, ready to greet us. As we struggled to find our few precious belongings, they set loose fierce dogs. I shivered with revulsion when one brushed against my hand with its wet nose.

After an hour of chaos, we were lined up and moved through the empty streets. The town was completely blacked out. I couldn't see my hand in front of my face. The guards had to call out to each other to keep the column intact.

The rain soaked me to my skin and made me shiver. The man

behind me inadvertently stepped on my loose puttee, a strip of cloth that wraps the leg from ankle to knee. I nearly fell. When I stopped to gather it up, a guard pushed me hard with his gun butt. I had to abandon that piece of my uniform.

All at once, searchlights switched on, and a prison camp seemed to materialize in front of us. We were marched briskly through its barbed-wire gate. Within the brightly lit yard, twelve hundred Yugoslav officers—all Serbs—stood at attention in orderly rows.

Then came the invariable roll call and the sharp voice of a German officer. He read out the do's and don'ts of the camp. The recitation of each rule was accompanied by an emphatic threat of death to any offender.

I tuned out the officer's welcoming words and looked around curiously. But he regained my attention when he announced that ferocious police dogs were to roam the compound at night. The dogs had been trained to attack us. With a sinking feeling, I began to realize one thing that the Germans truly believed: escape was practically impossible.

4

Offlag 5-D

MY NEW HOME in Offenburg, presumably for the war's duration, was Room No. 3, Barracks No. 17, Offlag 5-D.

A P.O.W. camp for Yugoslav officers, it had formerly been a German military training center. The buildings were aligned in three rows, surrounded by a nine-foot-high triple fence. Every 150 feet along the perimeter was a guard tower equipped with machine guns, alarm horns, and searchlights.

The entire grounds took up more than a half square mile. Cordoned off by barbed wire, the front section was allotted to the German camp personnel. In the rear section were ten barracks for prisoners, a mess hall, kitchen, and the unused classrooms.

Each barracks had twenty cramped rooms about a central corridor, plus a washroom and toilets. Somehow, Pachany and I managed to stick together, and we got in the same room. Despite having to share it with four other officers, the accommodations were better than we expected.

Along a wall were three wooden bunk beds with straw mattresses and blankets. There were two small tables, six stools, a stove, and three big chests—one chest held earthenware bowls, utensils, and a metal water pitcher for tea. A lightbulb hung over the tables. The floor was of solid wood. The sole exterior window, opposite the door, was secured by iron bars and more barbed wire.

My first few days inside Offlag 5-D were spent trying to adapt.

It was a miserable place. The spirit of camaraderie was missing, and many men simply withdrew into themselves. As for me, thank God for Pachany. We shared everything from my rusty razor blade to his last lump of sugar.

In our room, Captain Luba Jovkovich and his cousin, Lieutenant Zivan, were the principal proponents of the everyone-for-himself attitude. They guarded a food stash in a canvas bag, chaining and padlocking it under their bunk bed. The two other roommates were my old friend Captain Todor Kostich, former assistant to the infamous Lieutenant Colonel Trampuz, and an officer I hadn't met before, Captain Dragi.

Captain Dragi turned out to be the very personification of conformity. While the rest of us showed signs of wear and tear, he was always neatly attired. He favored strict observance of all camp rules as essential for survival. Our derogatory remarks about the Germans, our support for the Allied cause, and especially our talk of escaping disturbed him tremendously.

He constantly checked the room to make sure everything was in order and admonished us to obey the guards lest we be severely punished. Yet despite his fears, I can attest that he never betrayed our secrets.

In contrast, Captain Kostich, his bunkmate, was rebellious. He was always thinking of ways to challenge our captors and spoke openly for escape—so openly, indeed, that I began to question his actual intent.

To show me just how serious he was, Kostich sewed up a passable civilian overcoat out of a spare blanket. It didn't convince me of much. With his skills and imagination, Kostich was a good friend and a trustworthy fellow, but he was too full of his own braggadocio.

Pachany and I believed that Kostich lacked tenacity. For him, escaping was largely a dream, and the makeshift overcoat was his tangible token of belief. Like a religious medal, it gave him something to ward off hopelessness, but it did not give him the means to act.

We weren't interested in such dreamers. We were only interested in men with practical temperaments. Rightly or wrongly, Pachany and I decided not to include Captain Kostich in our plans.

Within a week, the camp was settling into a stultifying routine. The lively arguments, charges, and countercharges about the causes of our defeat were no longer to be heard resounding as in the early days of captivity. The round-the-clock poker games waned. Only smokers still crisscrossed the yard, searching for a stray butt.

For the first two months we were not going to be permitted to write or receive letters. Any news of the outside world came from Nazi propaganda rags provided by our jailers. With nothing to do, our waking thoughts centered on food.

The hours between meals seemed endless, and the meals were so scanty and inadequate that they barely made a dent in my appetite. The dietary staple was cabbage and beets. A few potatoes and a minuscule portion of horsemeat were occasionally thrown in.

Dinner usually consisted of an indescribable herb soup and a small piece of cheese that smelled so bad a hungry dog would have refused it. I had to hold my nose to get it down. I longed for the thin soup I'd found so distasteful in Belgrade.

The lack of real bread was hardest to bear. I was used to eating large quantities of bread, like people everywhere in the Balkan states. The Germans gave each of us less than a pound of "bread" per week. We never could figure out the ingredients, but we knew there was no wheat flour. I would wrap my portion in a wet towel to prevent it from promptly drying out and crumbling away.

Day by day, the collar of my uniform grew larger. My stomach growled continuously. I watched men eating grass in the yard and scavenging through the camp garbage for morsels. Some P.O.W.s traded their most precious possessions for a bit of real bread or some ersatz marmalade. A handful made deals with the

Germans. Little by little, the camp was turning us all into half-alive, emaciated men.

Almost as bad as hunger's physical effects was the psychological inertia it induced. I caught myself dreaming of the day when food would no longer occupy my thoughts. The lack of news from our families, the constant roll calls, the sudden searches of the barracks and our persons—everything contributed to a feeling of despair and humiliation.

The more Pachany and I talked about escape plans, the more skeptical I became. The camp was compact, well-planned, and superbly watched. Every inch was lighted at night and covered by the menacing machine guns in the towers. There were no outside latrines or garbage dumps to hide in. The perimeter barbed wire, thick and securely anchored to the ground, was nearly impossible to cut. To dig a tunnel beneath the barracks would have been sheer folly, as the foundation was cement. Only a fool would try to carve through it with a tablespoon.

I had to admit to myself that I had no good idea how we'd break out. Frustrated, I pondered the serious reservations some officers expressed. Why escape? What was there to gain? Where could you go?

Pachany was shocked to hear my doubts. "What's gotten into you, Bora? Don't you want to be a free man again?"

Of course I did. Like Pachany, I was yearning to be free. It was the strain of hunger and imprisonment that momentarily weakened me. My relationship with Pachany, though, was my salvation. We were always there for each other when it counted.

In those dark days of May, his pointed words snapped me out of my pessimism. It was our duty to escape. I also began to pray seriously for the first time in my life—reflections on my insignificance mixed with petitions to the Almighty. My prayers did give me the strength to bear the burden of hunger and to overcome self-doubts, but something more was needed, something to combat resignation, something to raise up the spirits of every officer in camp and to restore our faith in ourselves.

The idea struck me all at once. While walking through the yard one day, I noticed a group of prisoners gathered around a young man. He was dark-haired and broad-shouldered, with a handsome, smiling face. Playing an old *tambouritza*, a lutelike instrument, he began to sing a Serbian folk song. The audience laughed and teased one another, then little by little they joined in. Their faces beamed with life as the song rang out.

This was it. In the immortal words of the poet Zmaj: "The song has saved us—thanks to the song." There *was* a way to fight the frustration and despair of the camp.

When the group dispersed, I introduced myself to the singer. His wide grin and firm handshake made me feel as if we had known each other all our lives. His name was Ozren Bingulac, a schoolteacher and lieutenant in the Army Reserves.

In no time, we had agreed to present a series of camp sing-alongs. Lieutenant Bingulac volunteered to sing and seek out additional performers. I promised to take care of the general arrangements and spread the word in camp.

The preparation work was harder than I thought. With no previous experience, I had little idea of the endless details involved in preparing a concert. Besides securing the permission of the Germans (who were surprisingly indifferent) I had to find a suitable space, improvise a stage, and consult with Bingulac on the program. I found myself running from barracks to barracks enlisting volunteer helpers.

All the effort was worth it. The response to the premiere performance was overwhelming. The joy of the crowd warmed my heart.

Reflecting on this success, I realized that novelty was not enough. To continue attracting as many of the prisoners as possible we would have to broaden our appeal. Somehow we had to rekindle intellectual and cultural life in the camp. By bringing everyone together in shared activities, a new fellowship might arise in opposition to the apparent German plan to utterly demoralize us.

A well-organized group was needed, one accepted and supported by most of the prisoners. But someone had to do the spade work to get things started. With the encouragement of Lieutenant Bingulac and a few others, I was asked to try my luck.

I wasn't encouraged by my initial attempts to arouse interest. Many scoffed at my plan or were incensed with my "foolishness." Who needed more obligations? Who wanted to waste their energy? The regimen of camp life was already enough of a burden, I was told.

Perhaps it was my youth and inexperience working against me. What did I know, after all, about organizing and running a performing arts group? A casual friend in the room across from mine listened sympathetically to my apprehensions.

With a smile but no other explanation, he dragged me off to meet someone. He approached a middle-aged man. "Here is the solution to your problems," he announced, motioning me forward to be introduced. "This is Professor Milan Bogdanovich, Captain."

Bogdanovich was evidently a cultured man. Composed, quiet, and logical, he was a master of words. A gifted speaker, he chose to avoid controversy in his political views. As a result, he was liked by almost everyone in camp and proved instrumental in helping me win support. In addition, as the former director of the state theater at Novi Sad, he had the organizational and dramatic experience I sorely lacked.

My good fortune continued with the recruitment to our cause of Stanislav Vinaver, the newspaperman and literary critic. Renowned in prewar Yugoslavia for his satirical essays, he possessed a pungent wit and an eccentric personality that had made him a frequent target for jokes. Slightly stooped, Vinaver had a bulging stomach and a ducklike walk. His heavy-lidded green eyes always smiled, his appearance was slovenly, and his mild manners served to fool many a fast-talking, slower-thinking debater.

Always accompanied by a few admirers, Vinaver strolled the compound daily, pontificating on one subject or another. His knowledge was encyclopedic—even if he said so himself. Working behind the scenes, he was to select, write, and edit many of the pieces our group would present. It was his idea to include in our program a weekly report on world events.

We regular military types still thought of men like Bogdanovich and Vinaver as civilians, although they had been reserve officers when called to active duty. Offlag 5-D thus contained the best and brightest of our officers and the flower of the Serbian intelligentsia. In such a group, there had to be enough talented men to stage near-professional shows.

At a series of meetings, the instigators decided to found a cultural organization called the Barbed Wire Society. We planned to immediately sponsor an orchestra under the direction of Professor Mali, who was an experienced musician; a choir headed by Lieutenant Bingulac; and a theater group. An oral newspaper was to follow in the near future.

To underscore our commitment, performances would be given daily. For the first time since my capture, I felt some hope. I fell asleep exhausted that night and dreamed of theater, actors, and music.

Fortunately, the Germans did nothing to interfere with our plans, perhaps because they thought we'd be less trouble if kept preoccupied. They were partially right. The next two weeks we were so busy we even forgot about our hunger.

By pooling the last funds in camp, instruments were purchased, and soon Professor Mali could drill his musicians. The days were filled with auditions and rehearsals. Lieutenant Bingulac worked with the choir, while Vinaver and his team of newsmen diligently poured over the Nazi newspapers, extracting the few nuggets of truth in the mass of lies. They began preparing the oral news reports.

Professor Bogdanovich and I auditioned and trained actors for the comedy skits we planned to present. We found three excellent performers. Oddly enogh, two of them had the same name—George Petrovich. It immediately supplied a comic touch of confusion—an auspicious sign, we thought.

The initial performance of the Barbed Wire Society took place on Sunday, June 15, 1941, at 6:30 P.M. The following program was presented:

1. "Oh Serbia," sung by the choir under the direction of Mr. Bingulac
2. "We Know Fate," a poem by Aleksa Santich, recited by Mr. Milanovich
3. "Traumerei" by Weber, played by the Barbed Wire Orchestra conducted by Mr. Mali
4. "The Sparrow's Twitter" by Mr. Bogich, sung by Mr. Ilich and Mr. Stanojevich
5. Medley of songs from Srem, sung by the choir
6. "The Return" by V. Z. Masuka, recited by Mr. Stanojevich
7. Overture of *Rosamunde*, played by the Barbed Wire Orchestra
8. Imitation of characters in camp by Zarko Kapon
9. Solo singing by Mr. Bingulac
10. A gypsy from Meljak presents a survey of the war situation, written by Mr. Teodosijevich and performed by Mr. George Petrovich
11. "Poet and Peasant" by Soupe, played by the Barbed Wire Orchestra
12. Illustrated jokes performed by members of the theatrical troupe, Messrs. Veselinovich, Petrovich, Kapon, and Petrovich. Skits entitled "Prophecy," "In the Lunatic Asylum," and "In the Restaurant"
13. "Hi, Bugler," sung by the choir
14. "My Home, My Dear Paradise," sung by entire audience

Opening night was a complete success. All the men warmed to the popular folk songs. Listening to the laughter, cheers, and applause, I could hardly believe we were in the same camp. The music carried everybody beyond the barbed wire and watchtowers, above the hills and valleys of Germany, back to our native land. For a few precious moments, we felt free.

From then on, each evening after roll call, prisoners flocked to the assembly area and scrambled for the good spots near the improvised stage. Encouraged by the response, we redoubled our efforts. More P.O.W.s volunteered to perform or to work with us.

At a meeting of delegates from all the barracks, the Barbed Wire Educational and Cultural Center was formally reorganized. To my satisfaction, it was declared the cultural representative of the entire camp. A new board of directors of the expanded group was elected. Professor Bogdanovich was the chairman. I was elected general secretary.

At the urging of the professor, we agreed to open a school. It would offer courses in economics, politics, history, philosophy, and foreign languages. There was to be an area for painting and sculpting. Also, all sports activities would come under the supervision of Major Brana Popovich.

I was swamped with work. Entrusted with directing the theatrical troupe, I had to watch the rehearsals every day and work on writing new sketches. There were also meetings with Professor Bogdanovich, future programs to arrange, and a thousand other details to attend to. As it did with many of the men, the Society quickly became my own rallying cry against imprisonment.

Unexpected news from the outside world always struck the camp like a thunderbolt. In late June, we heard about the German invasion of its former ally, the Soviet Union. The camp buzzed with speculation. Surely the modern Soviet military machine would quickly crush the Nazis.

Long-suppressed feelings of brotherhood with the Russians surfaced. They were our fellow Slavs, even if one had a passionate dislike of the Bolsheviks. Brimming with optimism, some men even made plans to take command of the camp when the Germans capitulated.

I, too, was confident of ultimate Russian victory. But remembering how the Russians had gone about defeating Napoleon a century earlier, I doubted that it would be quick or easy. The first reports of crushing German victories sent the camp into a general depression.

The daily newspaper spoke of glorious Nazi victories, of enormous Russian territories captured, of the Red Army's disintegration. Rumors of imminent Soviet defeat spread through camp. Morale collapsed. In response, the Society redoubled its efforts with the oral newspaper.

Under Vinaver's supervision, cleverly written skits were presented at every concert. These put the news from the Russian front into perspective and, once again, lifted the men's spirits. Much care had to be taken, as a German N.C.O. who spoke Serbo-Croatian was always in attendance. Nothing could be said directly, so our point of view had to be conveyed subtly.

The Germans were otherwise content to leave us alone. Clearly, they figured the Society kept our minds distracted, as they wished. They could assume we had forgotten about disrupting camp routine, or worse, trying to escape. Perhaps it was true for some prisoners. But for me, it was far from the mark.

If anything, I hoped it was the Germans who were being lulled into bored inattention.

At the beginning of August, the newspapers we could get our hands on carried stories of unusual local "incidents" in Yugoslavia. There were armed bandits, according to the German papers, operating in the Serbian countryside. The editors warned that any resistance to the Third Reich was suicidal. Nazi power could wipe the Serbian people off the map of Europe.

From several Belgrade papers, we learned a little more by reading between the lines of the censored articles. On a back page, stuck between dispatches on the German Army's latest glorious victories, was a small item in which the name of Colonel Draza Mihailovich jumped out. The paper called him the henchman and leader of the bandits. A bounty of one hundred thousand gold marks had been placed on his head.

We knew who this "bandit" was. Like many other officers in camp, I had known of Mihailovich before the war. He was then attached to the Yugoslav General Staff, an impeccable officer and a good comrade. He was a man bold enough to state his opinions even when contrary to received wisdom.

The conclusion was inescapable. Colonel Mihailovich must be leading armed resistance against the forces of occupation. I couldn't have been more excited. Soon stories of his ability, bravery, and integrity were on everyone's lips.

The entire camp went into a frenzy of speculation about the nature and propriety of Colonel Mihailovich's resistance movement. Emotional discussions flared and arguments filled the air. One group, led mainly by older prisoners, claimed that armed resistance would ruin the Serbian people and pave the way for a Communist takeover. According to these men, things would have worked out if we had only cooperated with Hitler. They blamed the coup d'état, which took Yugoslavia out of the Axis camp, for all the miseries that followed.

Why was Mihailovich stirring up more trouble, they asked? Had he learned nothing from our defeat? They condemned any resistance as the foolish act of a few restless individuals who were insensitive to the threat of German reprisals.

I and many others profoundly disagreed. The Axis powers had never planned anything but slavery and exploitation for us. At last, some Serbs had again taken up arms. There were no words to express the feelings of pride this brought to my heart. The rest of Europe lay supine beneath the Nazi jackboot, while in my country the occupiers' blood was being shed.

The debate continued. The proponents of passive submission to the Nazis complained that the news commentaries presented at the Barbed Wire programs were attempts to discredit them. They reacted by vilifying the Society and, in particular, Vinaver and Bogdanovich.

In truth, the two men were well-known critics of the political situation in prewar Yugoslavia. They had formulated a coherent statement of what many progressive men felt. In their opinion, King Alexander's assassination in 1934 had dealt a blow to those who hoped for the reestablishment of parliamentary rule.

Since the king's son, Peter, was too young to assume the

throne, three regents had been appointed. One of them, Prince Paul, quickly assumed control. The quasi-democratic government he led continued to be a prime cause of the nation's internal dissensions, and its clumsy attempts to suppress dissident elements only made matters worse in the long run.

I'd shared such views, but career officers before the war were forbidden to participate in politics. If ever a word was uttered critical of the ruling government, our military oaths of allegiance were thrown in our faces. And there was much to criticize.

The mood of the nation as registered in the general election of 1938 had affected me deeply. Disregarding the expressed will of the people, Prince Paul's autocratic government had traveled the road to perdition. It had moved closer and closer to the Axis powers—until the March 27 coup d'état. Now the people were speaking again through Colonel Mihailovich. Deep in my soul, I believed he truly represented their will. The camp faction that so bitterly attacked his supporters had to realize this sooner or later.

From our censored sources we tried to glean every development in the activity of the "bandits." When Communist involvement became apparent, the arguments turned heated. From prisoner letters and news reports, we pieced together a story of two separate movements. One, led by Mihailovich, was named the Ravna Gora Movement, after the area in Serbia where he began his resistance. The other, dominated by the Communist party, named itself the Partisans. It was unclear whether the two groups were operating cooperatively or separately.

A tiny minority of leftists fully supported the Communists, while the rest of us debated the pros and cons of working with them. Bogdanovich and Vinaver downplayed the danger. They cited Winston Churchill's pronouncement that he would join forces with the devil, if necessary, to win the war against Nazism. Further, they argued that anyone who could should join in the struggle against the common foe.

Not everyone agreed by any means. The issue cut to the heart of political beliefs, provoking anger and resentment among

P.O.W.s only recently united by a common fate. While the summer labored to a close, these antagonisms within Offlag 5-D became increasingly pronounced.

Fresh news exploded in early September. At German prompting, a new civilian government had been formed in occupied Serbia. German recognition was granted on August 29. The head of the new government was General Milan Nedich, one of the leading Yugoslav military men before the war.

Everyone in camp knew him, many personally. Practically everyone considered him a good commander and a capable soldier. He had been renowned, while serving as minister of war, for his energetic efforts to modernize the army, and his resignation from the cabinet in the autumn of 1940 was still a cause célèbre. In the recent debacle, there were tales of his heroics on the Albanian front. We'd all heard of his fierce resistance against the Germans at the Kacanik Pass.

His resignation from Prince Paul's government was not, however, exactly what it seemed. General Nedich had left shortly after the Italians bombed Bitolj, a town in Yugoslav Macedonia, in December, 1940. Most people believed he had resigned in protest over the rejection of a plan that would have allied us with the Greeks in a combined counterattack on Italy. This view credited the general as a patriot.

Others, including myself, knew otherwise. Intimate sources had revealed that Nedich was in fact dismissed. With Greece on the verge of defeat, he'd actually proposed a Yugoslav attack to seize territory in Greek Macedonia. The Italian bombing, then, was a warning to Prince Paul, and the subsequent dismissal of Nedich was likely intended to reassure Mussolini.

Learning of the thwarted plan, I was convinced that Nedich was privately pro-Axis. His installation at the head of a collaborationist government made me even more skeptical. Why would any nationalist accept this role? He had to know he was without real power, a mere puppet.

The enemy clearly wanted to use Nedich's popularity to undercut Colonel Mihailovich and the resistance movement.

Why else did German propaganda proclaim Nedich the "father of the Serbian people" and his government "the people's salvation"? In my opinion, the new regime was a divisive force concocted to be an impediment to genuine efforts against the occupiers.

Unfortunately, only a few men shared my views, among them Vinaver and Bogdanovich. General Nedich, most argued, would heal the nation's wounds. Instead of being condemned, he should be admired. By curbing the senseless provocations of roaming bands of Communists and other irresponsible individuals, it was claimed that his government would prevent useless bloodshed.

Captain Dragi was one who took such a view. He would turn pale with anger, his lips tightly shut, whenever he heard me criticize General Nedich. On one occasion we nearly came to blows.

In no time, I was labeled a Communist by many in the camp. The name didn't bother me. Of far greater concern was that the Germans might be so informed. In that case, they'd watch me even more closely, the last thing I wanted. As the endless debate went on, I prudently withdrew to the sidelines.

After four months in captivity, I had grown accustomed to a P.O.W.'s life, but I'd never accepted it. There were many secret things on my mind. From the first day, Pachany and I had planned to escape for one basic reason, to regain our personal freedom. Then, with word of Colonel Mihailovich, we had been given a greater purpose.

There was a true resistance movement to join and a cause to serve. I could no longer remain calm. I wanted to participate in decisions more important than what entertainment to present at the concerts or which debate faction to support.

A world war was being waged, with the fate of my country held in the balance. That was where Pachany and I really belonged, out in the fight. We had to escape. The time had come.

5

Plans and Setbacks

THE ESCAPE PREPARATIONS that Pachany and I made were slow and methodical. At a minimum, we had to have civilian clothes, a map of the frontier, money, a compass, and a reserve of food. Without these things, any attempt was doomed.

Obtaining what we needed was to be far from easy. In view of my workload with the Barbed Wire Society, Pachany took the initiative. Clothes were the first priority.

Although civilian attire was confiscated and stored under guard, some prisoners were certain to have outfoxed the Germans. The trick was to find these men and convince them to deal with us. It took Pachany two months, but his persistence paid off. In exchange for my practically new military tunic, I received a pair of worn black trousers. Pachany also traded for a leather jacket and an old cap with a brim for me as well as a tattered suit for himself.

With my outfit complete, I had to beam inwardly, not daring to breathe a word to anyone. I hid the clothes inside my mattress and in the narrow yard between two barracks. Our luck was definitely holding when Pachany next found a German tourist book.

A guard must have lost it. His carelessness provided us, to our amazement, with maps of Germany. We dared not keep the book for long. There was too great a risk of its discovery in a surprise search. Working secretly, Pachany copied from the maps, paying particular attention to the border areas with France and Switzerland.

We also got details about the Swiss frontier from an officer just back from a P.O.W. hospital. He had information obtained from several French prisoners in his ward. They advised escaping to Switzerland, claiming it was easier even though the French border was a good many miles closer to Offenburg. Their advice appeared sound. The camp authorities would naturally expect us to head west, not south.

To merely see our own map excited me. I imagined us crossing the German border under cover of darkness, on our way to freedom. Yet I hadn't forgotten my previous experience. My enthusiasm was tempered by reality. Without a compass the map was worthless. Without German money we couldn't travel by train or buy food. And without a supply of food, we didn't stand a chance of surviving even a short trip. Our bodies were far too weak. We would collapse the first night.

Considering the situation in camp. I didn't know what to do. By mid-September, it all seemed hopeless again. Then, out of the blue, food packages arrived from the Red Cross. Even more miraculously, the Germans decided to let us have them.

This aid was allowed under the terms of the Geneva Conventions covering military internees. Oddly enough, the Nazis had not repudiated these humanitarian treaties. They even boasted of their compliance. True enough, they had sporadically complied with the letter of the law while consistently violating its spirit.

The packages were nothing less than a godsend. We could hardly wait a moment for their distribution. When Pachany and I ripped ours open, my eyes lit up.

The sight of real food was thrilling. But desperate and hungry as we were, we held off gorging ourselves. We deliberately put aside canned meat, chocolate, marmalade, and crackers into a cache for our escape. Then we pooled our coffee and cigarettes, which neither of us cared for, to use in future bartering. Finally, we indulged our aching stomachs with what was left.

We were not the only ones delighted with the Red Cross

packages. The German sentries and kitchen personnel, faced with increasing war shortages themselves, were anxious to trade with us. From them, Pachany obtained essential cash: 60 Reichmarks. We hid it in an empty marmalade can.

Outwardly devoted to Hitler, the Germans were often friendly and talkative when alone, and they liked to complain about the war. As soon as two of them were together, however, their manner changed completely. They became stiff and rude. Not trusting one another, they'd compete to express the most hatred of the P.O.W.s or Nazi enemies. It was as if Hitler's Gestapo had crept into the marrow of their bones.

Additional food packages gradually restored our physical strength. Life in camp perked up. The laughter at the programs became heartier, the applause stronger, the atmosphere in the classrooms livelier. Pachany and I pressed ahead with our plans.

When Captain Miljko Acimovich, a friend of Pachany's, guessed what we had in mind, he gave us a gift. With great generosity, he presented to us an officer's field compass. We hid it in the marmalade can along with the money.

Despite the odds, we had assembled everything needed. Our patience and Pachany's pluck had paid off. Next, we had to concentrate on devising a feasible escape route. After careful study, we concluded that jumping over or cutting through the barbed-wire fence was out of the question. There had to be another way.

We thought we saw one when the Germans asked for volunteers to work in the nearby town's factories. Pachany and I stepped forward. The whole camp was shocked, believing we wanted to help the German war effort.

Certainly we couldn't reveal our covert aim to anyone, much less a thousand fellow P.O.W.'s. The secret would never keep. We'd no doubt find ourselves caught in the act, and the guards were sure to shoot us.

Our instant notoriety didn't help, either. Pachany and I had no choice but to withdraw our names and look elsewhere for a means. Every day we reviewed new possibilities and every day we knocked them down. Was there no way out? Discouraged, we aimlessly plodded the grounds until one afternoon when Pachany spotted a large truck and trailer delivering vegetables to the camp kitchen.

Why hadn't we noticed it sooner? We observed the scene carefully. The kitchen workers unloaded large baskets of beets and cabbages from the trailer and returned the empties. The driver remained in the kitchen. He was still inside for a while after the workers finished, and during that time the truck went unattended.

When the driver reappeared, he got in the truck and drove slowly toward the main gate. The gate sentry checked his credentials and made a casual inspection. Then he was waved through.

For the next few weeks, we studied the truck's comings and goings. Sure enough, it arrived every Wednesday after the evening roll call. First, it delivered vegetables to the guards' side of the camp, then it came to the prisoners' kitchen.

The baskets were approximately five feet high, large enough to hide a crouching man. After the delivery, the driver stayed in the kitchen at least ten minutes. The trailer's rear opening—the perimeter guards never gave it more than a cursory glance—was secured with canvas flaps.

This was it. All we had to do was sneak into the trailer and hide under the baskets. Once through the main gate, we'd jump out before reaching the outskirts of Offenburg. Then, we'd walk to the train station, board a train for Freiburg, continue on to Donaueshingen near the Swiss border, and from there slip across to freedom. In theory, it seemed remarkably simple.

We picked the second week in October to go. With our preparations finished, I began counting off the days. I could already taste our success. But the day before the attempt, something happened that was completely unanticipated.

I received a devastating letter from home. My sister's children, a little boy of six and a beautiful little girl of four, were both dead. They'd been stricken by a mysterious illness. I was shocked and crushed.

Their faces were so vivid to me that I couldn't imagine a world without their laughter. For the first time in my life, I was unable to make myself work. All my great plans seemed vain and senseless, even the escape.

No matter how Pachany tried, I couldn't be consoled. Just when I should have been calm and sharp to concentrate on the details essential for a successful effort, I was at loose ends. My mind was preoccupied. It was as if the longings and feelings I had necessarily suppressed over the many months were triggered into release.

I couldn't go, not now. Not until my emotions were back under control. I felt I had no choice. In my present state, I would be a hindrance to Pachany and would only endanger him. I begged him to make the escape alone, without me.

Pachany was dumbstruck. He couldn't believe it. "I won't go without you, Bora. We need each other. Our chance of success is much greater if we go together. Please."

"I can't, Leonid. Don't ask me to explain. I just can't."

"Then we will wait until you are ready."

"No!" I insisted. "You must go now, without me. While you have the chance. It can't be put off. I'll join you as soon as possible . . . next week, or the week after. But you must go." I couldn't bear the thought of keeping Pachany from an opportunity that might be temporary.

With a heavy heart, he finally agreed, but he insisted he would wait two weeks for me at a Swiss village across the border from Donaueshingen. Wednesday, October 13—tomorrow—was the date we'd planned for, and he'd make the attempt.

To our dismay, in the morning the Germans told us to scrub our rooms and clean up—the usual signal of an impending inspection. After a long day's work, Lieutenant Dengler, one of the camp subcommanders, ordered us to assemble in the yard for a roll call. Just as it ended, I saw the vegetable truck drive into the compound.

I looked Pachany in the eye. There was no need to speak. As soon as we were dismissed, I strolled away toward the kitchen while Pachany went to pick up his equipment.

Most of the prisoners were relaxing in their rooms, awaiting the evening Barbed Wire program. It was due to start in a few minutes. Except for a crew unloading cabbages, the kitchen area was deserted. The sentry who usually stood by the fence was nowhere in sight.

The men finished their work and returned the last of the baskets. The driver went inside the kitchen. There the trailer stood, unguarded, a dark object in the pale light of the October dusk. The coast was clear.

Cautiously but nonchalantly, I approached the rear of the trailer. Lifting a flap, I inspected the interior. Just the empty baskets, as we'd figured.

I edged back a little. Prisoners appeared from the barracks, heading over toward the mess hall where the shows were held. Since I always attended, the German monitor would notice my absence. There wasn't much time left. Where was Pachany? It was now or never.

At last he emerged from the barracks. He wore an overcoat to conceal his civilian suit and kept his hat hidden in an inside pocket. The bag he carried held all his belongings and his extra food.

I signaled to him, and he joined me at the trailer. He looked pale and nervous. "Hurry up. You'll be fine," I whispered as we embraced.

"I won't succeed without you, Bora. Promise me again you'll follow."

"I promise. Now go." I can't describe how badly I felt.

I shoved aside one of the canvas flaps and helped Pachany inside. We shook hands. Then I covered him up with baskets. Letting the canvas drop, I quickly moved off. As I crossed to the mess hall, I heard the roar of the truck carrying him away.

With Pachany gone, I delivered my opening remarks to the audience in a trance. In my mind, I was following him out of the camp. Would he stick to the plan? Would he follow every step exactly? The smallest slip could lead to his capture or death. I prayed for his safety and success.

Back in the barracks, the curfew whistle sounded and the outer doors were locked.

"Where's Pachany?" everyone asked.

"Next door, playing chess with Acimovich, I imagine. He probably got locked in." Nothing more was said. The lights went out.

I lay on my bed but couldn't sleep. For the first time since my arrival in camp, the bunk above me was empty. There was no one to chide for moving too much and shaking pieces of straw down. *You should have gone. You should have gone with him* kept echoing inside my head. I would go next Wednesday, I promised myself. Without fail.

Around midnight, the door was suddenly opened and the lights turned on. A German officer, accompanied by several armed troops, ordered us out of our bunks. He zeroed in on me.

"Where is Pachany?" he demanded.

I pretended not to understand his German.

"Where is Pachany?" he shouted even louder.

I shrugged my shoulders. He asked again, this time in broken English. "I don't know," I replied in my most innocent voice.

"Liar. You know. You helped him escape, didn't you?" When I continued to profess my ignorance, the officer and his men left abruptly, slamming the door behind them.

In the morning the camp was bursting with excitement. It was obvious to everyone that Pachany had escaped. Scores of the younger officers followed me about, wanting to know about their hero. They were all full of plans and serious talk.

The commandant issued a statement: the entire camp would be punished. The majority of the P.O.W.s were ready to accept any reprisal, delighted in the loss of face for the Germans.

Knowing their acute embarrassment, we thought the threats mostly empty bluster.

But to my chagrin, not everyone approved. A group of senior officers with far too much concern for their own necks wanted us to demonstrate contriteness. They demanded that Professor Bogdanovich publicly condemn Pachany's escape as a selfish and shortsighted act that endangered our lives. Hard as it was for me to believe, Bogdanovich appeared ready to accommodate them.

Striding up to this man I had much admired as head of the Barbed Wire Society, I spoke bluntly and heatedly. "How can you even consider publicly condemning a fellow prisoner for attempting to escape? Escape is every soldier's duty. Pachany's courageous act is an example for all of us to follow. No honest man denounces an act of bravery just because he is threatened with punishment."

"A public statement denouncing, but not *condemning*, the escape will restore harmony in the camp and save face for the camp commander," Bogdanovich replied calmly.

I felt betrayed. I wouldn't listen to such nonsense. "To condemn Pachany is to commit an act of treason. Don't do it!" I shouted.

But he did. That night at the Barbed Wire program, Professor Bogdanovich made a speech denouncing Pachany. It caused a complete rupture between the senior and junior officers, since immediately following, I publicly resigned as secretary of the Society. I could no longer work with such a man.

Still smarting from my encounter with Bogdanovich, I found myself under armed escort to the German command office. Lieutenant Dengler interrogated me for nearly an hour. To my shock, he knew how Pachany had escaped from camp.

Someone—I never found out who—saw him enter the truck and informed the Germans. Lieutenant Dengler was also aware that Pachany had an uncle, a wealthy furrier, in Frankfurt. He obviously wanted me to confirm if Pachany had headed in that direction. Luckily, I thought, my friend was on his way to Switzerland. I hoped he was already there.

In response to all the lieutenant's questions, I simply stuck to my initial statement. I knew nothing about Pachany's disappearance. Dengler's patience soon wore thin. He threatened to send me to another, harsher P.O.W. camp.

When I still refused to say anything further, he finally released me. Back at the barracks, I discovered that all my belongings had been searched and ransacked. Fortunately, the Germans had miraculously overlooked my escape stash.

After lights-out, everyone talked of Pachany and tried to guess where he might be. "Maybe he is in Geneva, comfortably quartered in some hotel," Lieutenant Zivan suggested. I smiled at the remark. It was not impossible.

More than anything, I wanted to believe Pachany had succeeded. If only I had gone with him . . .

Early the following morning, a wild rumor spread through camp. Pachany had been recaptured. I refused to believe it. Surely it was just another German trick.

Then a guard came into the room and gave me a handwritten note. It was unmistakably from Pachany, requesting his blanket and other personal items. I faced up to the hard conclusion. Poor Pachany. My shoulders sagging, I gathered his things and followed the guard to the punishment block.

He was in a dark cell. It took me a few moments to spot him sitting on the wooden planks of a bed. Half-dressed in his civilian clothes, Pachany looked haggard and dejected. As I moved closer, I saw marks on his body. My God, he'd been beaten.

With a sad smile, he whispered, "Didn't I tell you I wouldn't make it alone?" I could barely hold back my tears as the guard took the things I brought and quickly pushed me outside.

After ten days of intensive interrogation, Pachany was released from solitary. When we finally managed to be alone, away from the other prisoners, he told me what had happened.

"When you helped me into the truck," Pachany began, "a feeling of uneasiness overcame me. I felt alone and terribly empty. Time stood still. A cold sweat dripped into my eyes."

Pachany's words made everything so vivid for me that I practically felt I had gone with him.

"After a seeming eternity, the driver came out of the kitchen and the truck finally rolled up to the front gate. I heard the footsteps of the sentry. When he lifted the flap and looked inside, I stopped breathing. I was sure I was about to be discovered. But the truck took off for the city."

I was satisfied to learn that the plan had proceeded as we'd expected. Pressing for details, I wanted to know everything. Far from being defeated, I was already thinking about another attempt.

Pachany had wiggled out from behind the baskets and peeped through the flap. There was no one in sight. When the truck slowed at an intersection, he jumped off. As planned, he proceeded on foot into Offenburg. Darkness was descending and the streets were practically empty.

He found the railroad station without any difficulty and took his place in a small line at the ticket window. When he happened to glance around, he couldn't believe his eyes. He froze. Standing not five feet from him was Lieutenant Dengler.

Stepping out of line would provoke attention. The only thing Pachany could do was pull down the brim of his hat and try to look calm and inconspicuous. When Lieutenant Dengler finally walked away, he breathed a deep sigh of relief.

Buying a ticket to Freiburg, he quickly boarded his train. His face buried in a newspaper, he still felt as if everyone were looking at him, even though no one really was. The train reached the city in two hours.

Freiburg was completely blacked out. Pachany didn't know where to go. Weakness was overcoming him. To wander aimlessly through the town seemed crazy, so he decided to hide in the railroad yard. Jumping a small fence, he walked cautiously along the tracks beyond the station. The place was deserted, and the empty cars on the sidings looked like phantoms.

He entered a passenger car and settled into a corner seat. Dangerously, he dozed throughout the night until bright lights woke him. At the opposite end of the car, a maintenance man had arrived to clean the train. Keeping calm, Pachany slowly slipped from his seat and eased out the nearest door, repacking his gear as he went.

There was a small coffee shop near the station. Since he was hungry, he took a chance and went in. A pretty young waitress greeted him pleasantly and brought him a cup of coffee. "Would you like a croissant?" she asked, smiling.

Pachany explained that he didn't have a ration coupon. The waitress said it didn't matter. He could bring it in next time. When she began asking friendly questions, he told her he was a foreign volunteer worker. He was stopping in Freiburg for only a few days. She seemed to believe him.

Quickly finishing his breakfast, he went back into town. The city was awakening. The clatter of streetcars and the backfiring of bus engines filled the morning air.

At a small store he bought a map of the city and a schedule of trains and buses. The next steps went smoothly. He caught a train, then took the bus until he reached a village near Donaueshingen. From there he hiked toward the Swiss frontier.

It was slow going. He purchased apples from an old woman in one of the local villages. She was very talkative and told him everything he needed to know about the area, then corrected his bearings to the border. He was only a mile and a half away!

There was a small forest on the outskirts of the village. Hiding under the trees, Pachany sensibly waited until nightfall before attempting to cross. He found a shady place and slept most of the day. When he awoke around five, darkness was setting in, but visibility was still good.

He went to check out the exact demarcation. All he had to do, it seemed, was walk across a clearing to its opposite side. The free Swiss side.

Everything was peaceful and quiet. There wasn't a soul in sight. Why wait any longer? Moving with great care, Pachany edged into the clearing.

"Halt!" a German voice shouted. From the brush, a border

guard emerged. His rifle pointed right at Pachany's heart. "What are you doing here? Don't you know this is the border zone? No civilians are permitted here."

Pachany couldn't believe it. How could he have been so stupid? If only he'd waited for darkness. But there he stood, motionless, as if struck by lightning.

Recovering his composure, he tried to talk his way out of the jam. He was going to see his brother in a neighboring village and must have lost his way. The soldier didn't buy the story and ordered him at gunpoint to a nearby post.

Marching ahead, Pachany weighed his option. He could make a run for it and almost definitely be shot. He could try to bribe the soldier, but he had nothing but his wristwatch to offer. Resigned to his capture, he thought about how astute I had been to not come with him.

It didn't take the border guards long to realize that Pachany was some sort of escaped prisoner. When he refused to say anything more, he was locked in the local Donaueshingen jail. By morning, the game was up. He was promptly carted back to Offenburg.

Despite his disappointment and the beatings he had received, Pachany was ready and willing to try anew. I was overjoyed. If anything, his adventure made us both more determined to escape than ever. His experience had taught us valuable lessons.

First, it was essential to have fake I.D. cards. Pachany felt he'd been extremely lucky. He could have been stopped much earlier for a check of his papers. With I.D. cards, we could travel through Germany posing as foreign workers. It was highly risky, but workable. Second, any border crossing should be attempted only at night. And third, the Swiss frontier was too well guarded. That was *not* the way to go.

Our plans were discussed and refined. We resolved to somehow get forged papers. We would make our next attempt at the French border. We would be more careful, and we would go together.

Of course, we also had to come up with another way to break out of Offlag 5-D.

For the remaining two months of the year, we lived in fear that Pachany would be transferred to a different camp. Thank God it didn't happen. Although the Germans watched him like a hawk, he proceeded to replace his lost equipment. He was now treated as a hero by most of the prisoners, and many were eager to help him.

One officer who was especially forthcoming was Second Lieutenant Ninkovich. Early on in camp, I had gathered that the lieutenant was somebody quite impressed by celebrity. He had a tendency to flatter those who could help him. Now, apparently, he had set his sights on Pachany and me.

He was a handsome man, tall and broad-shouldered, with unruly light brown hair and vivid brown eyes. He was young, only twenty-two, and had a number of appealing traits, although he was very ambitious, too. He craved recognition. Still, I couldn't fault him for his enthusiasm.

Despite my misgivings, Pachany seemed ready to take him into our confidence. The young officer guessed our intentions. He insisted he would join us in any new escape attempt or else try on his own. I judged his resolve to be genuine.

Although I was often irritated by Ninkovich and not completely happy with this turn of events, I acquiesced. But only on condition that he say nothing further to anyone. He swore solemnly to work cautiously and keep silent.

I little realized just how deep a thorn in our sides Ninkovich would prove. For the moment, there were more important things on my mind. As the new year began with all the ceremony of one dreary day turning into another, important news filtered into camp. In early January, a major change had occurred in the Yugoslav Government-in-Exile based in London.

The Prime Minister, General Simovich, had been forced out. He had been asked to resign by King Peter II. Peter, who was all of eighteen, had been installed by the coup against the regent Prince Paul. Not a month later, the young king and the new government had fled the country at the German invasion. The

Nazi papers portrayed Simovich's fall as further evidence that the Yugoslav people had turned against their old leaders and now supported German policy in the Balkans. In truth, the event was puzzling to everybody.

General Dushan Simovich had been the commander of the Yugoslav Air Force and the titular head of the coup d'état of March 27. At that time he had been easily the most popular, if not the most powerful, man in the country. He was a brilliant and progressive military leader with a clear vision and a tough mind. Practically everyone in camp supported him. His dismissal from the government to which we remained loyal seemed almost incomprehensible.

His successor, Professor Slobodan Jovanovich, was an elderly scholar of international repute. He had been a renowned professor at the Belgrade University Law School. A modest man, he was universally regarded as a paragon of integrity and political wisdom but thought to be without ambition or much initiative. After the coup, Jovanovich had assumed the post of second vice premier under Simovich. Well-respected as he was, he had neither the political skills nor the strong personality of someone like the general.

Whatever the cause, the change had occurred, and the camp was once more filled with disputation. The senior officers interpreted Simovich's ouster as a political plot, arguing that he was forced out because he was the one man strong enough to handle the Allies and control the politicians. Others expressed confidence in Jovanovich and extolled his virtues.

In view of the harmful discord, I reluctantly agreed to resume my duties as secretary of the Barbed Wire Society. Not only were the programs falling into disarray in my absence, but Professor Bogdanovich had enjoyed a free hand in disseminating his own views. Even though I wasn't anxious to associate with him, I couldn't let him speak out unopposed. In no time I began to present a series of analytical reports aimed at inspiring the prisoners' confidence in all the Yugoslav leaders.

I argued that nothing substantive had changed and that Simovich's removal was presumably a military necessity. Clearly, I exclaimed, General Simovich was to be assigned a new and more important task. In conjunction with Allied forces he would form a Yugoslav Army to restore liberty to our fatherland.

It was many months before I learned the real reasons for Simovich's fall. I was grateful the truth never reached the camp. It would have been a terrible blow to our courage and resolve.

The real story was a familiar one. The government-in-exile had been badly split between its Serbian, Croatian, and Slovenian members. As an intransigent Serbian nationalist, Simovich had managed to alienate all his colleagues. With the cabinet in disarray, the young king had reluctantly acted to oust him at his advisors' urgings.

My error was, I think, only natural. At the time I was far removed from London in distance and in spirit. My concern lay elsewhere. What I believed everybody truly cared about, as I did, was the fate of Mihailovich in the Serbian mountains. That was where I myself wanted to be.

I had resumed the duties of secretary for not more than a month when word began to circulate through camp of an impending transfer. In a matter of days, 250 "undesirable" prisoners were to be moved to a harsher P.O.W. camp in Nuremburg. Pachany and I were said to be on the list, along with Lieutenant Ninkovich and Vinaver.

A year prior, news of the coup d'état had come to us in March. Perhaps March would also be a good month in 1942. With that thought in mind, instead of feeling distress, Pachany and I were excited. This might be our chance. Again.

1942

FOR YUGOSLAVIA, THE triumph of the March 27 coup d'état was the one bright note in 1941. After that brief moment, the country knew only defeat, dismemberment of its territory, and the bleak reality of occupation.

Along with the main German invasion force, Italian and Hungarian troops had attacked. The Bulgarians arrived two days after the armistice of April 17, and they, too, shared in the spoils. The country was promptly carved up by Hitler, who hated and distrusted the Serbs more than ever, and the largest piece was reserved for the pro-Axis Croats.

The "Independent State of Croatia" was a misnomer in several senses. It was certainly not independent, but an Italian puppet. Further, it was not the "Greater Croatia" of the ultranationalists' dreams. The coveted Dalmatian coast along the Adriatic was handed over to the Italians, as were the coastal islands. The inclusion of all of Bosnia-Herzegovina, with its Serb and Muslim majorities, was seen as a Trojan-horselike compensation.

Slovenia was divided between Germany and Italy. From Serbia, the northeast Vojvodina region was delivered to Hungary. Bulgaria took Serbian Macedonia in the south, and the Kosovo area in the southwest became part of Albania—itself under Italian hegemony. Left was a rump protectorate as small as Serbia had been before the Balkan Wars.

The intent of the Axis invasion was predictable. But what had most shocked and stunned the Serbs was the betrayal of the Croats, especially in the military. In many cases they had abandoned their positions without firing a shot, surrendered, or

73

simply gone home. An entire brigade, including its commanding officer and staff, let themselves be captured by a German company on bicycle.

Two days before the actual Yugoslav capitulation, the Croatian Fascist Dr. Ante Pavelich rode triumphantly into Zagreb, the new capital. A lawyer, he had masterminded the 1934 assassination of King Alexander and had enjoyed Italian asylum for many years. Now he was the new leader of the Croats.

One of his first acts was to beef up his local armed troops. Besides increasing the Home Guard, he converted his own previously outlawed group into a paramilitary force. The ranks of the *Ustashi* (meaning "rebels") grew rapidly. Some ten thousand strong, they would carry out the forthcoming reign of terror.

As for the Serbs, they were reeling from the dramatic blows of the war. Far from shooting down many enemy planes over Belgrade, as Boris first heard, the Serbs had actually given the Germans a field day. Large sections of the capital were destroyed, and an estimated twenty thousand people were killed by indiscriminate bombing. Further, the Germans took two hundred thousand prisoners of war (all Serbs), looted and pillaged as they saw fit, and suspended civil liberties. With the parallel fall of Greece, the Nazis were the masters of the Balkans.

Occupation troops from Italy and Bulgaria took up positions in their respective areas as well, and the New Order made its priorities clear. The Fascists agreed. Their rule was to crush anyone who dared to resist them; but foremost they were intent on breaking the spirit of the Serbian people.

The news that had reached Boris in camp was sketchy but accurate. Two indigenous resistance movements had sprung up in Yugoslavia. One was led by Colonel Draza Mihailovich, a Regular Army officer. The other had a mysterious figure at its head, someone named Tito (which was in fact a pseudonym of Josip Broz) who was unknown. This group, the Partisans, were backed by the long-illegal Yugoslav Communist party.

Both groups were prepared to fight the occupiers but were

otherwise profoundly at cross-purposes. Despite some early efforts at cooperation that were aborted by Partisan attacks, they rapidly developed independently. Implicitly, a civil war was brewing from the start, a war of a kind which was later to become all too familiar—Communist versus non-Communist.

The presence of two formal resistance groups in one country was unusual in occupied Europe's underground movements and presented special problems to the Allies. Chief among these was that a choice had to be made in the long run to either support the Chetniks or the Partisans.

Since the British were not only seasoned participants in Balkan intrigues but had also retained Yugoslavia within their Near East military theater of operations, the choice was largely theirs. Defeated France, a former rival for influence, could not object, and the other Allies, America and Russia, were fully preoccupied with their own immediate concerns. By default, as the Chetniks realized, any near-term outside aid was going to be exclusively a British show.

It was also Mihailovich's Chetniks who struck the first blows against the occupiers. The name *Chetnik* stems from *cheta*, or "armed band," and had been in use since the nineteenth century, when Serbian guerrillas fought the Turks. The Chetniks had been an organized nationwide group in recent years, something like a fraternal order, and many Serbian officers had been leading members.

Ironically, after the defeat the head of the official Chetniks refused to resist. This split the organization, and many local units did as they pleased. Subsequently, the Chetniks' national leadership made a deal with General Nedich's quisling government. For this reason, Mihailovich originally called his group the "Ravna Gora Movement," but Serbian tradition supplanted it in time with the older name.

In the confusion of the early days of the occupation, Mihailovich's actions were unambiguous. He had been in Bosnia when the armistice was declared. From there he avoided capture, and with a handful of men he traveled to the Ravna Gora plateau in Serbia, an ideal area for guerrilla operations.

Boris had known of Colonel Mihailovich at the Belgrade Military Academy, for the decorated veteran of the Balkan Wars and World War I had served there as an instructor. He was a Serb, forty-eight years old, and had been a military attaché in Sofia and Prague as well as a member of the General Staff.

His outspokenness was on the record. He had actually been court-martialed for refusing to withdraw a report accusing politicians of diverting funds intended for defense. That cost him ten days imprisonment and banishment to an obscure post in Bosnia. But he continued to challenge the conventional military posture and to reaffirm his staunch anti-Axis views.

It is no wonder, then, that Boris in his P.O.W. camp already thought highly of the man. But he was unaware that in the summer of 1941 the Chetniks inspired a national insurrection that almost swept the Germans out of Serbia and the Italians from Montenegro. This forced the Germans into costly counter-insurgency efforts, and their campaigns to wipe out the "bandits" began.

In December, Mihailovich had been made a general by the government-in-exile, and he was shortly to be named minister of war and commander-in-chief of all troops inside Yugoslavia. Yet the London-based government had totally failed to deliver meaningful assistance. Discussions with the British were in progress.

The Partisans, unable to ignore all these developments, were preparing their own blast of vicious propaganda. In the new year they would declare to the world that General Mihailovich was a collaborator with the Germans and a traitor.

From the beginning of the war, the British had been convinced that they would eventually win. Their valiant prime minister, Winston Churchill, had often declared this. Yet for twenty months, no sober-minded Allied observer could exactly fathom how Britain alone could challenge the Third Reich's continental empire.

This had changed. The string of Germany military successes was still largely unbroken, but Russia and the United States had joined the fight, and the familiar triumvirate of the Allies was in place. Leading a block of countries that was christened the United Nations, the Big Three had the resources, manpower, and ideological commitment to prevail. The question was no longer simply how, but when and where and with what results they would win.

The Axis powers, however, were far from finished at the end of 1941. The Germans had caught the Russians by surprise in June. Even wily Stalin hadn't believed them when his spies reported the impending attack. Now the Germans stood deep in Russia, their invasion merely slowed by the first full-scale Red Army counteroffensive.

The United States, having lost most of its Pacific fleet at Pearl Harbor in December, was unable to halt the Japanese drive in the Far East. Only the bumbling Italians had suffered defeat, and that in the minor battle for Ethiopia. There the British had propped Emperor Haile Selassie back on his throne before turning their attention to the more serious matter of General Rommel and the German troops in North Africa.

Events in Yugoslavia were necessarily remote but not unimportant to Britain and Russia. Any difficulties the Germans faced in the Balkans could delay troops and matériel bound for North Africa and indirectly might relieve some pressure on the Russian front. For that reason, London sent a liaison team to General Mihailovich, and Moscow intensified its radio contacts with the Partisans.

The overall lines of battle in World War II had been set, and the coming year of 1942 was looked to everywhere as a possible turning point. For the Allies, this in some measure proved true.

6

Escape

WE WERE ORDERED out of bed at 4:00 A.M. and ushered into the mess hall. There we were searched. Knowing what was coming, Pachany and I had spent hours in preparation, concealing our secret gear.

As the German guards worked down the rows, grumbling about the early hour, my chief concern was Lieutenant Ninkovich. He kept flashing me conspiratorial looks. Did the man have no idea of the danger? I did my best to ignore him, and again I wondered if he ought to have been excluded from our inner circle.

At seven, having passed inspection, we marched off five abreast toward the Offenburg railroad station. Although it was refreshing to be outside the compound, my heart was strangely uneasy. After nearly ten months in captivity, I was leaving behind everything familiar, including many friends and comrades, and journeying into the unknown.

The sense of dislocation was offset by the golden opportunity that now presented itself. Our plan was simple and straightforward: We'd wait till the middle of the night, then jump off the train through a freight car window. Or we'd wait for a stop and escape from a bathroom. Then we'd somehow get to the border and into France. I was afraid to imagine what new hell might await us should this scheme fail.

When we arrived at the station, a passenger train was ready

79

and waiting. An entire battalion of 200 soldiers had been assigned to accompany a mere 250 unarmed men. What a dangerous group of officers they must have thought us!

Despite the zero-degree weather, we lined up for another roll call. A German officer began to read out a list of names. "Captain Todorovich, Captain Pachany, Second Lieutenant Ninkovich, Captain Vinaver. Step forward!"

I glanced quickly at Pachany and felt the blood drain from my face. My fingers went numb. The officer marched up and down in front of the four of us, his hands clasped menacingly behind his back. "We know all about your plans! Unless you wish to die, you must forget such foolishness! Escape from us is impossible!"

My shoulders sagged and my heart seemed to slow. We hadn't even boarded the train and already we'd been caught. I couldn't believe it.

I was certain, though, that Ninkovich was to blame. Despite my warnings, he hadn't kept his mouth shut. In his imagined heroism he must have boasted about our plans to others, in what he no doubt considered the strictest confidence, and somebody had informed the Germans of our intentions. I could have strangled him then and there with my bare hands. Especially since poor Vinaver, who had no knowledge of any of this and was hardly fit for strenuous activity, was being unfairly accused.

Despite my protestations of innocence, I was seized by several soldiers, dragged onto the train, and seated between two guards in the officers' compartment. Pachany and the others were taken to different cars.

Stuck as I was, I tried to remain calm and show no fear. I largely succeeded, until a German officer entered the car and gave me the once-over. "Hand over your leather jacket," he snapped. "It looks suspicious."

"I'll freeze without it," I feebly protested. He didn't care. When I removed the jacket and gave it to him, I knew my last shot at freedom was gone. Hidden inside the pockets were the hand-drawn maps, the money, and the compass—enough incriminating material to surely hang me.

The lieutenant looked at me, hesitated, then held the jacket out before my eyes. "Go ahead. Take whatever you want out of the pockets."

How I wanted to! But I didn't. It was clearly a trap. "That's all right. There's nothing in them," I said as politely and nonchalantly as possible.

Abruptly, the German left the compartment, the jacket slung over his arm. He hadn't bothered to search it . . . yet.

Shivering with cold, I wrapped my arms around myself and waited. Nothing happened. Then with a jerk the train started up. Offenburg soon disappeared behind us.

The trip seemed endless. I couldn't sleep, so I studied the tired faces of the guards beside me. They didn't look anything like the proud, ferocious soldiers who had conquered Yugoslavia a year ago.

Had the Germans had enough of war? We knew they were still fighting the tenacious Russians. I dared to hope that Russia's terrible winter had undermined the invincibility of the German armies. From what we prisoners saw, it was obvious that no one wanted to go to the eastern front.

As the train sped on through the day and into the night, the guards watching me grew less and less attentive. The rhythm of the wheels seemed to propel my thoughts along, and I couldn't stop thinking about escaping. I wondered how Pachany was faring—if they'd taken his coat, too, or if he'd been interrogated.

The guards dozed. I could slip away right then, I decided. No, without Pachany and the jacket, the risk was too high. My chance was slipping away. *Lost opportunity.* The words were stuck in my mind. *Lost opportunity . . .*

The train pulled into the Marzfeld station at Nuremburg at nine the next morning. We had reached our destination, and although we had traveled only 250 miles, it had taken us almost twenty-four hours. The German railroads were obviously being overtaxed.

Stepping off the train and into the cold, I shivered at the sight of the deep snow. Then I saw Pachany and the German lieutenant. He had my leather jacket with him. A brief glance from Pachany told me all I needed to know. As inexplicably as the jacket had been taken, it was being returned. Even before I put it on, I felt much warmer.

When the lieutenant was well out of sight, I checked inside the secret pockets. Miraculously, everything was intact. God had been with me once more.

My first impressions of Offlag 13-B were painfully depressing. The Nuremburg camp had blackened wood barracks, frozen wash troughs, and open-air latrines. The unbearable cold prevented anyone from washing, and lice were epidemic.

Worst of all was the condition of the P.O.W.s. They had pale unshaven faces, hollow cheeks, and long grubby hair. Their tattered clothes and feet wrapped in rags gave such a picture of misery that I shuddered at what was in store for us.

Pachany and I were assigned to a barracks in the seventh block. The room was in permanent semidarkness, the wind blew freely through the cracks in the walls, and the potbellied stove barely functioned. The prisoner kitchen was filthy and the food barely edible. It was no surprise to learn that the camp's mortality rate was very high.

Thanks to our previous experiences with German hospitality, we rapidly settled into the routines of the new, larger camp. I was again amazed at human adaptability to inhuman conditions. Somehow, life always continues.

Despite warnings of the consequences from our fellow prisoners, Pachany and I began anew to assess the possibilities for escape. This time, however, we excluded Lieutenant Ninkovich from our planning. From then on, it would be just the two of us.

Our first goal was to learn more about the immediate surroundings. We tried volunteering for work outside the camp, but no positions were available. Finally, we were forced to spend some of our precious money to bribe one of the regular workers.

Pachany was able to switch places with him and spend a day digging ditches.

After his foray, he was optimistic. "It can be done, Bora, if only we can find a way out of camp. The watch on the outside is very lax. But we must have identification papers, in case we are stopped."

That was our next task. We found a prisoner who retouched the photos taken from our military I.D. cards so that we appeared to be wearing civilian clothes. Another good soul, an engineer, ingeniously forged an official German seal using a pocket knife and a raw potato as the stamper. From a friend in the camp's command office, we got typed working papers. To these, we affixed our photos and authenticated them with the seal so as to pass for Croatian volunteer workers. Along with the I.D.s, an official letter was in preparation that would state that we were factory workers being sent from Nuremburg to Cologne.

Yet for all our progress, no matter how hard we tried, we couldn't find a way to get outside of Offlag 13-B. There were simply no openings for day laborers, and no other prison work would get us beyond the fence.

Stymied, we even took the incautious step of approaching a prisoner who worked in the hospital outside the compound. He wasn't willing to help us.

Then, in late March, opportunity unexpectedly arose. As evening fell, the lights along the fence failed to come on. It grew completely dark. And still no lights.

Pachany and I read each other's minds. Acting on the spur of the moment, we ran to the barracks, changed into our civilian attire, and grabbed our packed bags. Even though our phony papers were incomplete, we couldn't let another chance go by.

We made it over to the northeast gate undetected and waited for the guard to pass on his rounds. Timing his moves, we had maybe five minutes before he returned. There was no time to waste.

Crawling to the gate, we began cutting the barbed wire with a recently purchased pair of scissors. My hands were shaking. I was afraid even to breathe. We got through the first strand—two more left.

The lights came back on.

We lay still, petrified. A searchlight beam swept just over our heads. Slowly, so slowly, we edged away from the wire. Then we stood up and ran as fast as we could for the nearest barracks.

From building to building, we somehow scampered to our own room unobserved. Quickly, we changed back into our prison clothes and hid our escape gear.

My heart was still pounding, but my brain was icy calm. As I sat down on the crude bunk, I turned to Pachany. Tersely, I spoke: "We can't leave that wire cut, Pacha. Our attempt must remain a secret. We have to go back." He knew I was right.

Using all the stealth possible, we returned to the gate. The guard went by, and I crawled again to the fence to rejoin the severed barbed wire. Twisting it together, my fingers bled. When I finished, Pachany and I were like ghosts as we fled to the barracks.

Another opportunity, another failure. At night's end, we were no closer to escape than we'd been before. We needed patience, I knew, but the way things were going, the war would be over before we ever saw the last of German soil. The frustration was practically unbearable.

Good fortune did not completely desert us. A month later, a thousand prisoners—by German lights, the cream of the Yugoslav incorrigibles—were scheduled to be transferred, possibly to Osnabruck, Germany, or to a camp in Poland.

Pachany and I were on the list. To me, this was an unlooked-for reprieve. Fate had granted us another chance, and this time I swore everything would go right.

My resolve notwithstanding, everything at first went wrong. Time was already short. The transfer was set for May 6, and two days before, the fellow in the commandant's office still hadn't been able to type up our phony working papers.

Also, I had bought a civilian overcoat from another prisoner.

Unexpectedly, he came to me and begged to buy it back. I had no honorable choice but to return the coat. Disappointed and alarmed, I scoured the entire camp in search of a replacement but was stuck with my military-style leather jacket.

Perhaps because I knew fewer of the men in Offlag 13-B, the farewells were even more painful. Chief among my friends here was Major Mikota, my former battalion commander in Kraljevo. He was the one man I trusted enough to occasionally hint of our plans, but I don't believe he ever took me seriously.

"Be patient, Bora," he advised. "Why risk your life? In a year or so we'll all be free."

"I can't wait that long."

"Then, here, take this. It is of no use to me."

With that, he handed me his lucky U.S. dollar bill. During his retreat from the Germans, it had been given to him by an American military attaché he'd crossed paths with in Loznica. It was his only possession worth anything.

Tears rolled down my cheeks. I was so overwhelmed by Mikota's generosity that I couldn't speak. Silently, I hugged my old friend.

The next morning, a day before we expected it, the transfer P.O.W.s were separated out. We found ourselves confined in block one without any way to communicate with the rest of the camp. Pachany and I were frantic. We'd learned that our documents were finally typed and ready. But the Germans had labeled our group dangerous Communists and watched us closely.

We had to have those papers. At nightfall of an ironically beautiful spring day, we took matters into our own hands. Joined by several other prisoners (for reasons of their own), we all assembled surreptitiously near the barbed wire behind the central latrine. One prisoner with a pair of pliers knew what to do. He expertly cut the wire.

Easing cautiously through the gap in the razor-sharp barbs, one by one we passed into block two and the rest of the camp. While I hid in our former barracks, Pachany went off in search of the forger. Major Mikota was glad to see me one last time and insisted on preparing a final meal for us out of his precious food reserves.

Good old Mikota. I wondered when I'd ever again eat something half as good as his plate of beans. In a little while, Pachany returned, waving the long-awaited documents. He joined the feast. Then we bid the major a hurried last farewell and crossed back through the fence.

Four days passed. My nerves were on edge as we waited in block one for the Germans to do something. Finally, five days late by the original schedule, we were lined up and read the rules of transport.

Prisoners were to be transported in boxcars with two armed guards.

Prisoners were not permitted to leave the train, to move within the car, or to approach any door or window.

Prisoners were not permitted to address the guards.

Prisoners who disobeyed the instructions would be shot.

The Germans were nothing if not thorough. The next day, the transfer process commenced with an inspection. Nobody could exit block one without a complete scrutiny of his personal effects. This was a critical moment. The game would be up if our escape gear were detected.

When Pachany presented himself for inspection, I hung back. After he breezed through, he ran around to the latrine on the other side of the dividing fence between the blocks. I had meanwhile slipped between the barracks on my side and waited only for an opportune moment to toss the gear over the fence.

To my consternation, the guard on duty in that section lit a cigarette and stood by the fence smoking it. As I watched impatiently, I willed him to move away from the fence, but he refused to budge. If Pachany stayed much longer in the latrine, it was sure to arouse suspicion.

At last, the guard had barely walked off when I sprinted to the fence and tossed the escape gear over. Pachany immediately emerged to grab it. With only the slightest turn of his head, the guard could have caught us right in the act.

Thankfully, his eyes stayed glued ahead of him like some well-disciplined soldier on the parade grounds. I breathed a sigh of relief. Pachany and I had survived another step.

When it was my turn at the inspection table, one of the sergeants looked at me askance. Then he asked me in a low mutter, "Are you really a Communist?"

I wasn't sure how to answer. It was a question I never thought to hear from an ordinary German soldier without at least some accompanying profanity. Was this man perhaps a Communist sympathizer?

I knew there had been supposedly some nine million Communists in Germany before the war, and I'd heard rumors that the German Army was infiltrated. Should the Nazi war machine ever falter, I suspected these would be the first men who'd look to a different future.

None of the other inspectors had heard the question. I flipped a mental coin in my head. "Yes," I replied boldly, looking the sergeant in the eyes.

"Okay, pass on." He waved me by without another word and without looking through any of my belongings. I couldn't believe it.

In contrast to our bleak arrival in Nuremburg, our departure was almost joyous. From the camp, the transfer group marched to the Marzfeld station. The sun shone brightly as we trudged past peasants tending the well-cultivated fields and workers coming home from the factories.

It really was spring. We were outside the barbed wire. Life was going on as usual.

Everyone breathed more deeply and felt energized by the momentary release from imprisonment. When we reached the station and were milling about, some men actually broke out in Serbian song and danced the *kolo* until the guards clamped down on our "foolishness." Then the inevitable roll call commenced.

On a siding, we could see the dilapidated cattle cars of the transport train. They were of a typical European design that we knew well. On each side was a sliding door wide enough to load animals. Down the middle of the car ran a row of pillars supporting the roof, while high up on either side were small ventilation windows. These were flush to the roofline and abutted the front and rear walls.

When the train's whistle blew, armed guards crammed forty men at a time into these cars. In ours, Pachany and I found ourselves squashed toward the middle. There were a few benches, but most of us had to sit on the floor with the bundles that contained all our worldly goods.

The slatted door to our right was locked. The other stayed partly open but had an iron security bar to block the opening. Here the two German guards accompanying us took up their post.

As the men settled down, Pachany and I couldn't help but stare at the small windows at the car ends. They were barless, and through one we glimpsed a patch of blue sky and the setting sun.

The German guards ordered everybody not to speak or move about. An oppressive silence descended, and it made the air feel even heavier. With another long whistle, the train began to roll. It picked up speed. Soon only the idle conversation of the guards punctuated the wheels' monotonous click-clack.

Practically counting off each minute, I waited for the sun to set. It was taking forever, or so it seemed. At last, the light faded away, and most of the prisoners soon dozed off.

The night was black and moonless. It was so dark that I could barely make out the guards' silhouettes as they leaned against the half-open door. Save for the occasional flicker of their cigarettes, the car appeared lifeless.

I gave Pachany a shake. He understood, and we quietly started changing into our civilian garb. Afraid of making the slightest sound, I squirmed into my clothes inch by inch. The simple act of dressing took an eternity, but I finally managed to don my striped trousers, my sweater, and my leather jacket.

The train was moving at great speed. The rear window, our chosen target, was very small. And the guards were no more than a dozen feet away. Only a madman would attempt such an escape—the notion made me almost laugh aloud.

Around midnight, the whistle blew as the train entered a tunnel. The car was plunged into absolute darkness. This was it. The perfect moment.

Stepping carefully over sleeping men, Pachany and I made our way to the rear. There I gently woke two of our fellow officers. My request was simple: I asked them to spread their blanket like a curtain from the car wall to a middle pillar. This would partly conceal us should a guard strike a match to light his cigarette. They complied gladly, despite the risk.

The train had emerged from the tunnel. I could see a handful of stars through the rear window. Pachany and I were both ready, but who would go first?

With a supple move, Pachany took it upon himself to climb through. It was an incredibly brave thing to do. To just imagine such a thing—given the speed of the train, the pitch black conditions, the utterly unknown terrain—would send a chill down the spine of any reasonable soul.

After he disappeared, it was my turn. My whole body was bathed in sweat as I grabbed the lower edge of the window and pulled myself up. Above the improvised curtain I could again see the shadowy figure of the nearer guard. A strange fascination gripped me: he seemed almost close enough to touch.

Somehow, I couldn't move. With an act of sheer will, I made myself turn and wriggle through the window. I felt a sharp blast of air against my damp forehead. Then I was completely out.

I held on for dear life, suspended against the cattle car's side as the train hurtled on into the night. The speed was frightening. I judged it to be maybe 50 mph. There was no sign of Pachany. For all I knew, he'd fallen to the tracks and was already dead.

With a jolt of pain, I became instantly conscious of the severe ache in my arms and the cold sweat trickling down my sides. I didn't know what to do. If I simply jumped, I would certainly die. I couldn't hold on much longer.

As the train took a curve, I swung back and forth. The motion and the bitter night air sent another wave of pain through my body. I doubted I had the strength left to pull myself back through the window, even if I wanted to.

Suddenly, my right foot felt something. I stretched my leg to plant a toe firmly on the small protrusion. It must be a rung in the ladder fixed to the side of the car and running up to the roof, I reasoned. Now, if only I could get a hand on it. *If* it was the ladder.

I took a deep breath, let go of the window sill with my right hand, and grabbed out. My fingers curled around a metal bar. I was right. With the strength of desperation, I pulled my whole body onto the ladder.

Safely perched outside the car at the rear corner, I dared to look around. To my left, I could see the half-open door. One of the guards stood smoking, his cigarette a glowing red dot.

Around to my right, I could peer in between my car and the one behind. I knew that was where I had to go. Besides the massive center coupling beyond reach, there were large round bumpers that projected out from each car. From these, it would be another step onto the narrow wooden platform that partially extended over the coupling. That was the only place I could ride in some safety until I got a chance to jump.

Carefully, I climbed down the ladder, my face and body pressed tightly against the car. At the bottom, I held on to a rung and swung myself around the corner. I got a foot on a bumper and groped about with my free hand. There were gaps in the rough planking, but a secure grip eluded me, and I didn't dare let go of the ladder.

Just when it seemed hopeless, somebody took my arm and pulled me forward. It was Pachany. Standing together on the little platform between the cars, we hugged each other emotionally. Our luck had held so far.

Yet we had no idea where we were. Barely discernible to our eyes, thick forests stretched away on both sides of the tracks. At all costs, we knew we had to get off the train. To be discovered now or when the train stopped meant a death sentence.

Leaning out beyond the car from our perch, Pachany could see a red signal light in the distance. There must be a station ahead. Ten minutes later, the train began to slow.

Within our limited sightlines, a control tower appeared and was gone.

"Let's go," I yelled to Pachany over the noise. There was nothing more to be said. We embraced. Then we jumped from the moving train into the darkness.

I hit the ground hard and rolled onto some sharp gravel. The wind was knocked out of me, but I was alive. We were both alive.

Ignoring the pain from my scraped and bleeding hands and knees, I scrambled to my feet. Pachany was nearby, and I helped him up. Instinct took over.

Like wild animals pursued by a predator, we fled. The train had stopped at the station, the last place we wanted to be near, so we turned away from the tracks. Crawling under several parked trains, we emerged to find a brick wall blocking our way.

The wall was six feet high, but wings of fear made that of little concern. Pachany was already to the top and I was scrambling after him when somebody yelled in the distance: "Halt! Halt!" I had just gone over when a shot rang out.

A hundred yards further was some sleepy German town. We had to get our bearings quickly. Given what we'd seen from the train, we were probably on the town's southern edge.

"Walk, don't run. Turn to the right," I said in a low voice to Pachany, believing this would take us away from the populated area.

We turned onto a large, well-paved street that was very dimly lit. It reminded me of a ghost town boulevard. We kept walking, our shoes on the pavement the only sound in the still night.

The street seemed to go on forever. It was deserted, so much so that at first I thought the man approaching us was an apparition. Then I saw him clearly—a night watchman.

My whole body tensed. We could not run but had to continue

walking toward him. When we were a few feet away, I raised my hand and called out: "Heil Hitler!" Pachany followed suit.

"Heil Hitler," the man responded mechanically as he continued on his rounds.

I breathed a deep sigh of relief. We were soaked with perspiration, exhausted from our mental and physical effort, but alive with the sheer joy of escape. However, it was no time to relax or to let down our guard. We pressed on.

Past the last of the houses, the street became a path that skirted a plowed field and headed up a small hill. At the hilltop we found ourselves with a good view of the railroad station. We saw the train and heard shouting men and dogs barking wildly. As we watched, searchlights continually crisscrossed the area. They were looking for us.

We had to hide immediately. Not far away, Pachany discovered a ditch several feet deep. We hunkered down in this hole, covered ourselves with branches, and waited.

When I heard the sound of an approaching motorcycle, I had a spasm of shivers. We pressed ourselves into the damp ground as the headlight bounced around directly over us. The cycle prowled about the hill awhile, then sped off.

After an hour, the search began to peter out. A few more distant shouts, and it was over. Cautiously crawling from the ditch, we watched the train pull out of the station. I looked at my watch. It was 1:00 A.M.

Pachany handed me a hardened piece of marmalade. "To our escape," he toasted, smiling.

We both ate hungrily. Even though we were in the middle of nowhere and far from our goal, we felt intoxicated with our initial success. We were free of our captors and the oppressive P.O.W. train.

This time, luck really had been on our side.

7

On the Run

WE HAD TO figure out our next move. Looking at our crude map by the light of a match, we tried in vain to determine our position. Pachany and I didn't know it then, but on the early morning of May 13, 1942, we had escaped to the outskirts of Würzburg, Bavaria.

After a while, we gave up reading the map as futile. We were in agreement, however, that it was far too dangerous to head immediately for the border. That was just what the Nazis would expect. Since the stations up the line would also be swarming with soldiers and Gestapo, we decided our best bet was to follow the railroad tracks *back* toward Nuremburg. The Germans would never imagine that anyone was crazy enough to flee in precisely the direction of the prison camp he'd come from.

Traveling only at night, we'd hide out in the forest during the day. At the first station reached, we would catch a train for Frankfurt. From there, we had long planned to attempt the border crossing into France after help and counsel from Pachany's uncle.

Our decision was made. Confidently, we set out to return to the railroad tracks. But locating them was to prove no easy task. It was very dark, and we were essentially lost.

The paved road I thought would bring us close to the tracks went back into town, the last place we wanted to be. We tried again. Altering course, we reached a park where the road branched. We took the right fork, a worn road bordered with tall trees.

After walking for almost another half hour, I became uneasy. Instead of finding the train tracks or an open field, we were hearing the sound of water. Ten yards more and we realized our mistake. Directly ahead of us loomed a heavily guarded power plant.

Once more, we hurriedly turned to the right and began to cross a plowed field. A flickering red light in the distance had caught our attention. Perhaps it was a track signal.

As I strained to make out the terrain, we stumbled over soft furrows of soil and irrigation ditches. Pachany, his eyeglasses covered with sweat, tried to jump one of the bigger ditches and misjudged it. He fell headlong into the shallow water. In good spirits, we both laughed, but it wasn't that funny. Especially when I dropped my pack as I was helping him out. Retrieving it, I got as wet as he was.

Finally, we found the tracks. There they were, the signal we'd seen all along marking a switch on the main line. Using the compass, we checked and rechecked which was the way to Nuremburg. Then we started walking.

Soon the night ran its course and the first timid streaks of dawn brushed the sky. As the daylight spread, we could see the deep woods and the thick underbrush. For our sakes, I hoped the forest would live up to its folk reputation as the mother of fugitives.

Utterly drained, we left the tracks, went into the forest, and picked a hide-out for the day. I crawled into the middle of a thicket, cleared some ground, and spread my leather jacket. Pachany and I then stretched out on it and covered ourselves with his coat.

I lay there patiently, knowing I should sleep, but my wet body and excited mind were not conducive. We talked about our exploit. With satisfaction, we pictured the ire of the camp commander when he learned of the escape, and we readily concluded the worst was over.

As the sun rose higher, the forest started to buzz with activity. All around, I heard the sounds of farmers, of axes on wood, of dogs barking playfully. Perhaps the forest did have a protecting charm, for no one ventured near us.

The day grew warm. At least it would dry our clothes. My thoughts grew jumbled, and I sank at last into a sweet sleep and dreamed of my mother in Belgrade.

It was 2:00 P.M. when I awoke. My mouth was terribly dry, my lips cracked. We had not had anything to drink since we left Nuremburg. Yet until it was dark, Pachany and I had to endure our thirst.

The hours seemed to crawl. I could think of nothing but water. Around six, the forest calmed. Twilight came, and the first signs of night reappeared.

We waited another hour, then resumed our march beside the tracks. Crackling twigs beneath our feet made the only sound. Not more than a half mile farther, we spied a clear creek. Its waters were a gift of God to parched throats. We quenched our thirst, shaved, took some bites from the food reserve, and set out again.

Shortly after eight, the tracks led us to a nearly deserted station in the village of Strulendorf. The little train station reminded me of a children's book illustration.

In a few words, we decided what to do. Pachany went inside to purchase tickets, while I sat down on a bench by the water well and tried to look as if I belonged there. Some idling peasant women watched me curiously. I realized how odd I must seem to them, garbed in dressy trousers, soldier's shoes, and a pullover. I ignored their stares until Pachany returned.

"When are we leaving?" I asked at once, seeing the tickets in his hand.

"In several hours."

"What time do we arrive in Frankfurt?"

"We're not going to Frankfurt, Bora."

"What? What do you mean?"

"We're going to Nuremburg."

"Nuremburg?" I couldn't believe my ears. "What do you mean Nuremburg, Pacha?" For a moment, I felt we were about to deliver ourselves right back to the camp doorstep.

Pachany looked grim. "There isn't a Frankfurt train through here until late tomorrow. In Nuremburg, we can make a much earlier connection. We've got to get out of here."

Like a drunk man stepping into cold night air, I was suddenly sobered. Perhaps the search was called off, but we were still wanted men. I understood then the decision Pachany had been forced to make. No matter what, we must keep on the move, either by foot or by rail. Given that choice, Pachany was right. It was better to ride to Nuremburg than walk the local roads.

Our escape from the P.O.W. train had in reality been no escape at all. Rather, we had exchanged a cattle car prison for an entire country. We were on the loose in Nazi Germany, and every friendly-looking face could just as easily be someone glad to dutifully turn us in or too scared not to.

For the first time, I truly realized that the fate of our escape attempt was largely out of our hands. There was nothing more to do but pray. And wait for the next train.

The midnight train rolled into the little station with a deafening roar and came to a stop. Pachany and I were the sole passengers to board. Hurriedly, we entered a third-class car.

Although the window shades were tightly drawn, inside the car was brightly illuminated. As we made our way in search of seats, the other passengers hardly calmed our sense of unease. There were many soldiers who scrutinized us carefully, while the civilians glanced at us and turned away.

There were no seats together, so we were forced to split up. Sitting down beside a young, well-dressed woman, I accidentally sat on the edge of her overcoat. Angrily, she pulled it back, giving me the most contemptuous look. I mumbled an apology and tried to shrink into my seat.

Feigning sleep, I observed those around me. The noisy chatter when we first boarded had subsided to whispers. The officers in the seat behind me were talking about us.

Opposite me, a fat German with a Hitler pin in his lapel was studying my clothes disdainfully. Several rows farther down, I could see Pachany. His traveling companions looked no happier than mine.

The ticket collector went down the aisle. He exchanged hushed remarks with several officers and eyed me carefully as he took my ticket. Closing my eyes tight, I fought back paranoia and tried to doze.

I heard nothing else until the conductor barked "Nuremburg!" I could hardly believe we were back.

Pachany and I looked at each other, rose from our seats, and headed for the exit. The conductor blocked us with outstretched arms. "You must wait till the train comes to a complete stop," he said.

When the wheels stopped rolling, the conductor slowly opened the car door and went out. I followed him, head bowed, eyes fixed on the three descending steps. Pachany was right behind me.

As I stepped onto the platform, a heavy hand fell on my shoulder. My heart leaped into my throat. I turned and found myself dumbly staring at two tall Germans with Gestapo insignia on their sleeves. With the men were a pair of huge Dobermans, the dogs straining on their leashes.

This is the end, I thought.

"*Ihre papieren!*" one of them snapped at me. Without hesitating, I pulled my forged I.D. papers from my pocket and handed them over. Pachany followed suit.

Standing there with one foot in the grave, I trembled as the wet nose of a dog brushed against my hand. The rest of the passengers alighting from the train showed no interest in the scene as the Gestapo agents examined our papers intently in the dim blue lights of the station. (Thanks to the threat of British R.A.F. bombings, the station was under a blackout order.)

For the life of me, I couldn't understand why they didn't use flashlights. From time to time, the agents raised their eyes, comparing our I.D. photos to our faces. It was obvious they couldn't make up their minds.

"We need help, not harassment." I don't know where I found the courage to speak. "We left our home to work here."

"To contribute to the war effort," Pachany chimed in. "But instead you treat us like common criminals."

"We don't know the country or your language well," I added plaintively. "Please, help us find the train to Cologne and . . ."

"You must understand," one Gestapo interrupted. "We must be watchful. There are characters around who don't share our feelings about the Reich."

The two men examined the papers again and whispered to each other. Then their expressions changed. "Everything is in order." He handed us back our papers. "Pleasant journey." With that, they reeled in the dogs and were gone.

The forged documents had passed the test. It was a break few escapees ever dreamed of. Hiding any visible signs of relief, Pachany and I blended into the sparse crowd as quickly as we could.

At the information booth, we checked the timetables. The next train for Frankfurt departed at 4:00 A.M. We purchased our tickets and calmly left the station. We had about two hours to kill, too long to hang around the waiting room without tempting further suspicion.

The city was blacked out. We had nowhere to go. *Keep moving*, I thought. *Keep moving*. My whole body was crying out for rest. *Keep moving*.

Pachany and I were so exhausted we could barely stand on our feet. On a dark, quiet street around the corner from the station, we could go no farther. We sat on the cold ground and leaned our backs against a building wall.

We decided to take turns resting. I took the first watch, though what I could have done if anyone had come along, I don't know. Pachany slumped to the ground and in a second was sound asleep. I sat there watching the minute hand of my watch creep along.

When it was my turn, I woke Pachany and instantly took his place. The next thing I knew, his hand was shaking me. It was 3:45 A.M. We had to return to the station.

In the dead of night, military personnel were milling everywhere on the platforms. We managed to find our train. It was a *Schnell Zug*, an express, originating in Vienna and bound for Frankfurt and Paris.

Boarding, we walked up and down in search of an empty compartment. None was available. Passengers were already standing in the corridors. Finally, I spotted a second-class compartment where a couple of Luftwaffe officers were stretched out asleep. Although they took up two seats apiece, no one had dared disturb them.

Even after a brief nap, I was too tired to stand. Besides, out in the corridor, we risked having the train's conductors inspect us repeatedly as they went back and forth.

I opened the compartment door. The two officers didn't move. Leaning over, I touched the shoulder of the nearest one. He opened his eyes and looked at me in disbelief.

"We are volunteer laborers," I explained politely. "Can we share the compartment?" I remembered that, to our amusement, the Nuremburg station had posters plastered on its walls that glorified volunteer laborers. I was being bold, but German propaganda was not ineffective with its own brainwashed people.

Without a word, the young officer straightened up and slid over on the seat to the window. He woke his friend, who also moved, although he was far from happy about it. He looked at us as if we were scum.

After Pachany and I tossed our jackets in the overhead rack, we took our seats casually. Two days ago, we were in a German prison camp. Today, we rode pleasantly with officers of the German air force. With a strange feeling of unreality, I settled in for the journey to Frankfurt.

The huge Frankfurt train station was a maze of tracks, platforms, and underpasses. Thoroughly confused, it took us a while to exit this labyrinth and reach the city streets.

If we had been exhilarated by our success so far, our spirits now soared. In the bright light of an early May morning, Frankfurt looked like paradise. Shops were open for business, children were rushing to school along the wide and tidy avenues, and the townspeople appeared neat and friendly.

Everything seemed so normal. There was not a single trace of the war. The impression we got of a strong Germany implied that the Allies' troubles were far from over.

Pachany led the way across the city and I strolled some fifty yards behind him. We wanted no repetition of the Gestapo incident at Nuremburg. There was no sense putting both our lives in jeopardy if one of us was nabbed.

Our subsequent moves were greatly dependent on the helping hand of Pachany's uncle. As agreed, Pachany headed for his uncle's house while I ducked into a café. There I sipped ersatz coffee, buried my head in a newspaper, and waited.

When Pachany returned, I could tell from his face that something was wrong. Whatever it was, he wouldn't tell me in the café.

Out in the street, he confided distressing news. "I couldn't believe it, Bora. When my uncle saw me, he nearly collapsed in fear. He implored me to get out of town. Imagine, my own uncle." Pachany shook his head. "He was scared to death."

"The Gestapo?"

Pachany nodded slowly. "The last time I escaped he was questioned. Now they've threatened to imprison him if he doesn't cooperate and report any contact with us."

"He won't help us then." I said it flatly, knowing it left us in a real fix. We were almost out of money and food.

"For a moment, I really thought not." Pachany paused, waiting for some people coming out of the café to get out of earshot. "Bora, I was saying good-bye when my aunt came in and burst out crying. She fell to her knees and begged Uncle to help me. He agreed, on condition we leave Frankfurt immediately."

It was better than nothing. Everything considered, Pachany couldn't ask his uncle to take us in. The risk to him and his family was too great.

"What then?" I asked. We couldn't stand here talking on the sidewalk much longer, I thought.

"He advises we head directly to Metz and continue from there on foot to the French border," Pachany explained. "My cousin is going to meet me at midnight in the park opposite the city hall with food, money, and clothes for us."

"Midnight?"

"Yes. The next train doesn't leave till three in the morning."

That meant filling some very long hours without arousing suspicion or running into the Gestapo. Privately, I had another concern. I couldn't tell Pachany, but I prayed that his uncle wasn't actually setting us up for a midnight arrest.

In Frankfurt, there was no real place to hide. Even the city hall park was wide open to view. Buying a local map, we noted a forest area that should have been more secluded. It was in the nearby town of Offenbach.

We hopped a trolley and were there in a half hour. The "forest" turned out to be a beautifully groomed park with rows of pruned trees, flower beds on grassy knolls, and winding foot and bicycle paths. Very lovely and very German, an ideal spot for a Sunday stroll or a lovers' tryst, but an unsatisfactory hide-out for escaped prisoners. We were sorely disappointed.

Without any better option, we returned to downtown Frankfurt. The excursion to the park had left us exhausted again. After months of prison life, the normal physical reserves Pachany and I had always possessed just didn't exist. We were burned out.

Combing the area around the city hall, we found a movie theater. Thank God for double features. We slept our way through nearly four hours straight of Italian comedies.

By the time the houselights came back up and we had to leave, the streets were dark. That left an evening yet to kill. Feeling more dirty and grimy than ever, we returned to the railroad station and went to its public washroom.

In the washroom, I stood motionless in front of a mirror, mesmerized. I hadn't seen an accurate reflection of myself in over a year. The face in the mirror had hollow cheeks, a curved nose, and a well-formed mouth with a slightly drooping lower lip. It was like looking at a stranger. But it was my own blue eyes that held me the most. Although bloodshot, they glowed with a haunted intensity.

Having washed as best we could, we made our way back to the park to await Pachany's cousin. Separating to be somewhat less conspicuous, I stayed in a spot as far from the rendezvous point as feasible. On a secluded bench, I felt safe enough to stretch out and close my eyes.

Resting, I fell into a half sleep, but I woke instantly when a sudden weight settled on my stomach. I jumped up like a frightened animal, only to see a terrified couple running away, hand in hand. Poor young lovers, they'd chosen the wrong bench for romance tonight. In the darkness, they had sat down on top of me.

I would have laughed if I hadn't been so unnerved. The park no longer felt safe to me, and I paced aimlessly. *Keep moving, keep moving,* I told myself. When the occasional late-night stroller walked by, I shrank back into the shadows.

It was after 2:00 A.M., a scant hour before the train was to leave, and there was no sign of Pachany. I was worried. What if the cousin hadn't shown up? We didn't have enough money to get to Metz, our jumping-off point to the border.

Or worse, what if something had happened to Pachany? I wanted to race across the park and find him, but I knew we could easily miss each other in the dark. I had to wait.

At last, I heard a soft whistle. It was Pachany's. Thank goodness! I could just make him out as he came closer.

"Are you all right?" I said.

"Fine. Look."

He showed me food, money, and maps, then handed me a

hat and an overcoat similar to the ones he now wore. Never in my adult life had I worn a civilian hat. Well, there was a first time for everything.

"What took you so long?"

"My aunt insisted on seeing me a last time. I had to go to the house with my cousin." He did not elaborate.

I sensed he was troubled. The sight of his relatives must have evoked many memories of life before the war. I had to be a realist. Here was all the more reason for us to get out of Frankfurt, before sentiment clouded our judgment.

The huge train station was like a tomb so very early in the morning. Confident in our new outfits, we walked right up to a window and purchased tickets to Metz. Pachany was mostly silent and pensive, and I left him to his thoughts as we boarded the train.

By mid-morning, we had reached Vormos. There we had to change trains for Metz. Pacing the tiny platform as we waited, I noticed a group of laborers digging about the tracks. They had sunken cheeks and were dressed in worn-out clothes. I saw that for every actual swing of a pick or shovel, they took up endless minutes inspecting their tools.

I drew closer and heard them speaking Serbo-Croatian. These were fellow P.O.W.s. They were swearing like disgruntled whores, cursing everything under the sun. My heart went out to them.

The rest of the trip, I thought with pleasure of that work gang cursing the master race under their noses.

The Germans were no better liked in Metz. Although the town was officially absorbed into the Reich in 1940, when the international border was shifted some miles to the west, its inhabitants remained defiantly French in spirit.

Arriving in the late morning, Pachany and I went into the nearest café. We ordered our first hot meals in days, bowls of meatless potato soup served without bread. In Metz, we expected additional aid. The word in the Offenburg camp was to seek out the Café du Sport. There, it was said, we could find people who helped escapees.

As we were paying the bill, Pachany indiscreetly asked the proprietor for the café's address. Everyone turned to look at us. The owner stammered out a few unintelligible words.

Something was very wrong. A young man standing behind us whispered in French, "Café du Sport was closed long ago by the authorities." Without waiting for our change, I grabbed Pachany by the sleeve and urged him out the door.

As soon as we were outside, Pachany's long face showed remorse. He knew anybody could have been in there, a German or an informer, but the question had been on his mind. He had blurted it out before he could stop himself.

I told him to forget it. I'd felt my own suspicious guard slipping in the French ambience. But we had better shape up. On the plus side, at least we knew not to poke around in search of the Café du Sport. That might well have brought the Gestapo down on our heads.

Creatures of the night that we had become, we spent the rest of the day lounging. Thanks to the money from Pachany's uncle, we passed several hours in the public bath, had a shave and haircut at the local barber, and got our clothes pressed at a tailor's shop. We looked far more presentable, no longer obvious vagabonds.

A bookstore attracted my attention. We went in. While browsing the shelves, I discovered, of all things, a military map of Metz and the vicinity. I bought it at once.

The map showed everything: topography, fortifications, roads, streams, forests. And it marked out the new border. I couldn't have been more surprised if someone had handed me a top-secret German document.

As the afternoon shadows lengthened, we boarded a streetcar to the northern edge of the city, then continued warily on foot along the road to Thionville. Fortunately, except for a farmer or two, it was deserted.

After walking a half hour, we turned west on a side road. The unpaved lane wound through green fields and rose gradually into the hills. Even though it was the middle of May, the land reminded me of early spring back home. The smell of flower blooms was intoxicating.

As the sun's last rays faded out, we rested under the branches of a large tree. I spread out the new map on the ground and examined it. The names of the villages and hamlets were, oddly enough, familiar to me from my college study of the Franco-Prussian War of 1870.

Gravelotte, Saint Privat, Amanvillere, Leipzig, Metz. In school, they had seemed mythical, mere dots on a map that changed hands between the attacking Prussians and the defending French. Now they were all real places to be avoided if we wanted to get across the frontier.

I tried to guess where the border guards were least likely to be posted. A hilly area north of the village of Leipzig and south of Amanvillere seemed inaccessible and might be a good choice. I hoped so. We were betting our lives on it.

On the map, I targeted a border crossing point in that area, measured the azimuth, and using our compass I plotted a course. The terrain might get rough, but we'd have to chance it.

I calculated the border to be nine miles away.

Pachany and I waited until the full moon rose on the horizon. "Let's go," I said simply. Without another word, we got up and began the trek.

The ground ascended gradually and we moved without much hindrance. Higher on the hillside, we spotted barracks in the distance with several trucks parked alongside. Whoever was there, under the pale moonlight the buildings seemed sinister.

The climb became progressively harder. The woods grew thicker, and the moonlight was unable to penetrate the foliage. Pushing through the ground cover of thorny bushes, our hands and legs were soon scratched and bleeding. Crevices half hidden by brushwood made each step perilous.

Out of nowhere, a row of barbed wire stopped me cold. Slowly I eased through, but not without a few jabs. Following behind,

Pachany was swearing like a drunken sailor. He wanted to turn back and find an easier route, but I refused to deviate from the plotted course. We went forward.

The ground was hard and even under my feet. Too even. I realized I was standing on a concrete slab. It looked to be some artillery gun placement for one of the old forts around Metz. If we pushed on farther this way, we were bound to hit the main buildings, and they were probably in use by the German border troops.

Pachany was just coming out of the barbed wire. I said softly to him, "We are in an old fort compound. We have to go back immediately."

"I thought so," he panted. "Only I knew your stubbornness would keep us going. Don't deviate an inch, even if it takes us into disaster."

"You're absolutely right," I agreed snappishly. "I guess it was my turn to do something stupid."

Pachany grunted. Bleeding and bathed in sweat, we made our way back to the Thionville road. As we got there, some local church clock struck twelve. Precious hours had been wasted. For our efforts, we were back where we had started, much the worse for wear. I was terribly frustrated and angry with myself.

We followed the road awhile, detoured around a village, then started our climb anew. This time the ground was clear and the going much easier. The one obstacle that presented itself was a wooden fence. We clambered over it and found ourselves among a herd of cows.

At the top of the hill, we once more ran into dense forest. We tried to circumvent it. Two hours of walking later, we had not reached its end or found a trail. The moon had set and visibility was poor. We decided to call it a night.

Moving into the forest, we spread our overcoats under a large tree. In the damp cold, we huddled together and quickly fell asleep.

I opened my eyes at first light.

By day, the forest looked much less threatening and mysterious. I could see that here the dense woods extended only partway down from the hill crest. Hastily loading up, we began to descend.

Emerging from the trees, we came into tall grass wet with heavy dew. Fifteen minutes more and we had reached a large, level clearing. Below us, we saw railroad tracks and a paved road.

Pachany checked the compass and the map. We were right on course.

To our shock, we suddenly heard a military song being loudly bellowed out. We dashed back up into the woods. There we watched as a German infantry company marched into view, probably relief troops for the border. If we had been any lower, they'd have run smack into us.

When the soldiers were gone, we dashed down to the road. We crossed the tracks, jumped over a creek, and entered the sparser woods on the other side. The bottom of the hill wasn't much farther, and then we began to climb again.

Another hour and we reached the next summit. We decided to take a break. Pachany took the first watch while I slept. When he got me up in the early afternoon, the sun was hot. Trying to alleviate my growing thirst, I kept swallowing my saliva.

While Pachany slept I checked our bearings. The edge of the dense forest ran a few hundred yards away, near an abandoned watchtower. Orienting myself with the map, I picked out a church tower and the village of Leipzig. In the next foothills lay the main highway from Metz to Amanvillere, and far off I thought I could discern a trace of it. According to the map, beyond the highway was a minor secondary road that ran closer to the actual border.

I sat down heavily on the grass. I was terribly thirsty, and our food supply was exhausted. Tonight was it.

If we got across into occupied France, I felt our troubles would be over. Despite the German presence, the French would be friendly. We could make our way to Paris and be safe in the anonymity of the city.

It was dusk when I woke Pachany and we set out. After a few minutes, he fell behind. He was limping badly.

"What's the matter, Pacha?"

"It's my left foot. It's swollen."

From his face, I could see he was feverish and in pain. There was nothing I could do except relieve him of the burden of his overcoat and duffel bag. Without a complaint, he went on. Uphill, downhill, we walked in silence.

In under an hour, we reached the main highway. Taking cover behind a bush, we checked out the stretch visible some three hundred feet below us.

We could see two guard posts, fully equipped. They looked quiet enough but were no doubt manned. On the opposite roadside, a hundred-yard swath had been clearly cut, but the underbrush was already grown back. Then the thick forest resumed.

Somewhere in there was the border.

The evening shadows deepened. The posts' searchlights hadn't been turned on, and except for lights flickering inside and the occasional bark of a dog, everything was calm.

We could still see a hundred feet or so ahead of us. The moment was right. We crawled down the slope and hid in the ditch by the road.

"Can you run for it?" I whispered to Pachany.

"I can try. Just lead the way, Bora."

I did. I dashed onto the road with Pachany at my heels. Once across, we crouched behind a bush and caught our breaths.

A minute later, the searchlights powered up. They began to sweep the area. Timing the beams, we ran from one bush to another.

We had to get into the trees. Pachany began to drag behind. "I can't make it. Leave me here," he gasped.

"Nonsense! We escaped together, and if we're captured, we'll be captured together."

"Please, Bora. My foot is infected and my toes are full of pus. I'm burning up. Go ahead, I'll only hold you back."

I wouldn't listen. I grabbed him around the waist and slung his arm over my shoulder. "Just shut up and lean on me. With God's help, we'll be in France tomorrow. Be brave, my friend." With Pachany's sturdy weight leaning against me, we hobbled into the protective darkness of the forest.

The bugs were intense. With no room to walk abreast, Pachany had to go it alone. Thankfully, the slower pace made the pain in his foot bearable. He went first, holding the compass and checking the direction. I didn't want to risk losing him behind me.

Branches slapped at our sweaty faces, and my throat felt as if it were about to crack. We pushed on. After two more hours, we broke into a small clearing and collapsed on the ground.

I thought we were on course, but the secondary road had eluded us. Letting Pachany rest, I walked along the edge of the clearing. Only several hundred yards to the south, I stumbled on it. This had to be the road. I hurried back, and we were on the move again.

In the pitch black night, we followed the little road until the compass indicated a turn to the right. There was apparently a wide meadow at hand, so we left the road and crossed it. At its far end, a dirt trail continued west. Our luck was holding.

Head lowered, I marched on behind Pachany until he stopped abruptly. A huge ridge of earth towered before us. The sound of flowing water filled our ears.

"It's a reservoir," Pachany whispered.

Using my hat as a bucket, I drew water. We both drank eagerly and deeply. Then I put the hat, full of more cool water, back on my head, and I felt reborn.

A church clock striking the hour meant a village was close by. But on which side of the border? Pachany couldn't keep on much longer. Were we in France yet? Where were the *gendarmes?*

It was 2:00 A.M. Cautiously, we circled about. The next thing we knew, we were trudging through a cemetery, tripping over pots of flowers placed on the graves.

A steady rain began. The ground grew slippery and the footing unsteady. Soon we were covered in mud. Our clothes steamed, full of sweat from our hot bodies.

We had to find shelter. In a village field, we spotted an abandoned hut. It would serve until morning. Lying inside on its floor of beaten earth, we soon fell fast asleep.

At dawn, it was still raining lightly. Pachany could barely put weight on his foot, but we set off anyway. We had come too far to stop short of our goal.

Fifty minutes later, we came to a paved road. For no reason whatever, we turned right. *Keep moving*, I thought. We hadn't a clue as to where we were.

On the road we found a stone marker inscribed with an arrow. It read: "Bruville, 6 km." The arrow pointed the way we were going.

I hurriedly opened the map. My finger sought out Bruville. There it was. Here we were. Pachany saw it, too.

"France." We said it slowly. "France."

Then we jumped and danced around the marker like a pair of fools. We'd made it.

8

A Taste of Freedom

THROUGH LIGHT DRIZZLE, we walked into the sleepy village of Bruville early on a Sunday morning. It was May 17, 1942. We were in occupied France, the more northern of the two zones created after the French surrender, and the area under direct German control.

No one was in sight. Jubilantly, Pachany and I drank from the public fountain. The houses surrounding the cobblestone square were still and without signs of life.

We weren't planning to look around much, anyway. Bruville, as we knew from the map, did not have a train station, and we had to find one if we wanted to travel to distant Paris. That much was self-evident. But we were already at our map's limits, and to ask a total stranger for directions was far too risky. Standing out in the open while we waited for a better idea was not exactly prudent, either. There had to be a local station somewhere.

From the village, the road continued up a hill and disappeared into a patch of woods. *"Let's go."* Pachany insistently wished us to push on.

At a loss for a better option, I acquiesced.

My elation was fading. The dream of a sheltering France had helped sustain us, but the sober reality was a nation under occupation—an unknown condition. Moreover, it would be sheer folly to take our recent luck for granted. True, we had survived a week on the loose, but we were still escaped P.O.W.s with phony papers and no friends this side of anywhere.

We trudged off slowly, the rain growing heavier by the minute. I began to wonder what we were doing. Pachany was feverish and limped badly. The woods provided little cover from the downpour. Wet, dirty, and hungry, we fell to arguing and getting on each other's nerves.

Fatigue was taking its toll as I struggled to keep my mind clear. Sure, to head for Paris was our best bet. But how? By charging there like a bull at the sight of a red cape? I stopped in my tracks.

"Listen, Pacha," I said tiredly. "You're sick, and we both need rest. We don't have any idea where the local station is. And we can't travel to Paris looking like we do."

"You're saying I can't make it?"

"All right," I snapped, "suppose you can. Suppose we find the station. Who do we know in Paris? Can we travel without a pass? Please tell me."

"I tell you we should get to Paris right away. You've agreed all along. Look, we'll find help there. You know there are many Serbian expatriates."

"Yes. And more Lieutenant Ninkoviches?"

Pachany looked glum and frustrated. "All right, Bora," he said at last. "All right. If it's what you want, we'll go back to the village. Perhaps you can soon figure out what good that will do us."

By the time we got back to Bruville, I had done some purposeful thinking. I knocked at the front door of the first house we came to. A young Frenchman opened it. His face hardly concealed his suspicions or his fear.

"Monsieur, ou est le prêtre?" I muttered. With a sigh of relief, the young man pointed to a gray building across the square. His door shut firmly behind us as we turned away in search of the village priest.

We had but crossed the square when the priest himself emerged from his house. He was pushing a motorized bicycle, evidently off on some Sunday duty. I waved for him to stop.

"Father," I said carefully in French, "we are Yugoslav Army officers, escaped from a German P.O.W. camp. My friend can hardly walk. Please help us, I beg of you." Pachany nudged me. "We have papers to prove this."

I waited. The priest was a tall, middle-aged man with wavy hair and an ascetic face. He studied us intently with his sad, compassionate eyes, but said nothing.

"Why does he hesitate?" Pachany said to me in Serbian.

The priest broke his silence. "Knock at the brown door down there." He pointed. "The owner of the village bistro, Monsieur Boiteux, lives there. He is a good man. Tell him Father Pierre sent you."

"Don't you want to see our papers?" I stammered.

"I can tell a Slavic tongue from German," he answered brusquely, nodding to Pachany. "I shall come to see you in the afternoon." He mounted his bicycle and rode away.

Everything had happened so quickly that we weren't quite sure what to make of the Catholic priest. Regardless, the die had been cast. If he had gone to send up an alarm, our chances of getting away safely were already nil. With sinking hearts, we decided to follow his instructions.

At the brown door, a few hard knocks brought forth a tall man with slightly bent shoulders.

"Monsieur Boiteux?"

"Oui." He held us in a steady, dispassionate gaze.

I had barely started with my explanations when he threw the door wide. "Come in, come in," Boiteux said with a warm smile, and he led us inside.

Hesitantly, we followed him into a dark room and took seats around a large wooden table. "You are hungry, no?" Without waiting for our reply, he hurried off.

Pachany and I sat there in silence. If anything was out of place in that neat house, it was us—two muddy, exhausted men who looked more like common laborers than foreign military officers. If we'd shown up like this at my mother's house in Belgrade before the war . . .

My thoughts were interrupted by the entrance of Madame Boiteux. Bustling, she set places before us, then gave us a bright, welcoming smile. I thought I smelled eggs cooking. And was that bacon? I knew I must be dreaming.

A moment later, Boiteux himself returned with two plates. Deftly, he served us omelettes and bacon. I began to appreciate just how providential it is to have a bistro owner as your angel of mercy.

Pulling up a chair, Boiteux lit a cigarette and let us enjoy our meal. Polite as he was, I knew he was impatient to hear our story. We obliged him as soon as Pachany and I had finished our heavenly breakfast.

He knew about the Serbs from World War I, the brave combatants and allies of the French, and he was honored to have us under his roof. His attention was flattering, but as Pachany and I continued, I realized he was weighing our claims carefully and judging our veracity. I would certainly have done no less in his shoes. Helping two men from out of nowhere was not just an act of immense kindness but one punishable under the laws of the German occupation. Monsieur Boiteux might well be risking his own and his family's lives.

While we spoke, two teenaged sons came in and joined their parents. Overcoming their initial timidity, the boys edged closer to us, drinking in every word. The room soon resounded with friendly chatter. The boys wanted to clean our muddy boots, and Madame herself would attend to our soiled clothes.

"I am amazed you got through," Boiteux remarked. "The part of the frontier you crossed is very well guarded with traps, mines, and dog patrols. You gentlemen are very brave. And very fortunate."

Coming from this man, we did not take the words lightly. And something in my guts told me we could trust Boiteux implicitly. In wartime, this is what happens. You live by your intuitions, or die by them.

"Of course, you cannot leave today," Boiteux was telling Pachany. "It is impossible." I could see my friend was ready to make a good argument. "Even if you were in top condition," Boiteux added with sly Gallic humor, "there are no trains on Sunday, monsieur."

Pachany and I exchanged a look I wouldn't characterize in polite company.

"Both of you need rest. Your foot should be treated, Captain. How do you expect to walk to the station?" Boiteux had guessed our plan. "You want to go to Paris, don't you?"

I nodded.

"That's foolish. Assume you make it, then what? Eh? The surveillance in Paris is *formidable*." He lit another cigarette and gestured in the air. "Here is what you must do. Head south and try to cross into Petain's France. Yes, Vichy. The administration there collaborates with the Germans, true enough, but they are still Frenchmen. Many will look the other way, if you take my meaning. You understand?"

We did.

"Eh bien. Then tomorrow you can board a train at Mars-la-Tour, some five miles from here." He got up from his chair. "Now, my sister's house is empty. You will hide there and rest."

It was five before Pachany and I awoke. Wrapped in clean blankets, we had slept away the day on our beds of fresh straw. I blinked sleepily in the late afternoon sunshine flooding through a window.

The first thing I could make out was Boiteux himself slouched at the doorway. God knows how long he'd been there. A pile of our neatly folded, cleaned, and pressed clothes was beside him. Seeing me move, he nodded.

That evening, others joined us at the house. Father Pierre and several villagers arrived carrying large baskets of fried chicken, bread, and wine. Last to enter was a young man on crutches. His left leg was missing from the knee down.

It had been amputated, Boiteux explained to me, after he was wounded in the Nazi onslaught of France. It was a badge of honor. Everyone admired him, for he was a living symbol of resistance to the Germans.

The conversation flowed late into the night. Shouts of approval had greeted my expressions of determination to regain freedom. Even though we were far from our own land, these were men who thought as we did. They were like brothers I never knew I had.

I learned that Boiteux had fought the Germans, was captured, and escaped while in transport to a P.O.W. camp. He had not mentioned it himself. Around midnight, Father Pierre declared the party over. Tears ran down my cheeks as we said good-bye.

Back in my bed, I thought of a passage from the Book of Matthew chapter 25, verse 35: "For I was hungry and you gave me food, I was thirsty and you gave me drink, I was a stranger and you welcomed me . . ."

The next morning, we were up by six and prepared to move on. We said brief farewells to the Boiteux family. I wished we had something of value to give them, but they seemed touched by the gift of our pictures in uniform.

"Remember, do not ride the train all the way to Nancy," Boiteux warned us in parting. "The Germans are checking travel papers at the station. Go around, then pick up another train to Monchare. That puts you close to the border between our two 'nations' of France." His voice was tinged with bitterness.

Then he smiled. "Au revoir, messieurs." A bear hug, a kiss on both cheeks, and we were once more on our own.

"Bora, it's still six miles to Nancy. I . . . I can't walk that far."

Pachany would never have made such an admission much short of real immobility. Besides, I reasoned, the train ride to this point had been smooth and uneventful. There was no apparent danger. So on we rode.

When the train pulled into the station, it didn't take us long to realize our stupidity. I looked out and saw that all the exits save one were blocked off. There a quartet of French gendarmes and Gestapo officers were checking each passenger's papers.

All right, this was it. No place to hide. No way to break through the official gauntlet, or to explain papers that had us on our way to a German city hundreds of miles away. I gave up hope. Our fool's paradise was over.

Yet I did not panic. And neither did Pachany, even though his aching foot made him a sitting duck. Let them capture us, if that was our fate, but we were resolute military men, not terror-stricken civilians. Our spirits had been tempered after years of training, service, experience under fire, and captivity. There was no reason to disgrace ourselves now.

We hung back for a while, then quietly joined the exiting crowd. Everyone pushed forward, anxious to get through, and step by step we were carried along. Slowly, the security detail did its job.

There was only one man left in front of me. It was his turn to approach the guards, but the tall, fat Frenchman couldn't find his papers. As he nervously searched his trousers and his coat, he began stammering in confusion. It was almost comical, but a hush settled over the remaining passengers.

The Germans were definitely not amused. They closed in around the man and eyed him carefully. They signaled the pair of gendarmes to search him.

For a moment, the exit was left unattended. I saw it all in a flash—the fat man, the guards with their backs to me, the focus on the little drama, and the open exit. Without hesitation, I ducked my head, slipped past, and was out. Pachany followed as swiftly as my shadow.

Effortlessly, we were engulfed in the waiting room's milling crowds. I'm not sure if we deserved such good fortune, but we'd take it. And the sooner we were on another train headed out of Nancy, the better. I hoped that meant an hour or two.

Needless to say, the next train that went to Belfort and on to Monchare did not leave until the following morning. We would have to find shelter for the night. While this was annoying, certainly we weren't fazed. The problem of Pachany's foot aside, it was almost routine.

At a newsstand, I bought a map of the city. We took a local

trolley out to what was indicated as a wooded area near the northern suburb of Aisse. It turned out to be a cemetery.

Nearby, a small chapel attracted our attention. Its door was open, so we walked in.

Crossing ourselves, we approached the sanctuary. From the dark recess, a voice spoke. "Who are you?" The hunched figure of a priest emerged as our eyes adjusted.

"Escaped P.O.W.s," I blurted out. "Can you help us, Father?" The priest looked up at me, disbelieving. "My friend is ill. We're Yugoslav officers."

Unexpectedly, the priest reached into his robe and produced a key. "Go to the street leading to the trolley station. Number ten. This will let you in the gate."

I took the key. "And you are . . . ?"

"Father Antoine." He dismissed us with a wave. "You tell the old lady I sent you. Go with God, messieurs."

Our unexpected lodgings turned out to be a dusty attic storage room filled with furniture. It wasn't much, but we were used to lots worse. With a borrowed broom and a rag, I soon had the room livable.

Ordering Pachany to rest on a sofa under penalty of my personally smacking his foot, I went out to the courtyard to wash up. In the warm sun, I took off my shirt. I felt more content than I had in ages.

As I pumped up water into a trough, a young woman came out of the house. I smiled. She smiled back, then looked at my small pile of things to be washed.

"You've never done socks, have you?" she teased. "Perhaps I will show you how simple it is." She nudged me gently aside. "I am Francoise. I'm married to the old lady's son."

She was graceful and willowy, with large brown eyes. Her severe black dress only emphasized a milky complexion, and it could not conceal the lovely small curve of her breast. The touch of her fingers had sent shivers up my spine.

In the past year, I had spoken to rouse men to action, to rescue them from apathy, or to convince them of the truth of the cause we served. There in the yard of Francoise's in-laws, I spoke mostly to stifle my own desires.

She listened intently. "Why don't you let me take care of your friend?" she offered when I finally paused. She had a salve for Pachany's foot.

I was staring at her charming lips, but somehow I managed to say yes. When the two of us reached the attic, it was Pachany's turn to be surprised. I made the introductions and we soon were chatting like old friends.

Irascible as he'd been about his foot, he was willing to have Francoise attend to him. You'd think no one else had ever been concerned. When she then unexpectedly invited us to dinner, Pachany miraculously leaped up from the sofa, declaring he was quite ready. The hours of rest and the salve had done him more good than he'd admit.

In the evening, after a pleasant meal with the family, I went outside with Francoise and sat under the stars. For the sake of his foot, she had banished Pachany back to his sofa. We were silent awhile, the air filled with the scent of flowers.

From her heart, in a voice barely audible, she told me of her father and husband. They had been captured by the Germans and sent to camps. She wished they could escape, but perhaps it was safer if they stayed put.

"I do not know if I have the strength, Captain," she murmured, "to endure the desires of a wasted youth."

I did not know what to say. I took her soft, small hand in mine. She turned to me. We embraced, two survivors adrift in a shattered world.

The next morning Pachany and I slipped away quietly.

The day dissolved into a monotonous series of slow train rides. First to Belfort, where we endured a two-hour layover, long enough for us to find a bookstore with a recent map of France. The line between occupied France and Vichy was clearly marked. Then it was on to Besancon, another, shorter wait, and at last a train to Monchare.

A company of German soldiers was traveling on the same train. I supposed they were being dispatched to reinforce the border watchposts we were planning to sneak past. It was absurd, really, as if the train were delivering both hounds and fox to a forthcoming chase.

The sun was low on the horizon by the time we rolled into the Monchare depot. We again decided to put our trust in the local clergy. This time, however, a monsignor received us coldly at the parish house. He suggested we leave the premises immediately.

Shaken by the encounter, we quit the town in a hurry, passing the last row of houses in a matter of minutes. A path led south and we took it. Skirting around tilled fields, we walked until Monchare had disappeared behind us.

We stopped under a large tree and debated our next move. According to the map, we were about ten miles from the border. The most isolated route would take us through a large forest and over three streams. The map gave no indication of their depths.

At dusk, we were on our way.

The night was clear and a rising half-moon illuminated the land. Shortly before midnight, we reached the first of the three streams we had to ford. Nearly thirty feet wide, its waters glistened in the moonlight. Beyond the bank, we could glimpse the silhouette of a church steeple in the distance.

Being taller, Pachany volunteered to wade in first. He undressed and entered the water. It reached to his waist. That meant partway up my chest.

The situation was tricky. Wet boots and pants would slow us down and might prove suspicious later on, not to mention the possible damage to things in our pockets. There was no time to think of clever ideas. I would simply hold everything while Pachany carried me on his shoulders.

As Pachany eased his way across the stream, I scanned the opposite bank. We had only scant feet to go when I hoarsely whispered: "Stop. There's something moving out there. Maybe a guard dog."

We gazed through the darkness at the moving shadow. Leaves rustled. We heard sniffling. Pachany remained stock-still in the cold water, his shoulders sagging under my weight.

"I cannot stay here forever," he groused.

The animal came nearer and lowered its head to the water. A ray of moonlight caught the face. "It's only a calf!" I shouted in relief.

"Keep your voice down." Pachany tried to scold me but couldn't stop himself from chuckling. A few more steps and we fell in a heap on the bank.

By 2:00 A.M. we'd crossed the second stream and entered the huge forest. The going was very rough. It was pitch black, and every step was slow and dangerous. For two solid hours, we fought through the thick underbrush and the branches.

Reaching a small clearing, we collapsed into the grass, exhausted and dripping with sweat. The next thing I felt was Pachany's hand on my shoulder. It was now almost one in the afternoon.

"We'd better find out where we are, Bora."

"And on which side of the border," I grumbled. "The map has the border placed somewhere in here." Of course, I knew full well that any border crossing sensibly marked out was one with guards around who'd be happy to arrest us.

Without a reference landmark, the map was useless. I climbed a tall tree. There was nothing around us but trees, trees, and more trees. I had the nagging fear that we were lost.

Something had to be done. The night would only make things worse. We had to find out where we were, even if it meant a daylight march. The compass would hold our direction steady until we got ourselves located.

The day was warm and muggy, but we kept up a steady pace. Mid-afternoon found us at the third stream, a small creek that we easily crossed. We were back on course.

The forest thinned. We moved faster, then unexpectedly came upon a paved road. Cautiously, we waited, but the road was apparently without traffic. Finally, we sprinted across and slipped among the trees on the other side.

The woods ended abruptly. From there, a lush meadow stretched away as far as our eyes could see. Behind us, the sun was setting, the dying light making the forest glow with an eerie serenity.

We spied a group of farmhouses not far off. Approaching a middle-aged farmer raking in the nearest yard, I asked politely, "What's the name of this place?"

"Farm Rosier," he responded. Seeing my concern, he added drily, "In Vichy, monsieur."

The farmer smiled broadly but asked no questions. He treated us to fresh milk, then suggested we keep walking to the nearby town of Mont-sur-Vendreille.

What a joy it was to hike on a real road. Side by side, Pachany and I marched along singing Serbian songs or talking of our newly won freedom. We would seek out the American representatives in Vichy, the capital city which had bestowed its name on this rump version of France. Surely they could help us.

In peaceful Mont-sur-Vendreille, we discovered there was actually a relief center for escaped P.O.W.s. We went at once. The young man in charge gave us a hot meal, listened attentively to our tale, yet seemed noncommittal.

"My friends, I congratulate you on your escape. You are the only ones to have made it today. Eighteen others were captured." He glanced about casually, then lowered his voice. "But listen, my friends, you cannot go to Vichy."

"Why not?" Pachany asked. "This is free France."

The young man stiffened. "You cannot go anywhere openly. If you are picked up, you'll be dispatched to a work camp and maybe to Germany. Okay?"

"I see. The German leash is that short."

He smiled without humor. "I'm supposed to report you myself, you know."

Pachany turned to me and shrugged.

"What should we do?" I asked.

"First thing tomorrow, head for the American consulate in Lyons. They might help you. Avoid the gendarmes and never truly identify yourselves."

Such advice was already second nature to us. The young man rose from the dining table and resumed the role of unconcerned host.

"If I may show you your room . . ." We trooped after him. After a long bath, I fell asleep to the sound of raindrops hitting the windowpanes.

A cold shower brought me sharply awake the next morning. After a quick breakfast of oatmeal, Pachany and I set out for Lyons. The first leg of our journey was a bus ride to Poligny where we'd catch the train.

Waiting for the bus, an immaculately attired gendarme approached us. He asked who we were and where we were going. Right on cue, I fed him the line that we were escaped P.O.W.s headed for Lonse-le-Sonier to report in. That apparently made perfect sense to him, and he left us alone.

The railway station in Poligny a half hour later was a busy little place. Long lines of people stood patiently at the ticket windows. We had no sooner joined a line when a plainclothes cop made his presence known.

"You are the escapees who crossed the border at Mont-sur-Vendreille?" Evidently the word had gone on ahead from our first encounter.

"On our way to Lonse-le-Sonier," I responded.

"That's good. That's good," he beamed agreeably. "They are expecting you. I will escort you to your train."

He tagged along right up to the window. In a whisper, I requested tickets to Lyons. Concealing them, Pachany and I strolled over to the Lonse train's platform, trailed by our helpful watchdog. When he saw we were abroad, he gave us a last long look, then sauntered off. We immediately slipped out the other side and quickly boarded the other train.

Four weary hours later, we were there. Despite contrary

advice, we still thought the best bet for swift action was at the American Embassy in Vichy. We checked out the schedule, but no train ran that day.

Fortunately for us. Later we would learn just how strict that city's security was. We could never have made it to Vichy without being apprehended.

Sitting in a Lyons brasserie, we concluded that second-best might serve after all. The consulate was here. We were running low on money, and the authorities might well be on the lookout for us. We downed our beers and headed for 2 Place de la Bours.

The consulate gate was guarded by several French gendarmes. To our delight, they asked no questions. Passing inside, the building seemed deserted. The caretaker told us to come back after lunch. Everyone was out.

I thought, don't they know a war is going on?

Shortly after two, we were back. The receptionist told us to wait, and wait we did. No one paid any attention to us, despite our repeated requests to see the consul.

As we sat cooling our heels, the staff read newspapers and talked idly. Bureaucrats were a universal breed, I decided. At last, the senior officer was invited into the consul's office. That was Pachany.

Several minutes later, I, too, was ushered into the inner sanctum. Pachany smiled at me reassuringly. The consul asked for the names and addresses of anybody in London who could confirm our identities.

We complied, then he rose from his desk and walked us to the door. "Gentlemen, I'm sorry, but I can't do anything for you. Except to inform your government-in-exile of your presence here. I suggest you go to the Café de l'Etoile and ask for Mr. Becelich. He will take care of you, I believe."

So much for swift action. We thanked the consul, despite the disappointment we felt. He smiled affably. "After you settle in Lyons, do come back and see me."

His words rankled me all the way to the café. Was he serious?

I should have assured him of one thing. We had no intention of sticking around Lyons any longer than necessary.

The waiter at the café greeted us with a somber face and little interest. When we asked to see Mr. Becelich, he promptly disappeared into the kitchen.

"I didn't like it, Pacha. This looks suspicious. Let's get out of here," I declared, imagining some sort of trap.

I was almost to the door when a smiling, reasonably well dressed middle-aged man emerged from behind the counter. "Are you Serbs?" he asked in a pure Belgrade accent.

"Yes, for sure."

"Escaped P.O.W.s, if I am not mistaken?"

"Yes."

"Welcome!" He gave us both bear hugs. "I am Neiman. I am an architect. Follow me, please."

He led us into the back of the café. "Mr. Becelich is in Marseille, but when he gets back tomorow, he'll help you. We call him Cata, by the way." (The nickname, oddly enough, meant "pencil pusher.")

Neiman assumed we needed an explanation. "It's because our Cata is always cutting through red tape or writing petitions on our behalf."

He brought us into a room where a group of young men sat at a large table. They were engaged in lively conversation, and the sound of so many voices speaking our native tongue was like music to my ears. Seeing us, they stopped to regard the newcomers.

Neiman gestured to Pachany and me. "Gentlemen, fresh recruits for our Yugoslav colony here in Lyons." We weren't sure what we should do. He took us aside as the conversation resumed.

"You'll meet everybody soon enough. Many of these men are escapees, like yourselves. Thanks to Cata's help, our lives have been made tolerable," Nieman added.

"How long have they been here?" I asked.

"Ah, not a long time. Many are eager to move on." He saw in my face I wasn't about to be put off. "I think . . . well . . . about eight months."

9

Clandestine Affairs

THE LITTLE COMMUNITY of Yugoslavs in Lyons sorely lacked leadership and discipline. There was dissension between the older men, many of whom had been residents for some time, and the younger escaped P.O.W.s. Worst of all, no one was making any real progress toward returning home.

The most important member, "Cata" Becelich, turned out to be a pleasant, magnanimous man. He had come to Lyons before the war to study law and also play professional soccer, but the lure of the playing field won out. Well-liked by the fans, he had ended up marrying a French girl and getting a job in the police department. There he developed valuable contacts within city government and in the consular community.

After France was defeated in the spring of 1940, Cata helped many Yugoslavs who were fleeing the occupied north. Tireless, he ran around the city securing residence permits, ration cards, and jobs for destitute countrymen. He had quit his own position to devote his entire life to this work, and his efforts had won him the nickname of which he was rather proud.

Two years later, it was our turn to be helped. Cata secured Vichy documents for Pachany and me, based on newly assumed identities, and found us rooms in a run-down hotel. He then invited us to dinner.

Our meal with Cata evolved into a major review of the woes of the Yugoslav community. He thought the Serbs in Lyons a mixed

127

lot. Calmly at the beginning, and then with increasing animation, Cata explained the difficulties.

"All my efforts to keep us together seem to be in vain," he lamented. "These people . . . let me give you some examples . . ." The examples largely involved men we would come to know ourselves, and most of what Cata said about them proved all too true.

Among the older Yugoslavs, we'd already met the architect, Neiman. He was a witty but ineffectual man. When laughter was badly needed, he had a ready supply of jokes and anecdotes. Beyond that, he could not contribute.

Then there was Dr. Daca, the bald-headed physician who had become a naturalized French citizen and had no plans to return to Yugoslavia. A kindly man, he provided free medical attention and bought an occasional meal for some of the less fortunate. Under the present circumstances, he saw no rational reason for anyone leaving. Why trade Vichy for an even more oppressively occupied homeland? Genuinely interested in the plight of the escapees, Dr. Daca advocated that they remain in France until the day they could join the Allied rollback of the Germans.

Another of the older men given to pontification was Mr. Rothchild. A businessman from Zagreb, he was rich, Jewish, stout, and well-dressed. Perceptive and experienced in the ways of the world, he had stayed one step ahead of the Nazis.

His oft-stated plans for leaving Vichy attracted the interest of many of the P.O.W.s. They had flocked around him, eager to follow his lead. Yet his words never led to deeds. A crippling concern for his own personal safety lay masked behind his bold declarations.

These three older men were typical of the attitudes that demoralized the younger Yugoslavs. Offered diverting witticisms, conservative caution, or empty bravado, the P.O.W.s basically were unsure of what to do. So they did almost nothing.

As far as Cata was concerned, we were a godsend. "I am more a caretaker than a leader," he declared honestly. "All my time is consumed in maintaining the relatively safe life we have here.

But you are professional soldiers, not civilians full of hot air. You're the ones to take charge of our P.O.W.s."

His earnest plea was tempting. "You can make something hopeful out of our situation," Cata added, filling my glass and Pachany's again. "Let's drink to it."

As May gave way to June of 1942, and the heat of summer grew, the American consul's parting words took on a prophetic ring. Pachany and I did settle down in Lyons, at least for a while. There wasn't much choice. Getting into Vichy was one thing, but getting out was an elusive goal pursued by more resident foreigners than seemed imaginable. French officials (and their German overlords) were quite content to have it thus. You might get in, but you didn't get out without a proper visa.

Also, we had accepted the task Cata offered. I felt strongly that to make some contribution to the war effort, however minor, was better than postponing everything until a grander opportunity came along. Right in Lyons, there was a willing group of men who could be properly prepared for future service to our country. Somebody ought to do the job, and the somebody was us.

As senior officer, Captain Pachany assumed command of our ad hoc unit. Jointly we supervised the training, establishing a solid program, and we restored military discipline by the middle of June. I taught courses in military tactics and field fortifications. Pachany conducted the physical fitness activities and saw to it that I was left gasping with everybody else at the end of the daily session.

It felt good to be back in command of soldiers. I enjoyed the challenge of motivating the diverse types of men in the unit. Actually, a majority of my escaped P.O.W.s had been military cadets before the war and were hardly seasoned troops. They had been called up in the general mobilization and then caught in the German sweep. Cadet Sergeants Kosta and Zivkovich, former classmates, were two who stood out. The contrast of their natures often gave me some strictly private amusement.

Sergeant Kosta, resourceful and likable, was obsessed with

returning home and becoming a fighter pilot. Because he was very short, he took a terrible ribbing from his friends and lacked confidence, especially around women. With a little encouragement, and strict orders to the rest of the men to lay off, his natural leadership ability emerged. He was no longer the brooding youngster I'd met at the Café de l'Etoile, but a man you could really count on.

Sergeant Zivkovich, on the other hand, was tall and handsome. Always impeccably dressed, he was a confident ladies' man, a talent he practiced on the French belles. Although respectful and cooperative, he seemed enamored of the easy life and was fearful of pain. I made that discovery one afternoon when we both went to the dentist. He argued that he had to have an anesthetic for a small cavity, then fainted at the sight of the needle. Yet he, too, sincerely wanted to be a fighter pilot.

Besides these former cadets, my staunchest supporter was Master Sergeant Krstich. He was a veteran soldier, an experienced N.C.O. Regrettably, his cynicism and disdain for his inexperienced comrades in Lyons had made him generally disliked. He had tried to lead the group without success, then completely abandoned the effort before we arrived. With unconcealed relief, he greeted our decisive action. It was what he'd been waiting for.

All our classes had to be held in secret. The French security agents were on guard against "enemies of the national revolution." That meant anyone engaged in activities that might discomfit the Germans. We obviously qualified.

By and large, the local French people were passive sympathizers. Our guise as students went unchallenged, if not without knowing smiles. Even the middle-aged landlady of the apartment we gathered in every morning treated us in motherly fashion.

Our greatest problem was financial support. We had to rely on small monthly stipends provided by the "Committee to Aid Yugoslav Citizens in France." This was a flimsy cover erected after the German conquest for the continued activities of the

Yugoslav consulate in Marseille. The funds we received were barely sufficient to cover essential needs.

I felt we had to improve the living conditions of our men or risk losing their trust. With Cata's blessings, a confrontation with the consul general seemed in order. He held the purse strings, and in the opinion of those who had dealt with the man, he held them a lot tighter than necessary.

If the Yugoslav Consulate in Marseille did not legally exist, its physical presence was certain enough. Surrounded by massive iron gates and beautiful gardens, the consul general's villa was very elegant. With its antique furnishings and rare oil paintings, it exhibited a prewar luxury.

Ushered into a large paneled office, Pachany and I exchanged greetings with the villa's proprietor. Wearing thick glasses, he was a thin gentleman in his mid-fifties with green eyes, a limp handshake, and a faint smile. He kept glancing at us nervously.

So this was Consul General Gerasimovich, a Yugoslav diplomat, a man the genial Cata had characterized as caring more for his personal property than his countrymen's well-being. It didn't take us long to discover that he was even more uncooperative than we'd feared. As Pachany detailed our work in Lyons, he looked out the window. I could see his hands trembling, but the indifferent expression on his face never altered.

When I next bluntly requested more funds for our soldiers, a long silence followed. "I wish I could help you, Captain Todorovich," he finally said in a barely audible voice. "Unfortunately, the government has left me insufficient funds."

His monotone droned on. "The times are uncertain, you know, and I must be prepared for any eventuality. The news from the Russian front is not encouraging. And Rommel is advancing along the North African coast. Who knows what tomorrow will bring?"

Which had nothing do with funds for the soldiers, I concluded. Pachany was no more satisfied that I was. We exchanged a hard, calculating look. In one of those mutual moments of inspiration, like others we'd shared, I realized that the consul general was scared of us. We were exactly the stuff of his nightmares, military officers he couldn't bully or order out of his sight.

"Consul General, we did not come here to tell you stories, I assure you!" My outburst startled him, and I think he almost cringed.

Pachany jumped in. "We want your cooperation to help care for the escaped P.O.W.s in Lyons. What is going on in the rest of the world is not our responsibility!"

"We're not asking for much," I added.

"A reasonable amount," Pachany allowed. "But we must have it."

"We will have it, yes?" I was staring straight at Gerasimovich. "Yes?"

He turned his back to us again. "Yes." His voice was weak, but clear.

We returned to Lyons with the promise of an additional one thousand francs per man each month and a keener understanding of what we were up against. It was hardly a great victory, but we were satisfied. Our training program could go forward.

Predictably, Gerasimovich failed to live up to his promise. A whole month passed and we received not a single additional penny. The men were disappointed, rightfully, and we had a hard time keeping up morale. With Pachany holding the fort, I decided to settle this debate once and for all. I would make another trip down to Marseille.

At our next meeting, the old man hemmed and hawed theatrically. I pressed him as hard as I dared, reminding him of his promise. Seeing my determination, Gerasimovich changed his tack.

"Believe me, I wish to help you and your friends, Captain." He practically sighed like some frail maiden. "But my work load is crushing. Crushing."

I said nothing. What was he getting at?

"If you're so . . . so energetic, come work for me here at the consulate. You shall be secretary of the Relief Committee and my assistant in all areas relating to P.O.W.s. What do you say, Captain?"

The sly old fox had been ready for me after all. He probably guessed that the last thing I wanted was a desk job down the hall from his office. My refusal would let him wriggle off the hook. I was sure he would be delighted to refer to me as someone who shirked an official call to duty.

My mind was made up. I accepted.

To give Gerasimovich credit, his surprise showed only for an instant. Then he was all full of enthusiasm, encouragement, and vague plans I'd never be able to pin him down on. Yet as I thought about it, my decision made sense. In Marseille, I could lobby constantly on behalf of my soldiers. And I might be able to establish direct contact with London.

I was already growing tired of the squabbles and petty politics of Yugoslav expatriates. The day would dawn when Pachany and I would be ready to move on. We'd need all the resources we could muster to make our way to the last bastion of free Europe across the channel in England.

A discreet phone call to Pachany,' and I had his complete agreement. Ostensibly, my transfer would be for the purpose of organizing the P.O.W.s living in and around Marseille. I would coordinate the activities of both groups and try to provide for their needs.

Naturally, the consul general did his best to insure that I became angry and frustrated in my new job. It was hard for me to be among men who had never seen war and were still living indolently. While I worked day and night, the consul general and his cronies barely worked at all.

I went to meetings with P.O.W.s, filed reports, evaluated plans for fleeing France, and sought more contacts in underground circles. Gerasimovich never came to the office before eleven, never worked more than two hours, and never cared for anything except his precious paintings and his own safety.

One of my discoveries was that the Marseille P.O.W.s were in even worse shape than the men in Lyons. The oldest of them, Air Force Master Sergeant Milan Srdanovich, had been the first escapee to get this far. He had suffered terribly at the hands of the consul general.

Frightened at his unanticipated arrival, Gerasimovich had ordered the sergeant hidden for weeks. He had to live like a tramp in the tiny concrete cellar of the villa. When Srdanovich learned just how unnecessary this had been, his bitterness knew no bounds. He condemned not only the consul general of the Kingdom of Yugoslavia, but also the corrupt social order that produced such men.

Despite his inflamed Communist leanings, I grew to trust Sergeant Srdanovich and made him commander of the Marseille P.O.W. unit. He did not fail me in his military duties. With the training programs in full operation, early in July I turned my attention to other matters.

Given my situation in the consulate, I wracked my brains for a way to establish direct contact with the government-in-exile in London. Specifically, I wanted to communicate with the prime minister's Military Office. But how could I do it? I couldn't ask Gerasimovich to wire London a critical report on his own activities.

The answer appeared in the form of Vice Consul Majdanich. He was a tall, charming fellow in his late thirties, the only other man on the staff unfailingly interested in our efforts. He suggested I draft a report on the P.O.W.s that he would channel to London secretly via our embassy in Bern.

I knew I was taking a risk, but the welfare of the men was at stake. I was damned if I was going to sit back and let a selfish, petty man like Gerasimovich do as he pleased. The next few days I worked diligently. I tried to restrain myself, but I was a soldier, not a diplomat. My language was blunt, and the report was a virtual indictment of the consul general's practices.

The first part recounted the plight of the escaped men and the insensitivity in Marseille. The second part included recommendations for action. I suggested that the Military Office designate a commanding officer to oversee P.O.W.s. Further, with funds sent through Switzerland directly to this commander, the men should be paid salaries according to rank. Lastly, the government-in-exile must undertake energetic measures to arrange our departure from France.

Consul Majdanich seemed pleased enough with my draft, and he filed the complete report. Surprisingly, London responded several days later. By special order of the military aide to the Yugoslav prime minister, I was appointed military attaché at the consulate. My orders were to organize all the career and reserve military personnel in Vichy. I was also given control over a special budget.

Frankly, I was delighted and amazed. Although I hadn't dared hope for such a positive response, I received it as our government's strong vote of confidence in all the P.O.W.s. We hadn't been forgotten.

The consul general said nothing when he learned of my appointment. Fearing retribution, I tried to placate him by tactfully requesting his help. I wanted him to arrange the exchange of P.O.W. funds on the black market and act as custodian of the cash.

Graciously, he accepted yet another burden. Perhaps I wasn't such a bad politician after all. In these transactions he should be able to find some advantage for himself.

My one real concern was Pachany. He did outrank me, and he would have been a logical choice for attaché. When I told him the news, though, he congratulated me warmly.

Noting my awkward manner, my friend reassured me that he was much happier to be in Lyons. Hadn't I seen the success of his training program? We were sloughing off the prisoner of war stigma at last. Every escaped Yugoslav P.O.W. in Vichy would soon feel like an honest soldier again.

Sergeant Srdanovich wasn't the only man in Marseille influenced by Communist thinking. A journalist named Michael

Djulafich was a true disciple. He was a sworn enemy of the old political order in Europe, especially the Yugoslav monarchy. In his thirties, he had glowing brown eyes and disheveled hair, and his worn clothes had exactly the look of a freelance pen for hire.

I first encountered him in a fit of rage. Hearing shouting and a crash from the consul general's office, I burst into the room. Hysterically demanding the renewal of his press card, Djulafich was holding Gerasimovich by the lapels and shaking him like a little doll. It was something I'd dreamed of doing myself on a number of occasions.

After calming Djulafich and freeing the consul general, I heard him out. He swore his card had been allowed to lapse out of spite. It sounded plausible. Somehow I was able to convince the old man to issue a new one—perhaps because I threatened to leave them alone again.

It was the start of an odd friendship. A former Paris correspondent for *Pravda*, Djulafich saw the destruction of the Nazi war machine as the chance to effect social and political change throughout Europe. I agreed with him that the war was an opportunity for change. He saw Communism as the answer. I did not.

We often wound up having extended conversations in some Marseille bistro. "Djulafich," I'd say to him over a glass of beer, "we are in agreement over the national condition. The current order is corrupt. We have only to look at the consul general to see that."

His eyes would gleam as he waited. A sip of beer and I'd continue. "Let me tell you why Communism is not the answer. My father fought for Serbian liberation from the Turks in the first Balkan War. He died at Jedren in 1913. During the reign of King Peter I, our country enjoyed a measure of democracy and freedom. Then came World War I and everything fell into turmoil."

By this point, Djulafich could barely restrain himself. "But the Communist party is the only political force that can unify Yugoslavia and . . ."

I would look surprised. "I, too, have studied Communism. But, you know, my widowed mother raised four children on her own. That makes you cherish the value of the family and the home. In my view, democracy is the only political system that can bring us liberty, stifle corruption and nepotism, and preserve the value of the individual."

"You'll change your mind, Bora. Let me tell you why." The journalist would then take a long pull on his beer before starting in. It was his turn at the joust.

Although Djulafich and I differed in our politics, we shared a determination to return to our homeland. Both of us could never get enough recent news from our sources. Even with my contacts through the consulate and his in Communist circles and the press, information was always at a premium.

The clandestine arrival of two officials direct from Belgrade in August was a coup for me. The information they had about the city and the resistance movement elated me. Despite the occupation, the people were *not* crushed, enemy propaganda to the contrary.

Guerrilla organizations and secret precincts had sprung up in the cities and the small towns. The railroads were being sabotaged. General Mihailovich's representative was active in Belgrade and the resistance had a man planted in General Nedich's quisling National Security Government.

Other news was not so encouraging. From July on, Radio Free Yugoslavia had branded Mihailovich an enemy agent and a collaborator. I never accepted the nonsense of this Communist station at face value, but I was troubled by these reported broadcasts.

Obviously, General Mihailovich and Tito, the mysterious Communist leader, were not acting in full cooperation. Just how serious this internal strife was, no one in Marseille knew, but I longed to find out. In my heart, I numbered my days in France. I would not sit out the war here.

From our perspective, the situation in Europe grew worse. Every day, reports on the eastern front were more and more discouraging. The German General Paulus had begun his offensive on Stalingrad and the advance of the Nazis across Russia appeared unstoppable.

We were conscious that the war's outcome was hanging in the balance. With the Nazi victories, the position of foreigners in Vichy deteriorated. Still, the Germans had many items on their agenda to contend with. If everything went predictably, we would have more than ample warning should they ever resolve to pay more attention to us.

By summer's end, the local ranks of escaped P.O.W.s stood at twenty-eight men. The latest to arrive had found his way to my office on a sweltering day in August. He made a memorable entrance, for more reasons than one.

It was a day when, unable to concentrate, I had occupied myself with meaningless details and shuffling papers on my desk. A knock on the door came as a relief. "Enter!" I shouted. The door swung open.

In walked Lieutenant Ninkovich. His cheeks were rosy and he wore a new blue suit. I could hardly believe my eyes. "At last I have caught up with you, Captain," he said as we embraced.

For the moment, all my old doubts about the man fell by the wayside. His presence was proof enough of determination and initiative. In short order, I had him seated at my desk, words tumbling from his mouth.

"Right after you and Pachany escaped from the cattle car, the guards did a head count. Everyone realized what had happened. I was very disappointed that you left me behind, but I was determined to follow you. In all the commotion at the station, I tried to escape, too. I was caught."

The events of four months ago came flooding back into my mind. How long ago it seemed. Rambling on, Ninkovich barely paused for breath, he was so excited.

"When we reached the Osnabruck camp, I was locked in solitary outside the compound. What a blessing that turned out to be. The walls were so thin that I broke through and escaped that night. Somehow, I wound up stumbling across the border into the Netherlands and found refuge with a local priest."

Evidently, he was as lucky as he'd always been. The angels do perhaps watch over certain types. But how did he get from the Netherlands to Marseille? Given his talkative nature, I did not expect to be held in suspense. I was right.

"I was passed along," he went on dramatically, "from hand to hand like a precious reliquary. When I reached Belgium, I hooked up with a group of resistance fighters who smuggled me across the border. They turned me over to a French group who gave me an identity card that made sure my accent would not give me away." He held out his I.D. "See, I am Henri Dupont, a mute."

I burst out laughing. Ninkovich a mute! What a joke. Nonetheless, it was a clever idea, and it had worked.

"So here I am, sir. That's the bare bones. Now, you will want to know the details . . ."

I hastily begged off, congratulating Ninkovich on his fortitude. Then I assigned him to Sergeant Srdanovich's unit. I also swore him twice over to secrecy, with an added warning about being discreet.

Over the summer of 1942, I had considered various escape routes carefully. Gradually, the balance had tipped in favor of Spain as the way we should go. I even went so far as to casually probe Gerasimovich about it.

The consul general had been discouraging. "The Spanish people will not help you. The Pyrenees are too hard to cross on foot. Our chargé d'affaires in Madrid is powerless."

Thus he dismissed the idea. "The government in London is working hard to get everyone out legally. I have requested Portuguese entry visas for the lot of you. In the meantime, Captain, absolutely no one is to take it upon himself to cross into Spain."

That ended the discussion. Typically, the consul general hadn't changed my mind. Yet he had, unintentionally, confirmed one thing. What we faced was no less difficult than the passage of the German border. It was, Pachany and I agreed, an interesting challenge.

With the coming of fall, many of the men grew impatient to leave France. I commended their attitude but strongly opposed any foolhardy attempts. When the moment was right, I averred, I would not hesitate.

Meanwhile, every avenue must be pursued, whether legal— the consulate might yet obtain valid exit visas—or illegal. The latter included firming up our contacts with the Basque contraband runners. They were the only people who could guide us over the mountains from France to Spain—for a price, naturally.

Our goal, at least, was identified: to reach the British embassy in Barcelona. This would not be a fait accompli upon broaching the border. Spain, although not a combatant, gave aid and comfort to the Axis powers. The Franco regime tolerated a Yugoslav chargé d'affairs in our former Madrid embassy, but Gerasimovich was, alas, correct. Our chargé was powerless to assist us.

The British alone had the clout to throw a protective veil around fugitives and the means to spirit them away. In Spain without protection, an apprehended P.O.W. surely would be imprisoned. Or he would be handed back over to the Germans.

Pachany and I had learned to be patient. Others were not so disciplined. Despite my cautionings, my hand was forced by two determined members of the unit, Corporals Ilich and Ivanovich. They declared they'd go with or without my blessing.

"Why should we wait for someone to help us?" they argued. "We reached Marseille on our own. We can make it to Barcelona." Undeterred by the Pyrenees, they had their minds made up.

Resigned to their action, I outfitted them for the trip as best I could. Maybe they'd make it. I hoped so. They could then send back much-needed intelligence.

Within a week after the corporals went off, the British Consulate in Barcelona reported their capture by Spanish border guards. They were interned in the infamous prison camp at Miranda del Ebro.

This failure did not deter the desperate. Vichy was under pressure to deal with its Jewish residents. The Lyons prefecture ordered Mr. Rothchild to the San Sebastian detention center by September 18. He had spent twenty years in France as the owner of a tractor factory and an inventor of oil refining methods. It all meant nothing now. He was wracked with fear of the Nazis.

"Don't be frightened," I told him repeatedly. "There must be a way out."

"I know there isn't," he'd say dejectedly. "I've tried. You've tried. I'm trapped."

Rothchild was not much off the mark. I had tried. My efforts to persuade the consul general to issue a false passport and to plead with a Portuguese colleague for a visa had gotten me nowhere.

"He can wait," was the standard reply. "More important and pressing matters have to be dealt with first." Whatever matters he meant, I could well guess when Gerasimovich planned to get to this one—never.

Pachany and I liked Rothchild, and because he had promised to place his knowledge and abilities at the disposal of our country and the Allies, we refused to give up. One lead after another fizzled out. Only the Spanish option was left. He'd have to take it.

With only a day to spare, we dispatched Rothchild with a volunteer, Master Sergeant Krstich. They would use the main underground traffic route from Perpignan in France to Figueras, eighteen miles over the border. The mountains in that area were the most accessible and could be crossed at night, provided you had an experienced and reliable guide.

If the two men were lucky and Rothchild's money sufficient, maybe they could outwit the Spanish patrols and get through. Pachany and I crossed our fingers.

Several days later, a jubilant phone call came from Figueras. Rothchild was on the line. "We made it. Everything's fine. The people are friendly. And the police are protecting us." He sounded reborn. "We'll be in Barcelona in a couple of days."

Maybe the crossing was easier than I'd been led to believe. The temptation was great to follow hard on the heels of Krstich and Rothchild. The opportunity was there. Agonizing for hours, I decided to hold off until they reached Barcelona. Then I would act.

Two days went by. When I received a late-night message to return to the consulate, I was ready for glad tidings. At the villa, I was instead presented with the sight of our two Spanish adventurers sitting in gloomy silence.

Rothchild and Krstich were disheveled, their clothes torn. When I questioned them, Sergeant Krstich swore a blue streak. They had been undone by Rothchild's lack of stamina and their failure to abide by my warnings to the letter.

The difficult trek over the mountains, which Krstich admitted was a trial even for someone in his excellent condition, had left Rothchild utterly exhausted. After the phone call from Figueras, he'd insisted on resting. Their guide flatly refused, and he abandoned them. They did push on awhile, but there was this inviting bench in front of a small mountain house . . .

The house was a police station. Discovered on the bench, they were brought in for interrogation. Rothchild was confident the police would help, but they had merely extracted all his money with false assurances.

"You gentlemen are nice people," the head of the detachment had finally said. "So we couldn't send you to the concentration camp. You have heard of it?" The Spaniard had smiled broadly. "We will send you instead back to France."

London ordered us to cease any further attempts to reach Spain. The government-in-exile claimed to be working on an underground channel through Belgium. We had to realize, they explained, that proper planning and implementation took time.

But the war wouldn't wait on the plans of London's bureaucrats.

November 8 was a beautiful fall day and Pachany was with me on his monthly trip to Marseille. The consulate was locked tight. Allowing ourselves a rare diversion, we decided to spend that Sunday at the racetrack.

As a former competition rider, I picked the winners for both of us. Unfortunately, the horses seemed unaware of my expertise. When we lost, Pachany teased me mercilessly. It really didn't matter, as it was simply grand to breathe the fresh air of the beautiful park and escape from serious thoughts for a while.

We were in the middle of cheering on another of our losers when the public address announcer broke off calling the race. "May I have your attention, please," a strained voice crackled over the loudspeakers. "American military units have invaded French North Africa. Our forces are resisting . . ."

I grabbed Pachany's arm. We didn't need to hear the rest. At the end of October, the British had scored a great victory at El Alamein in Egypt. Rommel's forces must be in real trouble. And if the Americans were in North Africa across the Mediterranean, then southern France would become strategically vital to the Germans.

It had to be a question of days. Vichy was not going to survive. We Yugoslavs had to get out of France or fall once more into the grasp of the Nazis.

Pachany immediately departed for Lyons to assemble his contingent. He would return within forty-eight hours. In Marseille, I ordered Sergeant Srdanovich to gather all the local men. Sunday night I spent at the consulate destroying as many official files as I could.

I was burning documents in my office when the consul general burst in. I had never seen him so agitated. His face was ashen.

"What in the world are you doing here?" he screamed. "No one is supposed to be here on Sunday!"

"The Allies have invaded North Africa," I said calmly. "Haven't you heard?"

"Yes. So?" He was trembling.

"Business as usual is gone forever. We must move fast. Figure the rest out yourself!" Impatiently, I turned back to my task. I didn't even hear the old man leave.

The next day was a different story. Loud shouting greeted me as soon as I got to the villa. Somebody else was having an undiplomatic exchange of views with Gerasimovich.

Vice Consul Majdanich was the brave soul in the lion's den. Triumphantly emerging, he came into my office and produced a fat bundle of Swiss francs. "Here. This is rightfully for the men." He tossed the money on my desk. "I'm leaving today."

"What about the consul general?"

"The old fool will stay behind. But don't worry. He has years of experience. He'll survive." Majdanich gave me an ironic smile. "Yes, and some of us won't."

We embraced, then he was gone. Before I could close my office door, Lieutenant Ninkovich and Sergeant Srdanovich arrived with the rest of the unit.

Thank God we were prepared. Everybody had been issued a false passport with forged visas for French exit, transit in Spain, and Portuguese entry. The British embassy in Barcelona had been kept advised.

The men were divided up into teams of three or four. My own team included Pachany and the two other senior men, Master Sergeant Srdanovich and Lieutenant Ninkovich. We would leave Marseille only after everyone else was safely out.

I addressed the group as they stood silently before my desk: "Gentlemen, everything is arranged. Each team must move separately. Take trains heading for Port Boux, but get off at Argeles-sur-Mer. Continue on foot. Each team leader will be provided with money and the address of a contact."

They must have known my instructions by heart, but I methodically ran down the list again. "Act resolutely at all times. Otherwise, your border guide will not respect you. I remind you that his personal loyalty is dubious. Follow his instructions and handle your money prudently. Remember what happened to Mr. Rothchild."

When there was nothing further to add, I took a deep breath. "May we all meet safe and sound in Barcelona. Good luck to you." Then I dismissed them.

Tuesday morning, Pachany and his men arrived. As instructed, they were already in their small teams. Rothchild, who had been kept hidden for nearly two months, and Sergeant Krstich were ready for their second chance.

The months of training paid off. With clockwork precision, the teams were sent out from Marseille one after another. All that day and the next, everything went smoothly.

A state of emergency was in effect. Rumors spread wildly. The Germans were sweeping across the armistice line. Lyons would fall shortly, it was said.

The last scheduled train to Port Boux was Wednesday at 8:00 P.M. My team had to be on it. November 11 had to be our last day in Marseille.

At seven, Pachany, Srdanovich, and I met at the railway station. To our utter shock, Ninkovich showed up dressed for a night on the town. He wore a navy blue suit, white shirt and tie, a light raincoat, and dress shoes.

"What the hell are you wearing, Ninkovich?" I asked. This time I *would* strangle him.

"Oh, I can move faster like this, Captain," he quipped brashly.

Ever since his arrival in the city, Lieutenant Ninkovich had been a pain. He had bragged constantly about his conquests, his good looks, his fly-by-night escape plans. Besides spending money too freely, he still couldn't keep his mouth shut. I had reprimanded him more than once.

"We have fifty-five minutes before the train leaves. Go back and change your clothes."

"But, Captain . . ."

"Do you wish to be left behind?" He knew I meant it. "Change. Now!" Pachany and I looked at each other. We'd save this fool in spite of himself.

The Marseille station was a nightmare. Fear was in the air.

People were pushing and pulling, struggling to find room on the trains, dragging their worldly possessions around in heavy bundles. Conductors and gendarmes were helpless to control the waves of people moving in every direction.

Ninkovich returned. We four then wedged our way through the crowd and got to the platform gate. Without warning, it opened. Screams, shouts, curses, and sobs arose from an avalanche of humanity. Crushed together, we rode the thronging mass until we were jammed into the corridor of a car. Outside, the chaos continued. A conductor shouted, "No more room!"

The train inched from the station. The crowd surged forward, and I looked out on that sea of desperate human faces. There was nothing to be done.

The train began to pick up speed.

10

Over the Pyrenees

"EVERYBODY OUT! LAST STOP!" It was the middle of the night. The harried conductor pushed through the cars making his announcement. "Train for Port Boux leaves this afternoon!"

We were in Perpignan, many miles to the west of Marseille. The train had swept around the curve of the Mediterranean and deposited us within hailing distance of the Spanish border. But not close enough.

Unlike the scene we had left, Perpignan was a picture of nocturnal tranquility. Evidently, the panic hadn't reached here yet. The night was balmy with a gentle breeze. The pleasant scent of flowers teased my nose.

There were some twelve hours ahead of us before we could complete the short trip to Argeles-sur-Mer. Near the station was an outdoor café filled with people. Ninkovich, Srdanovich, Pachany, and I sat down together at a table.

No one seemed aware that it was two in the morning. Waiters were circulating among the tables, serving customers in this welcoming haven for travelers. Even if we'd had beds for the night, I would have been reluctant to leave.

It was also precisely the atmosphere to encourage Ninkovich's exuberance. To my annoyance, he was soon booming away. Dulled by fatigue, I wasn't quite sure what action to take. If I clamped down too aggressively, I'd just create a bigger scene.

People at nearby tables were already turning their heads,

looking at us. I was sure they were trying to guess what language we were speaking. My eyes bored into Ninkovich. For the third time, I quietly urged him to keep his voice down.

I might as well have thrown fuel on the fire. "What are you afraid of, Captain?" He laughed loudly, enjoying himself. "The Germans aren't in Marseille yet and we're almost to the Span—" He left the sentence hanging.

Pachany nudged me under the table. I turned my head. Two men were standing behind Srdanovich, staring right at the flustered Ninkovich. My jaw tightened.

"Your I.D. card, please," the taller man said. Despite the civilian clothes, both were obviously police. Everyone in the café knew it.

Like each of us, Ninkovich carried two false passports. He had the choice of being a Bulgarian or a Croatian student attending school in Marseille. Either identity would satisfy this pair. As he meekly produced an I.D., I assumed we'd have to do a little fast talking to placate the detectives, but I had as usual underestimated our bon vivant lieutenant.

"I see you have a very low opinion of our intelligence, monsieur," the detective remarked after examining the I.D. "Do you think we are idiots? For ten minutes I have listened to your loud voice blasting our ears in some foreign language. Yet your papers claim you are a mute Frenchman."

My God, how could Ninkovich be so stupid? I had told him repeatedly to destroy that old phony card. My blood boiled. To have come this far only to be undone by a fool!

I had to try something. "Please, it's a practical joke," I interceded in French. "It's just a gag he pulls in school. We're Bulgarian students on our way to Spain. Here's my passport."

"Yes, here." Pachany offered his, and Srdanovich followed suit. Even Ninkovich, coming out of his trance, managed to pull out the right passport this time.

The two detectives looked at our documents. Politely, they handed them back. They conferred. Ninkovich alone was surprised when one of them said, "I'm afraid you'll all have to come to the station."

It certainly was what I'd expected.

We rose from the table and were escorted out into the dark, winding streets of Perpignan. Walking beside me, Ninkovich whispered to me in Serbo-Croatian. "Why don't we jump them, Captain? There's two of them and four of us. We could get their guns and . . ."

"And what? Have the French police hunt us down? You have caused your last disaster, Ninkovich. Shut your mouth. Open it when I tell you. Or I swear I will leave you behind to rot in a cell."

For once, the lieutenant was subdued. At the police station, the gendarmes searched us thoroughly. They confiscated our belongings.

Luckily, my stash of money and second passport escaped notice. They did, however, find the other passports of my three comrades, and probably concluded we were Allied spies. My loud protests got no response, except for the information that we would be held for further questioning.

After an hour, I was escorted into a small interrogation room. "Who are you? What are you up to?" the police sergeant demanded to know.

I gave him our prerehearsed answer. "I'm a Yugoslav student fleeing from France to Spain. I only ask that you permit us to cross the border. We've done no harm to France. Please, let me speak to the chief inspector."

"You'll see him when he's good and ready. You're dismissed. Next."

After individual grillings, we were placed together in an underground dungeon. The cell was small, the cement floor dank, and the stone walls were wet and moldy. It smelled of filth and human excrement. A feeble light hung from the ceiling and left us in semidarkness.

I was dozing when the cell door jerked open. A streak of dawn sunlight cut across the cement. A gendarme sergeant ordered us out into the yard where we washed our faces.

We were running out of time. I repeated my request to see his superior.

"Forget it," the sergeant barked. "He has more important things to do. The Germans are due in town this afternoon."

As we were returned to the cell, our hopes faded with each passing minute. I began to remember life in prison camp—and the thought made my stomach turn. I didn't think I could endure it another time.

"What are we going to do, Bora?" Pachany sounded as discouraged as I was.

"Perhaps if I can talk to the inspector . . ." It wasn't much, but I had no better idea.

"And say what?" Srdanovich asked. "Considering how we got in this mess."

Pachany refused to recriminate. "We could ask him to get in touch with the consul general and try to send us back to Marseille. The prisoner in the next cell says the Allies are bombing Corsica. When the invasion comes, we could join the French underground."

"Yes, that's a great idea," Ninkovich piped in.

My face turned dark. "We're going to return home where we're needed. Going back to Marseille is out of the question. If we fall into German hands now, I imagine they would take one good look at our dossiers and order us shot."

As if timed to unnerve us, a voice cried out from the next cell. "The Nazis are here! The Nazis are here!"

I rushed to peer through the cell keyhole. Sure enough, a German captain stood talking with the gendarmes. He wanted all the prisoners. They were to be sent to work on coastal fortifications.

The day dragged on endlessly. We could overhear snatches of conversation. The German officer's visit had left the gendarmes agitated and upset. His arrogant manner had done nothing to encourage cooperation.

There was one gamble I could still take. It was a long shot, but I saw no other choice. All else had failed. I would try telling the truth.

My three companions agreed. We had little to lose, anyway. With crossed fingers, I called for the sergeant.

He looked through the small barred window in the cell door. "Yes?"

"Please, we're not students. We are escaped P.O.W.s and officers in the Yugoslav Army. You can't allow the Germans to take us. I must speak to the inspector."

The sergeant said nothing. We all held our breath. "I'll see what I can do," he whispered. I had guessed right. He had a true French heart beating inside his official uniform.

The rest of the day and another uneasy night were spent going over what I would say. We had to go for broke, put ourselves at the mercy of the French police, and pray they shared a common hatred for the Nazis. That was our only possible ace in the hole.

The next morning, the sergeant escorted me to the inspector's office upstairs. I was greeted by a tall, middle-aged Frenchman with a faint smile. His face showed signs of intense strain. He sat down and gestured for me to begin.

"Inspector, we're career officers performing our duty," I said in what I hoped was an impressive military tone. "We are guilty of one thing—our determination to fight the enemy of both France and Yugoslavia."

The inspector sat motionless, his eyes fixed on my face. I went on as forcefully as I dared. "Once before, our fathers fought side by side. In the First World War, we were together against the Germans. History now repeats itself." Was I imagining it, or were his eyes teary? "Inspector, for the good of your conscience and the honor of France, you must not turn us over to the Nazis. I beg you to let us complete our mission."

He rose from his chair and reached out for my hand. "Damn the *Boches*. Go, with Godspeed. The sergeant will return your passports and belongings to you and your men."

I couldn't have been more stunned.

"If my duty wasn't here, I would join you," the inspector said at the door. "You're not much of a dramatic actor, Captain, but we French always appreciate a sincere performance." Another faint smile, and he turned away.

Our original train was long gone, but our luck held. A local got us to Argeles-sur-Mer around noon.

The small town was buzzing with activity. German soldiers were digging trenches on the beach and setting up artillery pieces, preparing to repel the Allies someday in the future. We steered a wide berth around them, but they were preoccupied with their duties.

The place was undeniably picturesque. We walked up the main road past small, Moorish-style houses. Below, waves crashed on the shore, while a deep blue haze hovered over the neighboring hills.

I led the team in search of our contact, a man named Pierre Loge. When I found his house, the front door was open. I went in alone while the others waited outside.

"Anyone home?" There was no response.

As I was about to leave, a beautiful young woman emerged from another room. She was wearing the traditional Basque costume with a black kerchief and a long, matching shawl. Silently, she regarded me.

"I would like to buy some property," I said carefully. This was the recognition phrase.

Her smile was demure. "My father is waiting at the property on the hill, sir. I will take you and your friends there."

I breathed a sigh of relief. She must be Pierre's daughter. We had made our connection.

She led us single file up the side of the mountain, never looking behind, never slowing the pace. After a grueling two hours, we arrived at a little cottage hidden in the forest. A thin, smiling man came out to meet us.

"Welcome. I am Pierre Loge. You are late, but no matter. Come with me."

We were taken into a cozy room with a crackling fire and served a hearty lunch. Afterwards, Pierre had arranged a rendez-vous with a man who might be willing to conduct us across the Pyrenees. He was anxious to get started.

Another hour's climb brought us to a seemingly solid cliff. "Go ahead," Pierre ordered. He showed us the concealed entrance to a cave.

One by one, we crawled into the tiny cave. It was no more than ten by twelve feet, with freshly cut twigs covering the dirt floor and a fireplace built into a corner. We found ourselves joining the company of a group of tough, scruffy-looking men in Catalonian attire. They looked like underworld characters out of some French movie.

Pierre introduced me to José. His dark eyes were not friendly. When told my request, he started shaking his head.

"Too dangerous." He spoke broken French in a harsh Catalonian accent. "Path very rough. You not make it. Four too many." His dark eyes flashed menacingly. "We caught, they kill me. Maybe you."

He was bargaining, all right. I had to play tough. "We mean business, José. The man who helps me and keeps his word will be paid handsomely. The man who cheats me . . . will die."

I turned to Pierre and openly paid him two hundred Swiss francs for the introduction. A broad smile lit his craggy face. All eyes in the cramped cave were riveted on us. These illiterate men knew to the decimal the high value of Swiss francs on the black market.

José's attitude did a remarkable flip. At some imperceptible signal, his friends got up and left the cave. He began calling me "Chief," a sign of his respect, and suggested that I had misunderstood him. Maybe a hike over the border was possible.

"Chief," he said in much-improved French, "we have to climb all night. No stops, no matter how tired. I give the orders. I tell you when and where to rest. Okay?"

We had our guide. After bickering back and forth, I struck a bargain. I agreed to pay him five hundred Swiss francs. One-third in advance, a third more upon reaching Figueras, and the rest when he arranged transportation for us to Barcelona.

At nightfall, we began to climb.

From the first step, the Pyrenees were treacherous. The path was barely visible. There were loose rocks that were sharp and jagged, and the tall grass on the slopes often made the going slippery. A careless step could be your last.

Leading us, José climbed effortlessly like a mountain goat, while we struggled to stay with him. Several hours passed. Ninkovich began lagging. "Can't we rest, Captain?" he pleaded. "I can't keep up the pace."

José wouldn't hear of it. "No rest, Chief, or we all take a big risk. Leave the big baby behind. Fear make him catch up fast. You watch." I only wished I could. To ease his load, I relieved Ninkovich of his heavy knapsack.

Like four ghosts in the night, we continued climbing after José for hours. Sweat poured down my neck. The knapsack glued itself to my back, and the mountain breeze sent a chill through my aching bones. I felt I could hardly move, but my legs went up and down automatically.

Finally, we reached a vast plateau where the ground was practically barren. Mysteriously, José turned right, then left, following markers I couldn't discern. We reached a gently slopping hill where several trees loomed in the darkness.

"Wait here, Chief," José said. He disappeared while we stood there like dumb beasts of burden. The wind picked up and it began to rain. Fifteen minutes later, he was back.

Immediately, we resumed the march. But this time, mercifully, we moved downhill. When we saw the silhouette of some crude huts up ahead, José stopped and turned to me. "Chief, welcome to Spain. The sun rises soon. We rest here."

Welcome to Spain, I thought. I was too exhausted to think anything about it.

We had collapsed in one of the empty stone huts. I awoke early the next afternoon. José was busy stoking the fire and preparing beans. Then the sound of voices outside brought me to my feet.

Pachany and I didn't know what to think. Ninkovich was still asleep. I motioned Srdanovich to edge closer to the door, in case we had to jump an intruder. Irritatingly, José showed no concern whatever. He went on stirring his pot of beans.

In a minute I understood why. Two men appeared at the hut entrance. One was certainly a Basque guide and known by José. The other was a tall, distinguished-looking man in a black overcoat and a homburg. He wore glasses and leaned on a black cane.

In the shock of recognition, I wondered if I were seeing things. Was it possible? Could it be Monsieur Piche, minister of the interior in Marshall Petain's Vichy government? We all knew his face from pictures in the paper. He had been the infamous enemy of the refugees from Nazi-occupied Europe who had streamed into France. His aim had been to deport us all.

Indeed, it was he. The minister introduced himself, but I stared in disbelief. He was the last man on earth I would ever have expected to meet on the Spanish side of the border.

Why was he fleeing over the mountains? Perhaps he had decided that the Allied victories in North Africa meant it was time to switch sides. I didn't really care. It gave me pleasure to see the nervous twitch of his eyes behind the thick lenses and hear the slight tremor in his cultured voice.

While his guide conferred with José, the minister took it upon himself to make a small speech to us. "I hate the Nazis, you know. Yes, gentlemen, strange as it sounds. You probably believe I am a collaborator. Well, that reputation helped me do a lot of good for France and the Allies."

This was something new to me, traitors defending themselves on the grounds they had really prevented worse things from happening. Piche had caused a lot of actual misery to innocent people, but he didn't consider that. He had the same sort of moral relativism that had done so much to let the Nazis come to power in the first place.

Silence followed his last words. We had nothing to say to him, but the minister had no doubt guessed our status. To put off his curiosity, I admitted we were traveling toward Barcelona, while declining to specify exactly who we were.

"I have secure passage through Spain," Piche practically blurted out. "I would be glad to take you four along. A car is waiting for me at Figueras with clearance to Lisbon. Come with me."

"No, thank you," I declined politely. "We are obligated to our guide." I wanted nothing to do with him.

"Well then." Piche drew his coat around him. "I am off, gentlemen. Bonjour." He went out of the cabin to join his guide. The air inside, I thought, noticeably improved.

Steady rain washed the mountains as José guided us on the next leg of the journey. Down, up, right, left, we plodded a circuitous path that descended steadily. After countless hours, we reached the lowlands late that night.

We halted at a wooden shack in the middle of a cane field and spent the night. Rising early in the morning, I went outside. José was there. Together, we watched the first rays of the sun chase clouds across an azure sky. The field looked freshly scrubbed, the sugar cane dainty and silky soft against a backdrop of starkly looming trees.

"Let's go, Chief. Not safe here," José muttered. He roused the others and we left. Figueras was only seven miles away, but there were a hundred hard miles to Barcelona.

We crossed several fields and hit a twisting road beside a small creek. From there, we hiked along pleasantly until José stopped at a tiny stone cabin. He ordered us inside.

"Stay here, Chief," José explained. "Don't walk around or talk to nobody. I go to Figueras now to find a truck. Come back later today. You pay me in full now."

I shook my head. "That wasn't the deal. When we get on the truck, then I'll pay you. But here, take fifty francs." I held out the money to him and his face brightened. "Bring us back some food."

"Chief, you a good man." José stashed the francs away. Then he was gone.

I didn't like the position we were in, totally dependent on a guide. What would we do if he took off? The thought nagged at me. I hoped he wanted the balance of his money badly enough to see us through.

Our clothes were still damp and the cabin was too small. Despite José's warnings, I led everybody out to a grassy knoll. Ninkovich begged for some food, but none was left, so I suggested he sleep away his hunger. Shortly, all of us had succumbed and were dozing in the bright sunshine.

The barking of a dog woke us. As we rose to our feet, a golden retriever ran out of the grass, followed by an old Basque man pushing a bicycle. A shotgun rested on his shoulder.

We regarded each other warily. "Good morning, Uncle." I smiled broadly.

The old man smiled back. He handed us a large piece of bread. From his bag, he took a wooden dish filled with a bean puree. He was offering us his lunch.

It would have been an insult to refuse. Eating hungrily, we talked with him as best we could in a mixture of French and Italian. "Franco," he said, "non bono, non bono." He was proud to help us.

Although the old man had been friendly and harmless, I wasn't about to ignore José's warnings a second time. Another imprudent encounter might not go so pleasantly. With Ninkovich grumbling loudly, we moved back close to the cabin.

As promised, José did return that afternoon. He also had a friend along who never uttered a word to us. Our guide was very cheerful and very anxious to get his money. The friend, he claimed, would lead us to the rendezvous point with the truck.

I didn't like this setup. "I'm sure he's okay, but you agreed to personally take us to Figueras. Only when I see the truck will I pay."

"No, no, no!" José protested. "I live up to my bargain. Pay me now!"

I refused. We were arguing heatedly when the old Basque man reappeared, smiling and carrying a basket of food. José looked daggers at me. "Who is this, Chief?"

Before I could answer, José and his friend scrambled off into the woods. I was forced to send the old man away. It wasn't what I wanted to do, but in Spain we had to have a guide, like it or not.

Methodically, we all searched for José. The sun set, but there was no sign of him. The francs aside, my instinct was that he wouldn't abandon us. I was convinced he was just hiding, fully enjoying seeing us sweat.

When he came popping out of the woods like some demented rabbit, his anger hadn't cooled. "You broke a promise to me, Chief." I apologized profusely. It took awhile, but I did calm him down.

After sunset, we were ready to tackle Figueras. We filed along a river bank to the edge of town. "Move silently now, Chief. No noise."

The dark, narrow streets were deserted, ominous, and unfriendly. We walked swiftly until we reached a wider street. José stopped and pointed to a white building. "The police station, Chief. We go one at a time now. Move past the building, then turn right and wait. You go first, Chief."

I did as he ordered. The others hurried after me, and we had no trouble getting to the far side of town. There two men were working on the engine of an ancient pickup truck.

Considering the truck's age and condition, it seemed unlikely to last all the way to Barcelona. But there was no other alternative. I quickly negotiated a price. Then I paid José the last of his money.

"So long, Chief." I was satisfied with our bargain. He'd done his job well. Disappearing as quickly as a cat, he left us in the hands of the truck owners.

The two men climbed into the cab. The four of us had to ride in the back. As we bounced along, charcoal dust in the truck bed caked our bodies till we looked like chimney sweeps.

When we had to duck a checkpoint, we'd clamber out and walk across the fields. Then we'd meet the truck down the road and climb on again. As the night progressed, it began to seem oddly like some children's game of hide-and-seek.

Around four in the morning, the engine stalled out. Our pair of drivers tinkered feverishly, cursing all the while. Finally the engine came to life as dawn broke.

The sun was well up when we got to the outskirts of a small town. This time when we pulled over, there was nothing wrong with the engine. "We go no further," the driver shouted. "Too dangerous."

"But you agreed to take us to Barcelona," I protested.

"We cannot. Too dangerous."

The other man added, "You will be safer without us. It is not far into the city."

They refused to budge. I needed some local currency, so I made them give me ten pesos. Then they cranked up the old truck and took off in a hurry. We were on our own.

"Let's make ourselves more presentable, men," I suggested. At the roadside, we proceeded to change our filthy clothes. A few workers hurrying to early morning factory shifts looked at us in amazement. We paid no attention to them.

With renewed confidence, we spread out in a single file formation for security. I took the lead. Pachany trailed me by a hundred feet or so, then came Srdanovich, and lastly Ninkovich. We had agreed that the first man to spot a taxi would hail it and pick up the rest.

The streets became more crowded. People were hurrying about, running for the trolleys that clanged along. When I looked back for Pachany, I couldn't spot him. It would be a disaster if we lost each other at this point.

A taxi pulled to the curb up ahead of me and I heard Pachany's distinctive whistle. I ran for the cab. They were all inside.

"The British Consulate," I snapped as I climbed in.

"Si, señor," the driver replied.

The drab street turned into a beautiful boulevard lined with trees. Our taxi braked in front of a six-story building on Paseo de Gracia. "The British Consulate, señor."

We were so close now. I looked out the rear window at the two Spanish guards by the gate. "Look like you know where you're going," I whispered to my three comrades. "And don't hesitate."

I paid the driver in pesos, got out, and went up the embassy path. We breezed right past the bored guards. Inside the building, I stopped the first person I saw.

"The office of the consul general?"

"Fourth floor."

We flew up the stairs as if on wings. At the fourth floor reception area, a young lady greeted us. "What nationality are you?" she asked briskly.

"Yugoslav," I replied breathlessly.

"Welcome, friends." She smiled. "You are quite safe with us."

The subsequent days were a blur of activity. The men and women on the consulate staff were eager to help us and make us feel at home. To my joy, I learned that most of our men had arrived safely from Marseille.

We spent several days secretly housed in the apartment of the consul general's chauffeur, then we were sent on to Madrid by car. To avoid detection during the trip, the consulate gave us phony papers and outfitted us in British Army uniforms.

I felt funny in a new uniform. It was so different from what I was accustomed to. And every time I tried to pronounce the British name under my I.D. photo, "Captain Owen Thew-bridge," Pachany burst out laughing. I resolved then and there to master English some day.

The road to Madrid went through hilly countryside that looked bleak and dreary under a cloudy sky. I noticed the remains of burned-out farmhouses, trees ripped from the ground, mounds of debris. The peasants, wrapped in their blankets and carrying sticks of wood or pulling goats, seemed somber and lethargic. It was a landscape of modern warfare.

In contrast, the streets of Madrid were clean and lively. To our great surprise, a reception in our honor awaited us at the British Embassy. The ambassador, Sir Samuel Hoare, greeted us personally, and his staff shook our hands. We were congratulated on our daring many times over.

The Yugoslav chargé d'affairs, Mr. Visacki, was there. Tears rolled down his cheeks and he gave us all bear hugs. I, too, had trouble containing my emotions. It was a warm, heartfelt welcome that renewed our faith in the future.

The subsequent three days we spent in the luxurious Yugoslav Embassy. During that time I started a written report for the prime minister's Military Office in London. I also did oral debriefings to be transmitted to the foreign secretary.

Travel plans were worked out. Pachany and I were scheduled first on the train for Gibraltar, while Ninkovich and Srdanovich remained in Madrid. They would follow later.

After a long ride, we arrived in Algeciras, the last stop in Spanish territory. A friendly British Army captain and two noncoms were expecting us. They took us to a pier, and a motorboat ferried us directly on to the fortress.

Three additional days in bleak quarters were in store for us. While we waited for a ship, we were sent to the fort's hospital for a complete medical examination and a series of inoculations. I was shocked to learn I had ticks.

The cure was straightforward. Two medics worked with unconcealed glee on my midsection, scrubbing my skin down with disinfectant. The pain intensified with every stroke of their brushes. Next, an ointment stung almost as badly. While I suffered, I at least managed to figure out where I had picked up the nasty bugs. I cursed the Perpignan jail, Ninkovich, and my bad luck with equal abandon.

After my third treatment, I was pronounced cured. Our transport ship was due to anchor off Gibraltar any day, but it couldn't be soon enough for me. Pachany and I were impatient to get to London.

I worked on my report and thought fleetingly about the course of my life. Today I was looking forward to a Christmas in England. A year prior, I had been in a P.O.W. camp, a statistic of the invincible Third Reich. If, a year before that, anyone had told me that such remarkable things would happen to me, I would have scoffed at the very idea of such lunacy.

11

Hail Britannia

On November 30, 1942, Pachany and I boarded a troop transport off Gibraltar. It was a hastily converted ocean liner, bigger by far than anything I'd seen on the Adriatic. Until that day, I had never stepped foot on such a ship.

The spacious salons, huge dining room, multiple decks, and luxurious cabins were the stuff of imagination. I played it cool and tried to behave as I thought seasoned travelers did. The two of us shared a first-class cabin, our luggage conveyed there by an orderly who would attend to our needs during the voyage.

He helped us get settled, then we attended a shipboard briefing. The captain's orders were strict. No man was to undress before going to bed. Life jackets were always to be within reach. Peaceful as everything seemed to us, we were good soldiers and obeyed—at least for the first night.

Early the next morning, a knock at the cabin door made me jump. Who was it? "Tea, sir!" the orderly announced. He brought in a tray with two cups.

"What do you say, buddy?" I teased Pachany as he joined me. "Aren't we true English gentlemen now? This is the way to travel. First class." We were indeed being treated with the same courtesy given the several hundred British officers aboard going home on leave.

During the night, the ship had sailed west beyond the straits and out into the Atlantic. We were now on the open seas.

Cutting through heaving waves, the churning ocean made the decks pitch and roll. Oddly enough, Pachany and I weren't much bothered. We found the dining room almost empty and had all the food and service to ourselves.

A good many of the British officers were recuperating from wounds or from battle fatigue. They looked pale and exhausted.

While the two of us were roaming all over the ship, the British passengers sat quietly smoking and reading in the great salon. After the second day on the ocean, most of them remained in their cabins, drained by seasickness. No one made any effort to get acquainted with us, so we minded our own business.

The ship's captain did all he could to impress us with the danger of German U-boats, which were then at the height of their naval maraudings. We traveled without the customary convoy, but it didn't bother me. I figured that our great speed alone was sufficient protection. Yet each day, to my annoyance, we had to attend evacuation drills.

On the first sound of the alarm, we would run to our assigned stations. Then we practiced each step of the evacuation procedure. I was truly amazed at the seriousness with which the crew approached these drills.

As one uneventful day passed into the next, I was even more brashly convinced that the drills were unnecessary. What an innocent fool I was! I did not appreciate the constant danger, and it was a good thing the crew couldn't understand my sarcastic remarks in Serbo-Croatian. Otherwise they might have tossed me into the ocean or confined me to the brig.

Still, Pachany and I were very much interested in the methods used to outwit German submarines, even if we knew little of naval maneuvering. Our own speculations served as sobering thoughts before bedtime. In the dark, a sudden attack in the midst of a seemingly empty ocean was vastly more plausible. We were lucky to be spared that grim experience.

The ship had been moving at full speed but taking a huge detour around the Bay of Biscay. We were headed for the Irish Sea between England and Ireland, a backdoor route as far as our ultimate destination was concerned. It meant a long train ride for us down to London.

After four days, we sighted the hills of Scotland. The ship soon sailed into the port of Greenock, and the experienced hands on board smiled with relief. Another mission without any casualties. Ironically, for Pachany and me it had been the most pleasant and easy trip we'd had since leaving Marseille.

Perhaps that very ease should have given me greater pause. Especially in wartime, a false sense of security usually leads to surprises, and largely of the unpleasant kind. As it turned out, it wasn't only U-boats that I should have held in higher regard for their ability to do the unexpected.

Anchored in the dreary Scottish port, I anticipated after debarkation that the British would politely direct us to London. After all, aboard ship Pachany and I had been extended many courtesies befitting our rank as officers. I was so convinced of this applied logic that I thought Yugoslav representatives might even be permitted to meet us in Glasgow, the nearest major city. Our government-in-exile would immediately take charge of us, with British blessings.

The shore police were but the first to invalidate my naive hopes. After they had verified the travel permits of all the other passengers, they concentrated on the small group of foreign nationals to which Pachany and I, of course, belonged.

They asked us for our papers. We showed them everything we had, an astonishing collection of real, fudged, and outright phony documents. This called for explanations. Each of us was interviewed separately, and our belongings were searched.

Impounding our papers, the shore police then informed us that we had to stay on board until the following day. The other passengers had long since departed.

The next day we were finally allowed to land—under armed escort. Taken before British immigration officials, we faced another long and tedious interrogation. It seemed they wanted to know everything that had happened to us since the war began in 1939.

As the hours passed, I began to feel like a defendant in some Kafkaesque trial. What did they want? Could they not verify my identity through the Yugoslav Government-in-Exile in London? The repeated questions seemed totally irrelevant to our situation. Discouraged, confused, and exhausted, Pachany and I were among those finally led away by a shore police lieutenant and a few shore police soldiers.

To my great astonishment, we were next subjected to a search to our skins, a method I had last encountered at the hands of the Germans. Immediately afterwards, we were taken to a barracks in Glasgow, given supper, and then brought to the train station. Clearly, we were to be kept under British lock and key for some time to come.

I protested sharply. Contact our representatives in London, I urged. They could supply all the necessary facts. I stressed that we did not accept the idea of being treated like enemy prisoners, even if some British officials erroneously thought we possessed information that we were refusing to divulge.

The S.P. lieutenant in charge tried to ease our minds, saying that we would all be in London soon enough. Besides, didn't we realize they had to take security measures to deny the entry of enemy agents and provocateurs?

Yes, I responded, and in our case that was easy enough to determine. Of course I knew it was a matter entirely out of his hands. There was nothing for us to do but wait and fume.

The long overnight train ride from Glasgow ended at Victoria Station. A military van was waiting. It took us to a compound somewhere in metropolitan London.

After an hour's ride, we were ushered into a building that by all appearances might have once served as a jail or a mental asylum. The routine was eerily similar to the German P.O.W. camps, although our British hosts were certainly more courteous. And the food was better.

That first day, we were searched again, given medical exams, and spent the usual tedious hours just waiting. There were certainly no Yugoslav government representatives around, either to be seen or heard from, even if one asked—I did, to no avail.

During the next few days, Pachany and I learned more about our new lodgings. There were several buildings of various sorts situated on a large plot of land. The entire compound was fenced off by iron railings and kept under surveillance by armed guards. Secured with a heavy chain, the main gate was manned by two sentries.

Save for the absence of rows of barbed wire and machine-gun turrets, superficially it little differed from the camp at Offenburg. We could hardly believe our eyes. Having come halfway across Europe, were we supposed to sit out the rest of the war here?

Some ten days after arriving in Merry Old England, we finally were transferred to another section of the compound, the famous "Victoria Patriotic School." Greeted cordially by the official in charge, we were given a set speech designed to encourage our speedy cooperation.

"The Patriotic School is part of the Home Defense Command," the official explained, "and its purpose is to debrief Allied military and civilian personnel reaching England, and to prepare them for the life ahead of them."

The debriefing staff was particularly interested in escaped P.O.W.s, their motivation and methods. It all sounded logical, but somehow it did not add up in my head. No matter what explanations were given, it was clear to me that we weren't to be trusted. We were suspects. The cordial greetings, polite treatment, and decent accommodations could not remove that stigma. My pride was offended.

At any given time, the Patriotic School had several hundred detainees. Men from all the countries of Europe milled across the rooms and hallways of this clearinghouse. While walking around the compound, I could hear almost every European language. It was like some modern Tower of Babel.

I mixed among them with resignation.

Of the "students" at the school, the Polish military men were in the majority. Pachany and I struck up a quick friendship with several of them quartered in our building. These officers were neither disgruntled or dismayed at being confined, although some had been here for more than a month. They were full of optimism, cracking jokes left and right at the expense of our "custodians." Their attitude was contagious. I stopped brooding and began to look forward to the world still out there beyond the iron fence.

The school's basic subject was Endless Interrogation, conducted throughout the day. I was not at all surprised to be questioned by a gentleman who spoke excellent Serbo-Croatian. Irritated as I was, I couldn't hide my displeasure at the whole procedure, especially being asked everything five times over.

My attitude made no difference. Every second or third day, I was again interviewed by the official in charge of my case. As we proceeded, it became obvious that my interrogator was principally interested in my activities in Vichy France. So, to speed up my debriefing a little, I wrote up a full account of that period. It seemed to help both of us ferret out the points he was interested in.

Separately, Pachany was undergoing the same repetitive questioning, but otherwise we were allowed the run of the school grounds. The great formal English park within the compound had a number of long garden paths, and we often took to these to walk off some of our frustrations.

One day, we heard people speaking Serbo-Croatian up ahead of us. Intensely curious, we discovered several men discussing politics. Loudly. These new students at the school turned out to be Colonel Gerba, a former military attaché in the Lisbon embassy; an embassy clerk, Mr. Matich; and Mr. Mata Ruskovich, a member of the dissolved Yugoslav Parliament who'd recently escaped the country. Our initial conversation, polite but impersonal, revealed that they were all undergoing the same routine that we were.

At the time, my encounter with these fellow Yugoslavs cheered me up. In particular, Colonel Gerba and Mr. Ruskovich were men with connections and authority and were hardly nonentities to the British. The colonel, a former diplomatic and military representative in Portugal (a neutral country) had close contacts there with various British services, and was well-known. Mr. Ruskovich was not only a member of our last parliament, but also claimed to have come directly from General Mihailovich, the Allies' acknowledged leader of resistance inside Yugoslavia.

Yet here both men had to undergo the same "schooling" as Pachany and I. And we were, by British reckoning, two unknown Yugoslav P.O.W.s who claimed to have escaped from Germany and occupied France. Given our common plight, I felt I really had a lot less to complain about.

Yet if this chance meeting was no more unusual than a thousand other momentary encounters of wartime, it was also the faint inception, unrecognized them, of some of my most somber private thoughts. So it is that trivial incidents in our lives may eventually assume a profounder aspect. In my later thinking, these two men were to some extent embodiments of the plight of the Yugoslav peoples who had fallen to the Germans a year and a half earlier.

Colonel Gerba was Croatian, and the routine stereotype of Croats has always been their opposition to the Serbs. In the war, the majority of the Croats were indisputably allies of the Axis, and not only those living in the so-called Independent State of Croatia. The British apparently suspected that Colonel Gerba had maintained connections with the Germans in Lisbon, and so his internment was not without initial justification.

However, given detainment criteria based on a record of loyalty to the Allied cause, my internment, not to mention that of any Serbian like Mr. Ruskovich, was absolutely illogical. Naively, perhaps, we had expected a better reception from an ally. Mr. Ruskovich did, and he was angry.

He has risked his life to escape from Yugoslavia so he could bring his government, which the British themselves had recognized as legal and sovereign, important information on the current state of affairs. Before he could do so, the British insisted on knowing if he was also bringing secret messages to King Peter, or to other ministers. Openly declaring that he was not bound to answer such inquiries, Ruskovich had protested that the British government ought to obtain the information it sought directly from the Yugoslav government, once he was allowed to complete his mission. Diplomatically, his strong stand was perfectly correct, but with the British sense of fair play already badly frayed by the war, he had forthwith found himself at the Patriotic School.

(I never learned if Colonel Gerba was actually a traitor, though I did hear later that efforts made by the government-in-exile to extract Mr. Ruskovich were unsuccessful.)

As my own interrogation sessions continued, I sensed a subtle change in tone. By the second week there was cause for optimism. Abruptly, I was cordially thanked for my cooperation and told to be ready to leave. Pachany was reporting similar progress, and we hoped that our release was near.

This time we weren't disappointed. The next morning, we said good-bye to our Polish officer friends. Official certificates attesting to our successful completion of the Patriotic School course were presented to us. Then, half an hour later, Pachany and I strolled out through the forbidding main gate as casually as any tourists leaving their hotel for a look at the London sights.

It was two days before Christmas, and we were again free men.

There was a car waiting for us. An official of the Royal Yugoslav Government had come to pick us up, and we were driven across London to the prime minister's offices located at Kingston House in Kensington. Despite all that had happened to us, Pachany and I were still army officers on active duty, so I surmised that we'd be assigned to the Military Office.

Outwardly, I tried to maintain my best military bearing, but I was conscious that, however minor my own position would be, I'd soon be rubbing shoulders with some of the top leaders from prewar Yugoslavia. In my heart, I was elated that my dream was on the verge of being realized, to throw myself into the war effort and make whatever contribution was needed until the eventual liberation of my homeland.

At the ministry, my orders were already prepared. I was to serve as adjutant to Major Zivan L. Knezevich, secretary of the Yugoslav War Cabinet and chief of the Military Office. A clerk told me that within a few minutes, I would be ushered into his office and formally introduced.

Although I had never met him, I certainly knew of Major Knezevich. In military circles before the war, it was hard not to notice the tall, handsome blond captain with a row of medals set on his officer's tunic. Alternating between the General Staff and postings to field commands, he was being groomed for the highest positions in the military. Word was that the man himself was well-liked by his superiors and by the younger officers under him. None of this, however, quite compared to the national prominence he suddenly achieved as a participant in the famous coup d'état of March 27, 1941.

His older brother, Radoye Knezevich, had been a distinguished member of the Yugoslav Democratic party. The two men together had played a major role in organizing and executing the coup after our government had signed the Tripartite Pact, the 1940 agreement that teamed Germany, Italy, and Japan as allies. With counsel from Radoye, Zivan had persuaded the other plotters, notably Air Force Brigadier General Borivoje Mirkovich, to commit themselves to a political program that called for a coalition government composed of representatives from all the political parties.

The elation and exuberance of the coup had proved a badly needed shot in the arm for an embattled England and briefly overshadowed Hitler's furious response. With the German invasion and victory that followed, the new government and the young king it had placed on the throne had little choice except to go into exile. Zivan went with them.

Now here I was a year and a half later being shown into his private office. Not without some trepidation, I reported for duty and saluted. The major arose, an imposing figure in his tailored olive-drab uniform, and gave me a bear hug that was genuine and warm, as if at the reunion of two old friends. He could not have been more cordial, and he insisted that I address him by his nickname, Zika.

His broad smile could not altogether hide signs of strain. Full of optimism despite the difficulties he faced daily, Zika swiftly introduced me to the duties of my new position. As he bombarded me with a torrent of words, his eyes lit up, his enthusiasm recharged, and the tension-etched lines in his face faded away.

With this splendid welcome, it took me only a few minutes to feel at home. It was more than simply being back in harness with a military man of Major Knezevich's high caliber and ability. Here was someone I felt might well become a lifelong friend, an idealist and fighter for exactly the same things I believed in.

Without wasting time, Zika had arranged suitable accommodations for me at the Marble Arch Hotel. When I checked in late that afternoon, I found myself in a room that exceeded all my expectations. Pachany, too, was billeted here, and we agreed that the hotel vastly outshone our recent quarters in the Patriotic School.

The next day I was to get properly attired. It would hardly do for me to assume my new duties in the clothes I had worn since leaving France. An aide escorted me to a tailor shop on Seville Row, where Milan the tailor promised me the fastest service possible. Since he was an expatriate Yugoslav, I was even inclined to believe him. From there, my guide took me to Morgan and Ball, a well-known men's store on Piccadilly Square, and I finished my shopping. At least on a material level, things were definitely looking up.

The Christmas season was a muted celebration. For me, the one bright note was my reception at the Military Office by Major Knezevich. Other than that, I shared with all Londoners the ever-present threat of German air attacks and concern for the Allied armies battling in Russia and North Africa. Needless to say, the war had not taken a holiday.

True to his word, Milan completed his work in a few days. So, as the old year ended, I became the proud owner of a wardrobe consisting of several uniforms and two civilian suits. I also was learning my way around London and had plunged into the serious study of English. Since my new duties would likely bring me into contact with British officials, I wanted to be able to rely on my own proficiency in their language.

The last week of December found me immersed in my new position. In many ways, I had yet to adjust. This was not only because I was unaccustomed to the work and the local office habits. I was also confronting a sharply different perspective on the government-in-exile's activities and its relationship with the British than, frankly, I had been prepared for.

There didn't appear to be a problem initially. Of course, I had assumed that what I read in the newspapers or heard on the radio would not precisely tally with the truth revealed in inner circles. However, the development of events seemed largely in accord, whether from official or unofficial accounts, and certain main points were generally conceded.

First, there presently existed in Yugoslavia an organized armed resistance against the forces of occupation. It was of inestimable value to the Allied cause as it tied down thirty enemy divisions.

Second, the Yugoslav forces in exile were admittedly inconsequential, and had more of a symbolic than a military significance.

Third, nearly twenty months had passed since the Yugoslav government had quit the country and joined the other émigré governments in London. But it had left with tremendous moral prestige because it was the one government courageous enough to reject the Tripartite Pact, even though it knew it would provoke Germany to war.

Fourth, the prestige of the Yugoslav Government-in-Exile had quickly risen above that of other occupied nations with the start of the earliest open resistance. At the time, it was the outstanding example in all Europe.

It was not necessary to stress the results beyond the major

disruption of the German operational plans for the invasion of Russia. Yugoslavia had cost the Germans at least two months, and in losing that time, the Nazi war machine may have doomed itself. Surely British statesmen could never forget that the Yugoslav act of defiance had amounted to conscious national suicide on behalf of the Allied cause.

The present Yugoslav government had logically placed itself at the head of in-country resistance. It therefore ought to have devoted itself to the tasks of directing the guerrilla operations at home, providing matériel, and disseminating supportive propaganda. Naturally, as an exiled government on English soil, Yugoslav officials could only proceed with the assistance of the British. In practice, that required the closest cooperation with the political and military services in the Allied war zone to which Yugoslavia was assigned.

Key to all these goals was the development of constant and direct communications with the forces of resistance. Only then could important questions be properly decided. Otherwise, our operations could not yield the greatest results, or they might fail to coordinate with the general Allied strategy and would violate the old military rule of seeking success with the least possible cost in casualties.

But on the first day of active duty in my new post, I received a completely unexpected shock. I was informed by Major Knezevich that direct contact with the forces of resistance *did not exist*. All communication was handled through British services. It was immediately clear to me that the government-in-exile could not then possibly exercise any real influence over the resistance forces, nor could it directly help to ease their terrible position vis-à-vis the occupiers.

In his office, I almost shouted at Zika from rage and pain. "Then what, in the name of God, have you done here for nearly twenty months!" His blue eyes gazed steadily at me from under his bushy eyebrows as I continued. "Do you not realize that the people at home will hang you the first day you return? Nobody will ask you about anything. Everybody will look for the results."

"That's right," Zika quietly answered. "All is just as you say it is. But please, read first all the files that you will find here. Then come back, and we will talk about it."

Challenged by his words, I did as he asked.

After another long day, I closed the current file I was reading. There was still much material to digest, but I was beginning to understand something of the deeper nature of the war being fought around the world. It was not simply a matter of the Axis powers versus the United Nations in a struggle to the death. That conception mainly applied to the military side of the war with its vast armies and navies pitted against one another in desperate battles.

There was also a political war being fought. In this war, on both sides, diplomatic calculations had nearly infinite gradations. The shooting war would stop someday, everybody believed. Then long-range national interests would again be of paramount concern. Unsurprisingly, those interests did not necessarily coincide with present alliances.

I did not want to bother anybody, even Zika, with questions, believing that their answers would not satisfy me. I would continue to read dossiers to seek an understanding of the true intentions of the British based on the record to date. It was even possible that everything would become clear when I better acquainted myself with the facts. For the moment, I would be content to absorb everything I could.

The military aspects of the war I had been trained to understand. They defined a relatively forthright arena where soldiers either lived or died. Now I wished to understand the political war in all its dimensions. It would decide the nature of the world for the survivors.

1943

AFTER THE TEHERAN Conference of November 1943, at which the top leaders of the Allies (Churchill, Roosevelt, and Stalin) met to discuss the course of the war, the British did some serious soul-searching over the matter of Yugoslavia. Brigadier Fitzroy H. R. Maclean quoted the following to-the-point conversation with Prime Minister Churchill, when in one discussion Maclean opined that the country was headed for the Soviet camp:

> "Do you intend to make Yugoslavia your home after the war, Brigadier?"
> "No, sir."
> "Neither do I. And, that being the case, the less you and I worry about the form of government they set up, the better."

The British War Office, and certainly not just Churchill, had gradually become disenchanted with General Mihailovich. Notwithstanding their own praise a year earlier, the personal commendations of the general, and the claims for Chetnik activities that the Allies themselves had been quick to trumpet, a new position was evolving. It basically faulted Mihailovich on the simple grounds that he was supposedly not doing enough.

By comparison, the Partisans were actively attacking the occupiers. The Partisans were carrying out raids and sabotage. The Partisans were mounting important operations against the Germans and Italians. And how did the British know all this—especially considering that they had no formal liaison with the Partisans, and that the only field reports were based on sporadic

177

contacts made by British commandos who had parachuted "blind" into the country?

Because the Partisans said it was so, amplified by Radio Free Yugoslavia, the propaganda of Communist parties, and the sympathetic response of left-leaning individuals in the press and within the British government itself. Conveniently, there was no way anyone could have established the whole truth. (Even today, captured German records provide more reliable information than the Yugoslav Communist sources.)

At heart, the British wanted to believe that the romantic picture of brave Balkan fighters rising up against the Huns was true. It was as natural as the wartime American image of the freedom-loving Chinese resisting the cruel Japs. Unlike Mihailovich, who was a trained and experienced officer with a strategy of his own, the Partisans seemed exactly what the British had in mind.

And who was Tito to deny them?

Marshall Tito was, in fact, as skillful a political operative and propagandist as any Communist movement could wish for. Born in 1892, the seventh child of a Croatian father and a Slovenian mother, he went to work as a locksmith at the age of twelve but eventually became a skilled mechanic with jobs in Germany, Czechoslovakia, and Austria.

In World War I, when he was called up for military service, he joined a Croatian regiment of the Austrian-Hungarian Army. This, plus his excellent German with a Viennese accent, had confused the issue of his nationality in the West when he emerged as the leader of the Partisans. There were also other aspects of his life that he preferred to leave murky.

As an Austro-Hungarian sergeant, he was severely wounded and captured on the Russian front. He then spent five years in an empire that was dissolving into revolution and civil war. When he returned to Yugoslavia in 1920, he not only had a Russian wife but had also acquired his lasting allegiance to Communism.

He joined the Yugoslav Communist party the same year, and from 1927 on was a full-time functionary. Up until World War

II, he had put his cosmopolitan background to good use, moving in high international Communist circles, yet avoiding the great purges and power plays emanating from Moscow. If his upbringing was humble enough, his penchant for good food, attractive women, and foreign travel was hardly in line with popular notions of revolutionary asceticism.

But when it came to leadership, Tito was ready. He knew what he wanted to do, and he was prepared to accomplish it without anyone's help, even the Russians'. Thus, fundamentally, the Partisans were never working *with* the Allies, as General Mihailovich hoped to do, but always toward their own goals. It meant, practically speaking, that Tito had no compunctions about lying.

For example, the British, and later some Americans, believed that Tito was more a nationalist than a Communist. They pointed to the inclusion of many non-Communists in the ranks of the Partisans. According to this "Popular Front" model, all the patriotic elements in the country had banded together to fight the Fascists.

The Partisan leadership was doubtless opposed to the occupiers, but never at the expense of their own agenda. When the Germans invaded in 1941, they had actually stood on the sidelines, since the "second imperialist war" was not their concern. When the Germans rolled into Russia, however, the "great fatherland war" was another matter. Again, this hardly squares with unalloyed nationalism.

The fact was that Tito was a Communist committed to an international perspective and Russian hegemony, until nationalism provided his only refuge from Stalin's wrath. The core of the Partisans was solely Communist. The Party only had about six thousand members before the war (this rose to twelve thousand by 1941), so necessity was turned into a virtue. Greater numbers of fighters had to be recruited from elsewhere.

If anything, Tito did not provide enough "window dressing" for his movement, at least according to the Soviets. They upbraided him for not subsuming his revolutionary aims in a more cooperative posture—defeating the Germans was to be the top priority. Tito ignored the advice, as he was prone to do whenever his tactics were questioned.

When the Russians failed to provide the aid he wanted, he cautiously wooed the British in his adept manner. (But whatever his disappointments, at no time did Tito ever break with Moscow.) Needless to say, the promises he made to the British and the agreements he signed to respect democratic freedoms and allow a choice of government after the war were never to be honored.

Were the Partisans then carrying out attacks against the occupiers in the period from 1942 to 1943? Yes. Were they carrying out *significant* operations? It is doubtful. The temptation is always to award military merit on the basis of the human drama involved, rather than from objective assessments. But guerrilla forces, without a great deal of external assistance, cannot make headway against an army such as the Germans had.

Given the circumstances, Mihailovich's basic strategy was to prepare for a national uprising that would coordinate with the arrival of Allied forces near Yugoslavia. This could not have come as a shock to the British: it was what they themselves were urging other European undergrounds to do.

Two other developing arguments against the Chetniks involved charges of collaboration and ineffectiveness. The collaboration issue is too tangled to easily summarize, but several points can be stressed. The case against *some* Chetniks is as persuasive as that against *some* Partisans. Neither group ever "switched sides" in an ultimate sense. Both Tito and Mihailovich had German rewards placed on their heads, and both strove for the eventual ouster of all occupiers.

The Partisans did, however, develop their accusations against Mihailovich with thoroughness and propaganda flair. Yet it took a real effort to even convince Moscow. The Russians had continued to praise Mihailovich well into 1942 as the leader of Yugoslav resistance before they about-faced and declared him a collaborator.

As for the Chetniks' performance, one could well ask, what

were they supposed to do? Fight without guns and supplies? In 1943, Boris himself was to discover what an incredibly ragtag army they were.

The British had proved rather ineffectual at providing logistical support, granted the extreme difficulty of trying to undertake air drops. (There is also some evidence that in Cairo, where the supplies were assembled, the normal tendency for snafus was exacerbated by a British intelligence officer and Communist mole, James Klugman. True or not, British skepticism about high-level Communist penetration must be weighed against recent spying revelations from England.)

Probably the best evaluation of Mihailovich's efforts at a time when British support was already ebbing should come from his arch rival. In March of 1943, Tito wrote to one of his commanders: "Your most important task at this moment is to annihilate the Chetniks of Draza Mihailovich and to destroy their command apparatus, which represents the greatest danger to the development of the National Liberation Struggle. . . ."

A major factor in Mihailovich's calculations had to be the genuine danger of Serbian genocide. Hundreds of thousands of Serbs had already died. The standing German policy, which had been applied earlier and more severely in Yugoslavia than anywhere else, was to execute one hundred Serbs for every German killed by the resistance forces.

The full dimensions of Nazi brutality were not yet known by the Allies. Isolated incidents were reported, such as the slaughter in Lidiche, a reprisal for the assassination of Reinhard Heydrich. When Boris heard of it, he commented: "I deeply grieved over the German crime of Lidiche . . . But with us, a thousand Lidiches! And while the entire world was shaken over the case of one Czechoslovak Lidiche, with us it was considered an everyday happening, something that had to be."

That was only the beginning. The Ustashi of the new Croatian State had gone on a murderous rampage in 1941. Hitler's chief henchmen estimated that they massacred some three quarters of a million defenseless people, mainly Serbs, but also twenty-five thousand Jews and other minorities. From Bosnia-Herzegovina and areas in Croatia where Serbs had always lived, refugees desperately tried to escape into Serbia. The rivers were running with blood.

Mihailovich had no intention of risking more Serb lives for anything but the soundest reasons. (In fairness, the Allies often had difficulty believing the magnitude of Axis mass murders until after the war.) Satisfying the British call for unlimited guerrilla actions was seen as too costly.

Tito, on the other hand, had fewer compunctions.

The British capacity for operations in the Balkans was itself decidedly limited. Yet the region seemed to call forth their fondest dreams. Churchill, in 1943, could still argue for some kind of Allied action there, even if the Americans always adamantly opposed a southeastern front. This would have been Churchill's chosen way to roll up Nazi Europe in consort with the Russians.

The American choice was a cross-channel attack into northern Europe, the second front that Stalin had been demanding for months. That was their focus of attention. Except for North Africa and the Italian campaigns, the Mediterranean remained a British theater of war where Americans assisted but did not call the shots.

From Cairo, the British coordinated military missions throughout the Near East and tried to deal with a polyglot mix of soldiers from allied or occupied nations. In 1943, Cairo was a center of intelligence gathering and analysis. But it would still be five months before even the battle for North Africa was ended, and British attention to secondary matters was understandably sporadic.

The most critical event of 1942, and the precursor of things yet to come, had happened far from the deserts of North Africa. On October 20, 1942, the last German attack on Stalingrad had failed, and by the end of the year the Red Army was on a massive counterattack. The invasion of Russia had come within a hair's breadth of success, but it had fallen short.

In hindsight, the triumph at Stalingrad had perhaps been insured by the Yugoslav War in 1941. The Germans had lost precious time, delaying the planned start of their Russian assault. Winter had then come too soon. That, rather than the claimed thirty divisions the Yugoslav resistance was supposedly tying up, was the legitimate "bill for services rendered" the Serbs could place on the table before the Allies.

When Boris had arrived in London, he thought General Mihailovich and the Chetniks were receiving leadership support from the government-in-exile and enthusiastic backing by the British. What he discovered as 1943 began was a more somber picture of events. It was the beginning of a year-long education in international politics and Allied war policy, and a time of personal reappraisals.

12

London Politics

IT TOOK LONGER to get really accustomed to working for the Yugoslav Government-in-Exile than I thought it would. Except for a few people in the Military Office, no one seemed in much of a hurry to welcome me. I didn't know quite what to make of this.

On the one hand, my ego suffered a natural human letdown, while on the other I was grateful that I was not the centerpiece at stereotypical official receptions. I never did enjoy rubbing shoulders with perennial party-goers or answering meaningless questions.

Major Knezevich's genuine bear hug at our first meeting had been the best of greetings, I realized. It made me feel at home. Outside his office, I was a stranger in the big city as well as in the small enclave of my countrymen.

The few receptions that I could not avoid confirmed that fact. I did not know how to curb my tongue. In a clique nurtured on speculation, rumors, and innuendo, my plain talk did not fare too well. People were hardly prepared to hear of my disenchantment with prominent men in the P.O.W. camps and in the expatriate community.

That kind of talk labeled you as a rebel against the existing order, or as an agent provocateur. Whichever, it was of no benefit to associate with any such person. Or with me. Under normal circumstances, to placate someone of my blunt speech would have been unthinkable. In the anything but normal atmosphere of wartime London, it was doubly so.

The majority of our colony's members belonged to the diplomatic corps. They had gathered in London when the embassies in France, Italy, Hungary, Rumania, Bulgaria, and Greece were closed. Most of them had not been in Yugoslavia for a long time, and they seemed to me often more concerned with the fate of their relatives and their property than with the nation's freedom. I thought myself signally honored when they decided not to consider me a member of their circle.

To my consternation, their lives revolved around the politics of the government-in-exile, in which almost everybody participated. Nothing else seemed to matter but the information leaks coming from the ministers' offices. These had to be confirmed, interpreted, and compared with what had previously been accepted as the truth, and then the "truth" was adjusted accordingly.

By the time of my arrival in London, the leaks were often in direct contravention of the public pronouncements made by the British and other Allied governments. Listening to so many conflicting accounts, I did not know what to make of it all. Only in the official War Cabinet files to which I had access did I continue to make some headway.

As the new year began, however, I was not without optimism and some minor sense of success. After a brief stay in the Marble Arch Hotel, Pachany and I were fortunate to find a suitable flat in a house in Kensington. It was spacious and comfortably furnished, and the landlady agreed to see to the cleaning.

At last we had a place of our own, and we settled in for a long stay. It was a pleasure just to come there every evening and find the place impeccably maintained.

Not far from the flat was a station of the London underground, giving us convenient transportation to and from the ministry offices. At first I was reluctant to use it alone. The trains moved fast, and I had trouble catching the conductor's announcement of stations.

But I pushed myself to overcome this handicap, despite the troubles I still had with the English language. Soon, like a well-trained dog, I was swiftly and routinely traveling back and forth, as habituated to the underground as any Londoner. Neither the blackouts nor the station platforms lined with portable cots at night slowed my progress.

The underground stations served as bomb shelters, and I often found myself snaking between the rows of cots on my nightly return to the flat. They'd fill with well-disciplined Londoners whenever the air raid alarms sounded.

Luckily, the air attacks were not so frequent as they had been before Pachany and I reached England. (The terror of the German V-2 rocket bombs had not yet begun.) Still, the Home Guard insisted that the air strike rules be observed. This meant that we, too, were expected to join the other cot occupants at the sound of the alarm.

After a few compliances, I simply remained in my room. Our part of London was not a favorite target of the Luftwaffe anyway, and I was much more concerned with the proximity of the antiaircraft batteries in nearby Hyde Park. While they were firing, the house shook to its foundations. The noise was deafening. You couldn't have heard an enemy bomb coming in for a direct hit.

Even under wartime conditions, London bustled with activity. As a young officer of thirty, I was not averse to sampling some of the diversions. Pachany and I remained close friends, although he had been assigned to another section in the Military Office. When off duty, we spent much time together, and I shared with him many of the thoughts that sprung from my unofficial investigation of the War Cabinet files.

We rarely ate at home. The flat had all the facilities, but who wanted to bother with cooking? And neither of us could find a young English woman ready to make that sacrifice. Besides, she might not turn out to be a good cook anyway, so why waste the time? It was so much easier to eat out. Not only were we assured of a good meal, but there was always the possibility of meeting someone nice at one of the London pubs.

Or not so nice. One evening, Pachany and I stopped at the Lyons for a drink. Two good-looking young women were sitting at a nearby table. Our masculine egos brimming with confidence, we took them out to dinner and then to our flat for a nightcap.

Of course we hoped they would be even more cooperative, but all we got were a few hugs while sitting together on the sofa. Then the girls said they had to leave. We used every trick in the book to make them stay, to no avail. They went to the bathroom to tidy up and then practically ran out of the flat.

Deflated and still trembling with excitement, Pachany and I tried to figure out what went wrong. Perhaps our Balkan style was too much for the English ladies? The possibility that we had been taken in never dawned on us.

Only when I found our empty wallets on the bathroom floor did we realize how stupid we were. Neither of us was ready to accept the blame, however, and the recriminations continued late into the night.

My affairs at work progressed more smoothly. My office had become a virtual checkpoint for people coming to see Major Knezevich. Mostly these were military men inquiring about their status. The others, usually newsmen, wanted information.

Whenever Zika was not available, his visitors ended up airing their frustrations with me. The journalists, attached to (or working for) the Yugoslav Information Service, were usually after background material or leads to new developments. Of course, officially I couldn't help them even if I wanted to.

The newsmen were then writing stories woven around leaks from our own government officials and willing British sources. Contrary to the optimism emanating daily from Zika, they had a far different attitude to report. The gist of it was that the Yugoslav government must compromise, try to understand the British point of view, and not always insist on having its own way.

Rehashing this later on with Zika, we both wondered how anyone thought we could "compromise" without abandoning General Mihailovich and his fighters or undermining the sovereignty of our government. My journalist friends really didn't know the half of the insinuations that continued to circulate and multiply. The handling of the whole resistance forces situation by the War Cabinet's present members was at issue—and "present" was the word you heard stressed.

Yet with rare exceptions, General Mihailovich and his Chetnik fighters were still the pride of the Yugoslav community in London. More significantly, the General was seen by most of these people as a return passport to the liberated fatherland where they would resume their careers within the government, or with its assistance. He was their bulwark against those who advocated and fought for violent destruction of the prewar social order. Whatever their other complaints, anything affecting his efforts remained of deep concern to them.

Dissension within the ranks of the government-in-exile continued unabated. The Yugoslav Information Service, for instance, had never done much, if anything, to counteract damaging stories. Headed by a Croatian politician, Mr. Vilder, the service seemed to act more as an instrument of British policy than as a vigorous spokesman for its own government. It was not unusual for the staff to actually edit government pronouncements if they were out of line with British positions.

There was nothing to be done, either. The removal of Vilder would most certainly have led to the resignation of other Croatian ministers. That, of course, would have precipitated the fall of the present government, leaving the field wide open for all our adversaries to pursue their own goals.

The radio broadcasting branch of the service had proved even more useless. Its head, Mika Petrovich, was known for his extremely liberal views, and he fully cooperated with the agencies of the British government eager to disseminate bulletins on the operations of Partisan units in Yugoslavia. No one bothered to check the veracity of these bulletins. With repetition, the impression was being fostered that Tito's Communist-based forces, rather than General Mihailovich's, were the ones taking the fight to the occupiers.

I could do little to alter this ongoing Machiavellian political scene in London. In fact, Zika had already struck one of the few effective counterblows. The Yugoslav government had begun its own program over the BBC on March 1, 1942, when the "Vojne Emisije" ("broadcasts on the military situation") went on the air. Prepared by Zika, and in most instances delivered by him, these broadcasts were the only direct voice of the government heard in Yugoslavia.

Initially, the British had cooperated. But General Mihailovich was a stumbling stone for Tito and those Partisans who quested for control of Yugoslavia and the imposition of a new social order. For them, Mihailovich had to be discredited and then destroyed by whatever means. I could not have understood this priority had I not had recourse to the historical record in the War Cabinet files.

In the middle of January, I was suddenly ordered to prepare for an audience with King Peter II. Pachany and several other escaped P.O.W.s were also given the same word.

The next day, the small group assembled in my office. Dressed in our brand-new blue dress uniforms, we were escorted to the King's quarters by one of his adjutants, Major Rozdjalovski.

My curiosity was soon satisfied by the appearance of a slender young man of medium height. This was the king. We all bowed in a military salute, and his pale face flashed a welcoming smile. As we were formally presented one by one, the aides flanking His Majesty answered his questions about us. One of them, Major Vohoska, made a real effort to dispel the air of rigid formality. His jokes about us made the king laugh, and we joined in.

The king wanted to know more about our experiences. As I was talking to him, I had to keep reminding myself that this young man was the sovereign head of government to whom I had pledged an oath of allegiance, and not just another well-behaved teenager on the verge of turning twenty. He appeared deeply interested and enthused. To him, we were perhaps the tangible proof of a spirit that could overcome all adversities, and he was genuinely proud of us.

Perhaps it was my imagination, but it seemed the king was being particularly partial to me. True or not, I enjoyed talking to him, and I wished I could see him often. I wanted to imbue him with the ideals that warmed my own heart. He looked so impressionable, so ready to respond to any noble thought or brave proposition or . . . I knew my daydream was impossible. And how foolish of me to be so pretentious.

To the king, the escape Pachany and I had made was an act of bravery. All my arguments to the contrary failed to dissuade him. Then to my great surprise, and to the delight of the other men, the king presented Pachany and me with medals—the White Eagle with Swords, the second highest Yugoslav decoration for bravery.

I was dumfounded. All along I had told anybody who asked that escape was the basic duty of every P.O.W. Now I was being treated as a hero. It only reminded me that my firsthand account of the hunger, privation, and suffering of thousands of officers and Serbian civilians in German prison camps (men who a year and a half later were still imprisoned) had not made much of an impression in London, aside from an outward expression of sorrow. It certainly had not produced great effects.

Still, I had sense enough not to persist in my arguments. There was nothing to be gained by creating false impressions in the minds of the king or his adjutants about my views and interest in diverse political ideologies. Later, though, when I found myself alone with Majors Vohoska and Rozdjalovski, I could not resist telling them that I was reluctant to accept the medal. They looked at me in utter disbelief and burst out laughing. I must have looked chagrined by their reaction, for both gave me friendly pats on the shoulder and dismissed my feelings as undue personal modesty.

I had mixed emotions about these two. I'd known both of

them when we all served briefly in the same artillery regiment. Major Rozdjalovski had been personally better liked by the younger officers, even as they flocked around Major Vohoska to enjoy his barracks wit and sharp tongue. I had never had a chance to hear either of them discuss serious matters, and I could only guess about their intellectual capacities.

The gossip in London was that they lacked any real qualifications for their positions. Admittedly, the choices were limited under the circumstances, and the king's adjutants had always been career officers. There was no doubt about their utter devotion to the king, as both had participated in the March 1941 coup that had brought him to the throne.

The king, I repeatedly heard, *was* impressionable. Like most young men at his age, he was bound to think that an overindulgence in the pleasures of life and the use of coarse language were signs of maturity. Rumors persisted that the two majors did nothing to discourage such notions.

In truth, Major Vohoska always referred to the king as "master," a distasteful expression. I talked about it later with Pachany. Neither of us could reconcile such talk with the role of a king in a constitutional monarchy. The last thing we wanted to condone was absolutism of any sort whatsoever.

I could only rely on the fact that the king's closest advisor, Professor Radoye Knezevich, had selected the two majors. There was never any doubt that Zika's brother was himself intent on guiding the king to an understanding of true democratic principles. Yet here again, I found my dream of heroic men who were body and soul with the fighters in the fatherland dissolving into the reality of petty intrigues around an exiled king and his self-satisfied adjutants.

That January, my Communist friend from Marseille, the journalist Michael Djulafich, also arrived in London. I was glad to see him safe and sound.

To his credit, Djulafich volunteered for military duty, but was turned down for poor health. Using my influence and that of others, he worked his way into the radio branch of the Yugoslav Information Service and became an assistant to its chief, Mr. Petrovich. At first I thought he could actually do some good there, but he turned his talents to reinforcing the changes in policy already underway.

The onslaught of information leaks from many sources, the war-induced unease many exiled Yugoslavs felt, and the open activities in London of men like Vilder, Petrovich, Djulafich, and their proponents gave credence to the worst rumors about the British government's intentions.

Were the British actually considering withdrawing support from Mihailovich and the Chetniks? Were Tito and his Communist Partisans coming into greater favor? It was unthinkable. Yet without any decisive action, the drift in British policy—if not that of the Yugoslav government—was undeniable. The mood of the community was changing, and endless speculation had ensued.

For myself, by February of 1943 I had finished my unofficial investigation. What I had learned from the official files and from the Yugoslav community in general was a story of political war being waged on several fronts. Its outlines seemed reasonably clear to me. I also realized it was driving honest and self-sacrificing men like Major Knezevich into an ultimately no-win position.

How had this happened? I remembered very vividly the day in the Offenburg camp when we first heard of the beginning of guerrilla warfare in Yugoslavia. My reaction was that our allies now had a chance to offer effective aid by supplying ammunition and matériel to the resistance forces, something they had failed to do during our short period of war with the Germans.

Allied propaganda not only succeeded in spreading the word of the great assistance being rendered to the guerrillas in Yugoslavia, but also conveyed to the public the firm belief that this help was sufficient and uninterrupted from the onset. I, too, arrived in London with that belief. And in my case, I had supported it with military logic.

The uprisings in Yugoslavia were clearly of great value to the Allies. It was definitely in the Allied interest for this struggle to continue without ceasing. The obvious conclusion was that the Allies, and certainly the British, would immediately want to organize a steady flow of sufficient support to the Yugoslav guerrillas.

On the other hand, the moral value of the Allied support to the resisters was vital because it made them feel they had not been forgotten. This gave them the strength to endure in the unequal struggle with the occupiers. It gave them a sign that their efforts would someday end successfully. In essence, the Allies had willingly made a moral commitment.

The guerrilla war in Serbia, already begun in May of 1941 by then Colonel Mihailovich, assumed the character of a national uprising in July. The resistance forces, using supplies hidden among the people, had brilliant success. Accounts quickly reached London, and the British responded favorably. Help would be sent as soon as it could be properly arranged.

By September, when the Chetnik resistance forces made radio contact with Malta and asked for help, nothing had been undertaken. The first Royal Yugoslav Government-in-Exile, headed by General Dushan Simovich as prime minister, was mired in its own problems. The British government was without initiative. The result was that our resistance forces were spent futilely against the far better equipped occupiers.

Preoccupied with settling in its London quarters, the Simovich government was satisfied to exchange messages with General Mihailovich via British services out of the Middle East Command in Cairo. Repeated memoranda did, however, attempt to prod the British along into providing some desperately needed supplies. Yet throughout 1941, after all the pleadings, the negotiations, and the promises, Great Britain managed to send just 20 Tommy guns, 680 hand grenades, and 10,000 rounds of ammunition to Yugoslavia—certainly poor evidence of Britain's status as a Great Power.

Deeply convinced that plentiful aid would be available, the

Serbian peasant, backbone of the Chetnik effort, was greatly disappointed. Sweet words over the London radio had urged him to fight on. There were expressions of admiration and the forwarding of congratulations, but he saw once more the truth of that old Serbian proverb, "A foreign hand will not scratch your itch."

In the meantime, the British were working diligently to establish reliable communications with Mihailovich. In their effort to limit access to themselves, they were indirectly helped by General Simovich's ambitions to assert his leadership within the government-in-exile. As the months passed, the general was becoming more and more enmeshed in his own political infighting, leaving practically a free hand to the British.

Finally, General Simovich maneuvered himself into an untenable position and had to resign. A new government, headed by Professor Slobodan Jovanovich, took over on January 11, 1942, and General Mihailovich was named minister of the Yugoslav Army, Navy, and Air Force in its War Cabinet.

The newly reorganized cabinet moved resolutely to resolve the key issues with the British. It petitioned Anthony Eden, the British foreign secretary, and Prime Minister Winston Churchill himself for assistance. More ambitious plans were formulated.

In early February 1942, Jovanovich's government proposed the creation of an in-country communications network under General Mihailovich's command. It was important to have such a network in place by early spring so that the expected intensification of guerrilla activities could be properly coordinated. Further, it was noted that communications without control had been allowed the Poles and Czechs.

Also, in an aide-mémoire, the government requested the formation of a Yugoslav bomber squadron of sixteen aircraft. These planes, as previously discussed with British Air Vice Marshall Medhurst, were to carry badly needed matériel to Mihailovich's forces. They would be flown by Yugoslav airmen who had escaped after the German invasion and now sat idle in the Middle Eastern theater, principally in Cairo.

The response of the Foreign Office was positive in principle. On the other hand, granting these requests would reduce the British ability to control communications with Mihailovich, or to use promised aid as a carrot to insure that his Chetniks would undertake military operations the British deemed important. Besides, since the British already *had* a direct link to the general via their own liaison officer, they could deal with the Yugoslav government from a position of strength. To sacrifice all this to the principle of national sovereignty, which they championed otherwise, was unthinkable.

The delaying tactics adopted were compounded of bureaucratic objections and technical issues. The opening note was sounded by Major Long, chief of the Foreign Intelligence Office. Expressing his sympathy with the Yugoslav government's requests, he flatly stated that his office could not spare a powerful radio transmitter for direct communications with General Mihailovich.

When the Yugoslavs questioned the credibility of that statement, another negotiating point was tossed on the table by Colonel Lord Glenconner, chief of the "Saboteurs" in the Ministry of Blockade. He insisted that the only way the Yugoslav government could have its direct communications link was through adherence to a policy of absolute secrecy. According to Lord Glenconner, only King Peter and the prime minister should have access to the dispatches.

Another argument to be dealt with—and precious time was passing. Frustrated but not discouraged, the Yugoslav government was not ready to throw in the towel. To the contrary, it resolved more than ever to pursue its rightful goals.

The "Cairo Affair" then erupted. Brigadier General Borivoje Mirkovich of the Yugoslav Air Force, one of the leading plotters in the 1941 coup, had never truly liked the idea of a civilian government. He accepted the political program drawn up by Professor Radoye Knezevich, but after the government settled in London, he expected more personal recognition.

When General Simovich was eased out as prime minister,

Mirkovich began an open campaign against the politicians, particularly the Knezeviches, from his base in Cairo. He took his case to the rank and file of the Yugoslav military in the Middle East, and almost all airmen and some naval personnel rallied to his support. The local British military commander was also sympathetic to him. Mirkovich felt ready to test the will of the London government.

At first, he began delaying the execution of orders from London. Then he rejected the authority of the newly appointed commander of Yugoslav Middle East forces. To prove his seriousness, Mirkovich ordered his troops to seize the Yugoslav Middle East headquarters and eject everyone loyal to the government.

These acts of open rebellion did not buckle the Yugoslav government's determination. It refused to invite Mirkovich to London for consultation, as he insisted. A series of strong protests were lodged with the British government condemning the attitude of their representatives in Cairo and insisting on the full observance of Yugoslav sovereignty.

Slowly, painstakingly, the British government complied. Brigadier Mirkovich was stunned. His followers, bitter and betrayed, dispersed. Yet the real loser in the Cairo Affair was General Mihailovich and the Chetniks. Now his repeated calls for help remained unanswered because the British Middle East Command was "preoccupied with the unsettled situation among the Yugoslav military personnel in Egypt."

Despite everything, during the rest of 1942 the Yugoslav government kept up the pressure for meaningful Allied support. His Majesty King Peter was personally enlisted to pass on requests, and he had an audience with the British King George VI on April 23. In June, he visited the United States and held discussions directly with President Roosevelt and Colonel "Wild Bill" Donovan, later head of the American Office of Strategic Services (O.S.S.).

The Yugoslav government asserted its readiness for cooperation, stressing the understanding that all operations in Yugoslavia came under the compass of the Allied plan. Nothing was ever intended to be done without consulting the High Command of the Middle East, but it could not be tolerated that the Command could act without the Yugoslav government's knowledge. It was a question of national prestige, justice, and Allied responsibility.

Through all of these political maneuverings and the dozens of other minor incidents, a steady barrage of propaganda was maintained by everyone with an interest in the affairs of Yugoslavia. The British had never ceased publicly proclaiming their support for the resistance forces in Yugoslavia, though just who was actually their leading protégé was wrapped in a frothy cloud of contradictory remarks. The Americans honestly proclaimed their support for Mihailovich, but were constrained to follow the lead of their British ally in the Middle East. The Russians vacillated. They were ready to throw over the general on Communist principles, but they were not yet willing to embrace Tito with his practical uncertainties.

As for the Communist Partisans, they maintained their own voice, independent of their sympathizers in London. As I had learned in Marseille, this was Radio Free Yugoslavia, which pretended to emanate from the mountains of Partisan-held territory. It actually beamed its signal from Russia and was currently housed in the Comintern building in Moscow.

The thrust of its 1942 broadcasts was to brand General Mihailovich a traitor and a collaborator with the Nazis. First he was reported to be working with General Milan Nedich, the head of the German-installed government in occupied Serbia. Then came accusations of collaboration with the Ustashi, the paramilitary units of the puppet Independent State of Croatia. To anyone who knew of the large-scale massacres of Serbs living in Croatia that were conducted by the Ustashi, such a charge against a patriotic Serbian general was ridiculous. Yet Radio Free Yugoslavia kept repeating it shamelessly.

Although subject to increasingly vicious personal attacks, General Mihailovich at the end of 1942 received full recognition from the highest military authorities for his excellent performance, including commendations from the Imperial British General Staff, the main British commandants in the Mediterranean, General Charles de Gaulle, and the chief Allied commander in Europe, General Dwight D. Eisenhower.

As 1943 began, General Eisenhower sent General Mihailovich a New Year's telegram. It read:

> The American forces in Europe and Africa send greetings to their comrades in arms, the resourceful and gallant Yugoslav military units under your splendid leadership. These brave men banded together on their native soil to drive the invader from their country are serving with full devotion the cause of the United Nations. May the New Year bring them full success.

Such was the overall state of affairs by the time I made my entrance into London and began my crash course in disillusionment. There was one overriding fact: General Mihailovich and the Chetniks seemed as far from being adequately supplied by *anybody* as ever. Meanwhile, the Russians were effectively directing aid to the Partisans, who at the time had barely managed to hold on to the northwestern part of Bosnia.

Dismayed and confused, I finally turned to Zika for another chance at an explanation. He was brimming with the usual optimism. All we had to do, he told me, was to remain firm in our attitude. Sooner or later, the British would side with our views.

After all, who else could they count on but General Mihailovich? What could the British possibly expect to gain if postwar Yugoslavia was governed by a regime tied to the Soviet Union? That's why Zika was confident of the final outcome.

Perhaps he was right, I thought. But personally disgusted with everything I saw in London, I decided a month after my arrival to volunteer to return to Yugoslavia. There I expected to find true and sincere fighters for liberty and democracy. There my dream was alive.

13

Around Africa

EARLY ONE EVENING, the routine pattern of my journey by sea suddenly changed. Two British corvettes, which were lightly armed warships built for speed, broke away from their position in the middle of the convoy. As I watched, the U-boat chasers sped quickly out of sight. Then I noticed a larger ship, a destroyer, trailing after them.

No one else on the small freighter I was aboard seemed to pay it much attention. Glued to the deck railing and holding on to my life jacket tightly, I gazed out into the distance. On the horizon, the sun was setting slowly, moments before its final, unexpectedly swift plunge into the Atlantic and the fall of night in the tropics.

Far away to the south, in a last flash of daylight, I spotted the silhouette of the destroyer. It had turned. The ship was moving back to its normal place in the convoy.

I breathed a quiet sigh of relief. Another false alarm, I deduced calmly. My mouth was dry, and even without the oppressive heat, I now welcomed the thought of cocktails at the daily gathering of officers in the upper deck bar.

All officers wore full evening regalia in the ship's bar, regardless of the temperature. When I got there somewhat after six, the usual shipboard news-and-gossip session was well underway, but the tone was somber. The ominous sea drama I'd witnessed at sunset had not gone unnoticed, after all. It had *not* been another false alarm.

A U-boat pack was known to be in the area. The word was that our corvettes had intercepted two of them and had managed to chase them off. Or perhaps the subs had declined to tangle with the destroyer.

The convoy just ahead of us had been hit as it was entering Freetown harbor, our next port of call. We heard that one of the ships sunk had been carrying a battalion of Women's Army Corps nurses. The women who managed to abandon ship were attacked in the open water by sharks, apparently attracted by their white uniforms. There was a terrible slaughter.

We had two days yet to go before reaching Freetown, the capital of Sierra Leone, then a small British colony on the West African coast. The port city was more than thirty-five hundred miles from London and some six hundred miles above the equator.

After twelve days in the open sea, I was suffering from the terrific heat and terrible mosquito bites. I longed to put my feet on dry land, but I'd have to wait. Even though the convoy was scheduled for a two-day layover, no one was to be permitted ashore.

Still, my assignment to a ship expressly designed for tropical waters was a stroke of good fortune. Built by the Dutch before the war, the 14,000-ton ship was basically a commercial freighter. However, the upper deck did have cabins. They were comfortable enough that a hundred officers could live in cramped but bearable conditions.

The rest of the ship had been jury-rigged to carry troops, eliminating the bulk cargo space. Including the complement of officers, there were about three thousand of us on board, most of whom were rank-and-file British soldiers. The Tommies, along with their equipment, had embarked as a unit from England, their destination a military secret.

In all, twenty-one ships made up the convoy, carrying a total of some thirty thousand men. Besides the troop carriers like the one I was on, there were initially four destroyers and the two corvettes to shepherd us along. Later, an aircraft carrier and a cruiser joined the group. That additional formidable firepower came as welcome news to everybody and had lifted our morale.

In the middle of the convoy, the commanding admiral's vessel flashed signals day and night. These directed the other ships, so that even though the convoy stretched for miles over the ocean, everyone was linked together like giant floating beads on an invisible thread. When one ship altered its position, all the others adjusted.

Ordinarily, I liked to observe these skillful nautical maneuvers while I walked about on deck. I could fill my lungs with pure air and sometimes get a glimpse of a flying fish. I also knew that one day I might see something else. Or worse, not see anything at all until the first torpedo exploded. But I didn't dwell on it, even after a day when I'd seen our ships on high alert. A distant brush with the enemy hardly seemed to count.

Prior to the cocktail hour, I had made the required change of uniform in the cabin I shared with eight other Yugoslav officers. One of my cabin mates had been waiting for me—Captain Leonid Pachany. Yes, Pachany had volunteered to return to Yugoslavia. I hardly needed to convince him, for we saw eye to eye about our reasons. If we were to do our best for our native land in this war, we had agreed, it wasn't going to be from behind office desks in London.

Luckily, in late March of 1943 we had managed to ship out together. We were still comrades in arms, as we had been since the days of the P.O.W. camps. Rapidly adjusting to yet another new environment, Pachany and I soon got to know many of our fellow passengers.

Nowhere, perhaps, can quicker friendships be formed than while traveling in a convoy. While in London, I had met only a few English people, and my association with them was always on an official basis. I frankly did not have a very positive impression of the average British officer, based on my limited experience and secondhand reports.

I had remained skeptical, but the officers I met on the boat were different. They were friendly and understanding, the type of men you felt could be depended on in time of need. Here there was no overriding sense of social rank, of upper and lower classes—a British trait I did not appreciate.

Except for the daily emergency drills in preparation for a possible attack on the ship, we officers were left to ourselves. It was up to us to make some constructive use of our time. For me, it was a chance to work on my English, my life in London having been too busy to allow serious study. I asked my new British friends to mercilessly correct my errors, and they good-humoredly obliged.

One of them was particularly interested in my efforts and freely offered to help. First Lieutenant George Rothey had been a professor of economics at a London college. He was extremely interested in Balkan culture and its peoples, and happily traded language lessons with me.

We nicknamed him "Djoka" in Serbian, and he and I were almost inseparable. Short and wiry with an engaging smile, Djoka looked more like a professional soccer player than a college professor. He was most pleasant company, and our conversation ranged freely from the causes and consequences of the war to music, sports, and the opposite sex.

Early in the morning, Pachany, Djoka, and I vigorously exercised to keep ourselves physically fit. Then, into the afternoon, I would sit in a remote corner of the upper deck with an English book in hand. Often Pachany and Djoka would be nearby, also reading, until another uneventful day drew to a close and it was time for the officers' cocktail hour. That became the testing ground for my daily dose of English self-study, aided greatly by Djoka's tutelage.

Gathered nightly in the bar, it seemed that everyone lived and felt for the moment. Nobody believed in tomorrow, thinking it might well never come. And it was certainly true that few of us were likely to cross paths again, once the convoy reached its destination.

Yet we could never stop wondering where we were being sent. With such a large number of troops, it had to mean that a major Allied operation was in the works. That much everybody guessed. We Yugoslavs had a premonition that our convoy's destination was in fact Cairo. Only to get there, we were making a small detour of over twelve thousand miles around the continent of Africa.

Given the German capabilities in the Mediterranean, even in 1943, there really wasn't much choice. Pachany and I and the others were not so important as to warrant direct British air transport. This was the only option we had. Anyway, our notions about Cairo delighted Djoka, and he was happy to pass them along to his fellow Brits.

The next day, as I lay on deck and enjoyed the sun that grew warmer and warmer, recent events in my life somehow seemed a million miles away. Although life at sea proved monotonous, I'd discovered that its rhythm was seductive. Had it been merely two weeks since Pachany and I had boarded, a stiff breeze chilling us to the bone? I calculated mentally, remembering our departure.

After finding our cabin, we'd acquainted ourselves with the upper deck facilities, noting with pleasure the reading room and the adjoining well-stocked bar. Further on was the modern dining room. It was a far cry from railroad cattle cars and the like.

By mid-afternoon of that dreary day, the embarkation process was practically complete. The ship's decks swarmed with soldiers, and if no one knew where they were being sent—by order of His Majesty the King and the Royal British Army—there weren't any signs of dismay, either. Across the bay, other troop ships were being loaded. Interspersed you could see the battleships riding at anchor. From a distance they almost appeared to be dancing on the incoming waves.

Precisely at 1800 hours, the upper deck bar opened for business on our first evening aboard. Pachany and I, properly attired, tentatively joined the group of officers there. The commanding officer, a British colonel, came in. He welcomed everybody and expressed his pleasure at having us Yugoslavs in his company. Easy chat and banter quickly filled the room.

Dinner followed, and soon afterwards I retired for the night. I fell asleep immediately. By the time the morning light penetrated the cabin, the convoy was well underway, steaming away southward at a steady pace. From my porthole, only gray skies and foaming Atlantic waves were visible.

It seemed like an eternal seascape those first few days, never to change. Within a week, though, we were nearing tropical latitudes off the African coast. The sea grew calm, as if content and happy with the weather. The endless surface was majestic, the convoy insignificant in comparison. There were no more of the cold swift waves that earlier had come at us with such seeming supernatural force that we feared for our safety.

The sky, which had been very cloudy and dark, was blue and bright. The wind softly tagged about the ship, a reminder that it really was spring. It was next to impossible to recall the dank and foggy weather of the London winter. And who would want to?

Otherwise, my memories remained as intense as ever of London's political intrigues and the expatriate community. I couldn't forget the surprised faces of my colleagues when I'd told them I was going back to Yugoslavia. They thought I was simply crazy to leave England and its comforts to go into uncertainty and grave danger. The only one who approved with real enthusiasm was Major Knezevich, who confessed he was thinking of joining me.

I had never dealt with any political party or with politics in general. In London I showed no preference and could have joined any group that I thought might best influence the future of my country. However, before I made up my mind, it was my nature to proceed carefully and first analyze everything I could learn.

In the Military Office I had discovered much, and it left me more skeptical. I even forced myself to consider whether the accusations made against General Mihailovich had some measure of truth. I wondered if I should ever have the luck or the opportunity to find out all the facts.

"Collaboration with the enemy." How terrible those words sounded. I could not conceive that the Chetnik guerrillas, who already had been fighting for two years under impossible conditions, would now decide to break bread with the very oppressors who had driven them into the mountains. I saw no sense or logic in this charge, if it were simply a matter of Chetniks and the foreign occupation forces.

To be truthful, I really did not know either General Mihailovich or his military confidants well. I had had slight contact with him before the war when he was a professor at the Belgrade Military Academy, but beyond respecting him as a national leader, I had felt no special interest at the time. It was his later acts of defiance in the wake of our defeat by the Germans that had won him my admiration and devotion. Moreover, it had seemed to win him the moral respect of the entire free world.

Frankly, however, I was not concerned with *who* led the Yugoslav people in these most tragic days. It was the people themselves who had pledged their allegiance and who had sacrificed their goods, their livelihoods, and sometimes their lives to oppose tyranny and fight on. My real duty was to follow and obey my people's wishes.

I knew one thing, the Serbian people weren't going to collaborate with their greatest and most vicious enemy in modern history. This was very clear to me because I felt it myself in a way that transcended politics and political thinking. The accusations against General Mihailovich, chiefly inspired by the Partisans, had caused me to consider the source. In this regard, just before we left London, I had had some fresh knowledge of my own.

After Michael Djulafich arrived in London, he had wound up in the Yugoslav Information Service. At first I thought this sensible, considering his reporting talents. I expected that one of his goals would be to undertake an exposé against Gerasimovich, the Yugoslav consul general in Marseille. Indeed, the basis of our friendship had been our mutual disgust with the man.

Djulafich did make an extensive report, but when I received a copy, it completely astonished me. It was absolutely contrary to everything that I knew had happened and to what Djulafich himself had thought at the time. His report highly praised and defended Consul General Gerasimovich and his actions.

It was then that I realized that my principles of decency and honesty were alien to the Communist conception of "tactics." That word meant for them the right to act as they saw fit, and without scruple, as long as they achieved their ends. Under such pressure, Djulafich, who fully knew about my own report on the inept Gerasimovich, was quite willing to malign my prestige and character.

But he was after something more important. He wanted to develop friendships with some of the men who were now very influential in government circles—and who were friends of Mr. Gerasimovich. For his future personal goals, he no doubt let his Communist associates advise him on tactics, adopting them as his own. I could well imagine that the Partisans in Yugoslavia were receiving a similar education.

The question remained as to Tito's ultimate position and effectiveness as a leader. To date, that was what no one really knew. Still, I had my suspicions . . .

Lost in these thoughts, a whole day had slipped away aboard ship in the North Atlantic, without much attention to my English studies. We were nearing the African coast. Tomorrow, the convoy would anchor in Freetown harbor, and I looked forward to the change.

Walking around the deck, I paused to observe a most beautiful sunset. Its fiery colors reflected off the ships, somehow giving me a feeling of spiritual security. I stood there watching until the sun had completely disappeared.

In the twilight, a destroyer off to our side broke into a zigzag pattern at full speed. It began to toss depth charges into the ocean. Before I could think, other destroyers joined in the pursuit of an unseen opponent, and our ship sounded its general alarm.

This was no drill. We donned our life jackets and prepared for any eventuality. As the destroyers set off their massive depth charges, huge waves from the explosions rocked our ship. Then the battleships veered away and were rapidly lost from view. The night was very quiet.

Our ship steamed ahead without the convoy's protection, the lurching changes in its direction attesting to more evasive actions. Later, in my bunk and still wearing the life jacket, I couldn't sleep a wink. No one was sure if the danger was behind us or about to strike again.

Several days out of Freetown, the official report on the incident was delivered. We definitely had been stalked by U-boats. Only the alert detection of our naval escorts had prevented a torpedo attack.

The German submarines did not come away completely empty-handed, unfortunately. After we scattered, and before the convoy could regroup, one of the other transports had been hit. Eight hundred lives had been lost. We had simply been the lucky ones, and we knew it.

Leaving Freetown, we dropped steadily away from the African coast, setting a course across the South Atlantic, southeast by east. I was relieved to be moving. The moment we had anchored, the tropical heat had become unbearable. Now the fresh sea breeze had returned.

War or no war, tradition is tradition in the British Navy. That included the ceremonial "baptism" at the equator, which we were fast approaching. Anyone who had not previously gone through it had to take part.

Our only concession to wartime was that the convoy would not stop on the equator line for the ceremony but would perform it on the fly. None of us Yugoslavs had ever crossed the equator. We were all duly interested in this ritual fun, though not quite realizing that *we* were to be included.

The following day, every ship in the convoy had its Court of Neptune. Presided over by the god himself and his assistants, it was hard to recognize anyone under their decorated masks. It soon became clear, however, that the assistants were selected from the strongest and most able-bodied men aboard.

Their task was simple. They selected the victims and brought them before Neptune. The god questioned the unfortunate supplicants and then decreed their fate. We laughed, watching other officers being submerged in a basin of water, hoisted up, tossed around, and splashed with paint.

Then it was our turn. When they got to me, two bruisers held me fast before the ruler of the sea. I pleaded for permission to cross the equator and got Neptune's answer, to everyone's delight but mine. The balance of the day I spent rubbing myself with turpentine to remove paint blotches, the visible signs of my "legitimate" crossing of the zero parallel.

The other men in my cabin met the same fate at the equator ceremony. I knew most of them well by now, except for Lieutenant Brana. He had been in the Yugoslav Air Force Reserve and was in his early forties, an old man compared to most of us. His prematurely wrinkled face accentuated his age, and we called him "Dad."

Most of "Dad" Brana's time was spent in the bar. He was the first to enter and the last to leave. Everybody knew him. Nonstop double whiskeys without soda were nothing to him, even in the heat.

Lieutenant Brana was happy to be with us. He wanted to join our fighting forces in the Near East, despite a previous taste of the bitter fruits of war. We liked him, constantly teased him, and marveled at his good-natured disposition, despite all that had happened to him.

A Serb with a modest inheritance, he originally went to Paris in 1923 to continue his law studies at the Sorbonne. There he ran across a group of Serbian perpetual students who eventually bilked him out of his last penny. Unable to continue in school, he'd taken a job as an artist in a film studio. His artistic talents bloomed, and he decided to devote his life to art.

He loved Paris but never became a French citizen, and had gladly served in the Yugoslav reserves. When the war came to France in 1939, he reported for voluntary service to his second homeland. Without any experience, he was placed in a French cavalry unit and then sent to join a battalion of the Foreign Legion. The capitulation of France to the Germans left him stranded in the south Sahara. Forced into labor duty, his release did not come until after Allied military action in Africa.

It didn't take me long to see that under his surface calm, Lieutenant Brana was deeply troubled. His sufferings in the desert war, a war fought so far from Europe, had left a deep and lasting mark. Frequently, in the dead of night I could hear him groaning and sobbing, calling strange names as he turned and tossed in his bunk. The man needed to open up. After weeks of gentle coaxing, he began to trust that I would listen.

He spoke of long marches in the desert with sand in his eyes and ears, in the food, everywhere. He spoke of the agony of the wounded in the scorching sun with no way to relieve their pain. When an Allied unit finally reached his post and freed him, he could hardly believe it was over.

Lieutenant Brana was grateful for my patience, and gradually we began to talk of other things, to even laugh freely at our fears. His scars would never totally heal, but this opening up had made his life easier to bear. I would not forget, despite everything, that his Serbian spirit had never been crushed. It was how I would personally remember crossing the equator.

As we sailed into Capetown harbor, I could easily have concluded we were somewhere on the French Riviera, had it not been for the imposing mass of Table Mountain rising in the background. It was a beautiful land. Whitewashed villas perched on the slopes around the bay, secluded behind flowery bushes and unusual trees. I couldn't wait to get ashore.

A month out of England, the convoy had reached South

Africa. Here some ships separated and went on to Durban, while the rest, ours among them, made port in Capetown. The timetable allowed us three to four days, with shore leave. It was a break in the shipboard life we all needed.

For Pachany, however, the layover would be a different matter. Prior to our arrival, he had injured himself during, of all things, a foot race on the upper deck. In the lead, he'd taken a turn too closely, brushed an exterior cabin wall, and fallen heavily. The accident left his whole leg and foot considerably swollen.

At Capetown Hospital, X-rays were to be taken to determine if any bones were broken. Pachany was quite worried about it, since his fitness for military service could be on the line. To keep his spirits up, I tried to make light of his "war wound," but I think he knew I was really as concerned as he was.

Leaving Pachany at the hospital, my stay in Capetown was a whirl of activity. I received an invitation from Lieutenant George "Djoka" Rothey to join him and friends for dinner at the Armed Forces Club. His friends included some young blondes, and while they were not the prettiest girls I had ever seen, this was wartime.

I groomed myself as best I could, brushed up on a few relevant sentences in English, and was ready to go. After dinner, I expected we would take the girls out to a night club for drinks and dancing. Instead, George had us all settle into a corner of the club's reading room where he and his friends conducted a lively discussion of British policy in South Africa.

There were still elements of the English character I obviously did not understand.

The next day, I was relieved to learn that Pachany's leg was not broken. He had received treatment at the hospital and was declared fit for limited duty. His complete recuperation would take longer, but if he took it easy, he'd be fine.

Pachany's good sense of timing had certainly not been impaired: I had just received a special invitation from the Yugoslav consul for a tour of the city and a reception in our honor. I suspected that someone in London had been thoughtful, but I appreciated the courtesy. It would be pleasant to be among fellow countrymen who lived here. Besides, Pachany and I were not averse to seeing the Capetown sights. It might be our only opportunity.

True to his invitation, the consul arranged for a wonderful day, including a cable car ride up Table Mountain. The ascent took longer that I anticipated, and the size of the mountain was not really apparent until you were in the small car climbing almost parallel to the rock face with dogged determination. From the top, the immense panorama took your breath away.

Our ships in the harbor were small dots and the city a miniature. Beyond it, you could see the Cape of Good Hope where two great oceans embraced—on the right, the green South Atlantic, and on the left, the blue Indian Ocean's waves. I thought our Yugoslav compatriots residing in Capetown must be pleased to live amidst such natural splendor, and I was astonished to hear later that some thought it the dullest place on earth. As for me, I thanked God just for the chance to put my feet on dry land again.

The reception that night was at the consul's villa, not far from the city limits. Most of the guests had already assembled when Pachany and I arrived. His wife led us to the reception room for a formal introduction, a far cry from the casual military style we'd grown used to.

Everyone was gracious, trying to outdo one another in pleasing us, but they were hungry for fresh news from London. As the evening wore on, they bombarded us with questions, intensely interested in any scrap of information that might bear on their own personal situations. Many of them were not in Capetown by accident. The Yugoslav Government-in-Exile had assigned them here to insure that their influence on its affairs would be nonexistent.

These men spent their days shuffling unimportant papers, while they believed they deserved to be center stage. In this jewellike city far from the real war, they felt they were the victims. With diplomatic caution, I was told they could identify with us, could understand the government's "mistakes" and the definite stand we officers had taken. It was really self-justification and didn't impress me very much.

There was nothing Pachany and I could do to revive their hopes, so they settled for stories about our experiences in London and at sea. It was better than telling them what I really thought— namely, that with regard to their present obscure posts, the government had not misjudged them.

The party broke up soon afterwards. On that note, and with many farewells wishing us the best of luck, we left the reception and caught the last shuttle bus back to the port.

As we once more settled into a familiar routine, the convoy sailed on around the tip of Africa and into the Indian Ocean. Pachany's leg continued to mend, and except for his declining to run any more races aboard ship, he soon seemed his old self.

The weather again grew steamy, and it was hard not to feel bored after Capetown's livelier pulse. I continued my English lessons with Djoka, although to do six hours of intensive effort daily was difficult. At times I was convinced that I should never learn the language anywhere near correctly.

Heading up the East African coast, our fear of U-boat attacks diminished. Soon we were using our life jackets mostly as deck chairs or pillows. After all, the ship's standing orders required us to keep them handy.

At dusk one evening, Pachany noticed that the Western Star appeared right in the middle of the horizon. After eighteen long days at sea, we deduced by its position that we had almost reached Aden. We were not wrong. The next day we anchored in that British-held Arabian port city.

The heat was almost unbearable as we took on supplies for the final leg of the voyage. The convoy's ships would enter the Red Sea one by one, headed for Suez. Ours was not the first to depart, but when we left Aden alone, three days later, it was somehow a great feeling of freedom to dispense with the convoy that had surrounded us for nearly two months.

The mouth of the Red Sea was very narrow, requiring several lighthouses to provide accurate guidance. Our ship had no trouble, but it would have been a different story for any Axis vessel. No U-boats were able to penetrate these waters.

I marveled at the wonderful military organization responsible for making an ordinary British lake out of the Red Sea. Such was the lack of concern that we were finally permitted to leave our life jackets stowed in the cabins. The ship sailed onward to Egypt without incident.

The Yugoslav Army Command in Cairo was housed in a beautiful building in Zamalek, the best part of the city. This was the most modern and European-like section.

To reach it, however, Pachany and I first had to pass through a confusing web of dirty, narrow, and crowded streets. We were glad when we finally reached our headquarters and were met by Colonel Dimitriye Putnik. The British Supreme Command had told him we were coming, and he received us most cordially.

The Colonel then told us he was absolutely helpless to assist us.

14

To Return

WHAT COLONEL PUTNIK meant when he declared he was help-less was that Pachany and I could expect only minimal aid from the Yugoslav Command in Cairo. Only through his British counterparts was there any chance of Allied assistance. This he would try to arrange.

In a few words, he gave us a vivid picture of the situation. The British, coming off their great victories and the resounding defeat of the Axis forces in North Africa, were firmly in charge of the Near East theater of war. They were the "dog" and we Yugoslavs were a "flea"—irritating at times, to be scratched on occasion, and in general not of high priority.

Most of our officers were pilots attached to the R.A.F. (Royal Air Force), delegated to the supply transport of fighter planes from the West African coast to Cairo. Others served in adjunct positions in intelligence or in various administrative roles. What we did *not* do was provide any direct support for our guerrilla forces fighting in Yugoslavia.

Such were the realities of practical cooperation with our ally. Lieutenant Brana and the other Yugoslav officers who had traveled with us were from the Air Force. They had jobs to do here. Pachany and I were another matter entirely.

The day before yesterday in Suez, I had left the ship for the last time in high spirits. I had assumed that the final stage of my journey was already planned. I remembered how many officers, in the last-minute flurry of packing, had exchanged addresses and promised future meetings, a ritual of shipboard leave-taking that denied the unpredictability of war.

Now I realized that I, too, faced a future of greater uncertainty than I had wanted to admit. (Months later, I was to learn that my British officer friends and their troops were part of the invasion of Italy and its bloody campaigns.)

It was nearing the end of May. I did not know exactly when my trip would continue, but I was closer to my homeland than I had been in a long, long time. Across the Mediterranean, beyond Greece and Albania, Yugoslavia was waiting. I would get there somehow. I had not come nearly fourteen thousand miles to be defeated in Cairo.

Despite the setback to my plans, my initial days in the city were exhilarating. Colonel Putnik ordered a twenty-day leave for Pachany and me, after which we'd take temporary assignments under his command. During my leave, I looked up many of my old friends and met other officers who were extremely nice. Several were frank enough to give me valuable information on headquarters "protocol," that is, who to trust, how to behave, and when to be cautious.

I began to learn my way around, both in the city streets and within local military circles. Everyone went to the popular club Djezira. That was where the pilots who flew the Cairo-Khartoum-Lagos round trip once a week would spend a goodly part of the two or three days they weren't on duty.

I appreciated that theirs was not an easy mission. The weather conditions along the way were notoriously changeable and the desert a deceptively featureless landscape to fly over. So although I was an army officer, I had seen a bit of Africa, and they forthwith accepted me.

At the club, the airmen always teased me about my good relations with Colonel Putnik and another officer, Colonel Dushan Radovich. Most of them seemed to rather despise and distrust the latter. At first I didn't understand their animosity to Colonel Radovich. Indeed, Pachany and I made his acquaintance on our first day in Cairo, and we'd liked him right off. He was very much interested in our plans and enthusiastically encouraged us to press onward.

It turned out this was yet another demoralizing residue of the infamous Cairo Affair of the previous year. Up until then, the younger set of Air Corps officers had idolized the Colonel. When he chose not to support Brigadier General Mirkovich's short-lived rebellion against the government-in-exile, they were bitterly disappointed.

In the politically charged atmosphere, Colonel Radovich had been judged not on his sense of military duty but by a Byzantine code of relationships. Thus it followed: Mirkovich's good friend was ex-Prime Minister Simovich, whose dismissal had helped to trigger events. General Simovich had a longstanding personal dislike of Colonel Radovich.

Moreover, one of Brigadier Mirkovich's first acts was to reject the authority of the newly appointed commander in Cairo, none other than Colonel Putnik. His good friend and assistant was Colonel Radovich, and that was enough to condemn them both, at least in the eyes of Mirkovich's chief supporters, a small group of influential senior officers.

These officers, many with R.A.F. contacts, did not lose their taste for intrigue with the Mirkovich debacle. Even before my arrival in Cairo, I was accused of being a dupe, or perhaps an agent, of Major Knezevich. This assertion, wholly false, was apparently based on no more than my brief stay in London.

Most of the junior officers had participated in the Cairo Affair and were thoroughly discouraged. I never agreed with their fundamental disobedience, but I also wanted to pacify them for the good of the cause we all served. Yet it proved impossible to convince them to follow my lead—it seemed the corrosion of their esprit de corps ran too deep.

Whatever the opinions about him, Colonel Radovich remained chief assistant to the commanding officer. Much of his time was spent preparing bombing target information for the Balkans and Central Europe. His work was always highly respected and well-received by the British. At one point, Air Chief Marshall Tedder, head of the Mediterranean Air Command, had the colonel attached to his own staff to supervise advance targeting.

Radovich, it turned out, had his private motives as well. All he wanted to do was find a way to go home. He knew a spot in Italy where, he claimed, the Adriatic could easily be crossed in a light plane. He had tried to sell this idea to the British.

They did not turn him down altogether, but they thought the moment had not yet come for such an experiment. Discouraged, he had left the British staff and returned to his old job with the Yugoslav Command. Lately, he had placed himself at the disposal of the American air forces in the Near East.

After Colonel Radovich told me of his own futile efforts to return, I realized that practically speaking there were no options. The only way to get back to Yugoslavia was by airplane and parachute jump. Of course, we had access to no Yugoslav planes. And I did not know how to step out of an airplane and float to earth.

I went to work on the problem.

I started going to Colonel Radovich's office nearly every day. There I gained considerable knowledge from his insightful comments and access to official reports. I also discussed with him my own observations of the situation in the Near East and what I knew about the government-in-exile in London.

Sometimes, without warning, he would spring a question on me to momentarily confound me. "Captain Todorovich, are you in reality representing an *idea* of Yugoslavia?" he asked me out of the blue one day.

Not fathoming precisely what he meant, I decided to answer confidently enough. "Of course I am. But not the nation of Yugoslavia we had before the war." As I continued, I groped to articulate what I felt deeply to be true.

"If I had the slightest suspicion that the nation would be restored exactly as it was before the war, then I would never go back. I hope that the guerrilla fighters know what they are fighting for. Yes, despite what the Croatian Ustashi have done and the other crimes committed against the Serbian people . . . It is indispensable that we should unite again . . . Even as these war criminals should be brought before the courts to answer charges and be punished."

I paused, then added simply, "I feel a future Yugoslavia should be founded and organized on a federal system in which each ethnic area and religious group is represented."

Colonel Radovich was attentive to what I had to say, but I could see he didn't agree with me. He handed me a document. It was entitled "The Croatian Crimes." Although I knew a great deal about this matter, I read it carefully.

"Do you wish a union with *them?*" he asked. "Isn't it clear to you now that the Ustashi are the greatest enemies of the Serbian people?"

"This is regrettably true," I replied, "but I cannot accuse, nor hold responsible, the whole Croatian people. I repeat that Yugoslavia must be united."

As I was not responsive to his attitude, Colonel Radovich switched the subject. "Have you decided to which part of Yugoslavia you will go? Mihailovich or Tito?"

It was not the first time I had been asked that question. "Both as individuals do not count much," I told him. "Insofar as they are representatives of the people, that is their greatness and strength. I have read General Mihailovich's dispatches and the government's reports. I know where he stands with the Serbian people."

"And what of Tito's reports?"

"How can I read Tito's reports when they are only sent to Moscow, Colonel?"

Radovich frowned. "Since April, there are the direct dispatches from the British mission to the Partisans."

Forthrightly, I got to the real point. "From what I saw in London, I believe the British do not consider it an opportune moment to render support to General Mihailovich, although they have yet to declare this."

"It seems, Captain, you are not familiar with recent events there."

He handed me an official dossier. I noted immediately that it was dated after I'd left. Inside, I found a copy of a British document that presented their latest position on aid to the Chetniks. There was a rehash of the collaboration charges that echoed the Partisans and the Communist press in London. The British government asked for any such activity to cease. It also seemed that Mr. Churchill himself had changed his mind. General Mihailovich was no longer the great man he had been up until a few months ago.

Particularly enraging to the British was a speech that the general had supposedly made in late February. According to the report of Colonel Bailey, head of the liaison mission, General Mihailovich had accused the British of exploiting the Serbian people. He had declared his real enemies to be the Partisans and Ustashi, then the Germans and Italians.

Far from being a major pronouncement to the world, this speech turned out to be some remarks to a few followers on the occasion of a baby christening. But conveniently, it was what the British wanted to hear. For the sake of their national conscience, it would be so much easier to abandon an ally they could paint as ungrateful.

A military order had been issued to limit support to the Chetniks until British demands were met. Despite all the promises of help, it was evident that the British all along had lacked confidence in General Mihailovich.

"What can you say now, Captain?"

I remained silent.

"I can only come to the conclusion," Radovich continued in measured tones, "that a British order like this has no foundation and is perfectly absurd. It will not alter the situation in Yugoslavia and will help foment a civil war." He looked at me steadily. "You are lucky. I believe you will soon be on the spot and can easily verify all we have talked about. I only regret that I shall not be with you."

"The British cannot really believe their best interests lie with the Partisans," I insisted.

"And destroy all those unwilling to join the movement?" Colonel Radovich was bemused. "Really, it's enough to force anyone to become not only a Communist but also . . . an anarchist."

Abruptly, the colonel ended our conversation. My own opinions had been clarified. The Chetnik cause was plagued by misinformation and misunderstandings. It was the victim of poor communications with the government-in-exile, the acceptance of unverified Partisan claims at face value in British circles, and Radio Free Yugoslavia's constant droning propaganda.

Nothing was to change my mind about this.

Weeks went by, and my appointment to paratroop training school had not been confirmed. I would inquire of Colonel Putnik almost every day, and always he'd wryly echo the laconic British response: "The Yugoslavs are not the only ones to be assigned to this school."

Then one day at the beginning of July, Colonel Putnik called and asked to see me immediately. When I got to his office, Colonel Radovich was there, and both were in a very cheerful mood.

"Congratulations!" Colonel Putnik began. "You're going to Palestine. I have succeeded in getting the British to assign you to the school."

I was delighted, yet I also felt dismayed. It meant, I was certain, that Pachany and I had come to a parting of the ways. He might be allowed to go to Palestine, but he would no doubt be rejected for paratrooper school because of his foot. It had never fully healed and was still swollen, although without pain. The single most important requirement of the school was to have healthy feet.

Knowing how he would feel, I kept my thoughts to myself. We had come through so much together and had traveled so many thousands of miles. I was accustomed to his good companionship and our firm friendship. And we had shared a dream. It would be a hard parting, when and if that day came.

"It is my duty as your commanding officer," Colonel Putnik went on, "to warn you how dangerous this training is. No one can force you to go and you will not offend me in the least if you decide against it."

With utmost seriousness, I answered. "My decision has not changed."

"I see. All right, then." He glanced over at Colonel Radovich. "Lieutenant Colonel Baletich and Captain Micovich are also assigned to the school. Perhaps they will go along with you to the homeland." This was the first I'd heard of other volunteers. "Please be discreet and do not speak to anyone about this. To your friends, you can say you're going to Palestine for a short rest."

I was not happy with the company I was about to keep. I knew Captain Micovich and personally distrusted him. He had struck me as a man of no integrity, someone who would be unreliable in difficult moments. As for Lieutenant Colonel Baletich, I really did not know him well enough to form an opinion, but I was not encouraged to see his age listed as forty-two. This seemed physically too old for the rigorous training we were about to undertake.

Several days before we were to leave, Captain Micovich joined me for lunch. He radiated discouragement but hesitated to admit it. He glanced around the dining room. "Look at these people here," he confided to me. "Not a single one would want to undertake the task we have chosen. Everyone thinks it is better to remain in Cairo and watch developments. And you and I have to sacrifice ourselves for their sake." Captain Micovich ended with a sigh.

"We are not sacrificing ourselves for them," I replied curtly. "When the war is over, everybody will have time to do some explaining. At present, there is no value to criticizing their attitude or allowing their opportunism to be an excuse for our inactivity."

"I am not retreating from my decision," Captain Micovich eagerly added, "but it makes me sick when I think I have to face all the danger, while they can remain here and enjoy life in peace."

Since I was hardly enamored of Micovich, I decided to try and get better acquainted with Lieutenant Colonel Baletich, if I could. He seemed eager to begin the course. As we took the train from Cairo up to Haifa, a twenty-four-hour ride in miserable conditions, my estimation of the man steadily rose. I learned to my surprise that he had previously tried to return to Yugoslavia in October of 1941.

Luka, as he encouraged us to call him, told us how his spirit had soared when he heard about the Chetnik movement. He had been trained as a saboteur and asked to be sent back as soon as possible. With just a few hours warning, he and several other men had been plucked out of Cairo by a British submarine. They hoped to land somewhere on the Yugoslav coast in a few days, but instead, for "operational reasons" they remained in Malta for forty days under intense German bombardment.

Finally, the sub went back to sea. One night, it surfaced off shore near the town of Petrovac, south of Boca di Cataro. Before the Yugoslavs could land, however, the sub commander announced he had received new orders. They had to return at once to Malta. All their protests and pleas were to no avail.

The next thirty days found the sub engaged in naval skirmishes all over the Mediterranean. It had almost driven him insane. Finally, they docked again in Malta. A few days later, Luka was delivered back to Cairo. He had never found another opportunity to attempt his return, and he felt that this was his last chance.

In contrast to Luka's anguished revelations, Captain Micovich's big concern was his weight. He really did weigh about 220 pounds, which perhaps might preclude parachute jumping. In elaborate detail, he also told us how his leg and been hurt while on parade. He'd been in the hospital for a month, and ever since it had bothered him. He was afraid he'd be denied the privilege of entering the school.

Luka listened to all this carefully and said nothing. I gathered what Micovich was aiming at. "This is a serious matter, considering your weight," I told him. "By all means, you must tell the doctor during your examination."

The suggestion pleased him very much. "You reason very sensibly, Bora." Then Micovich added, "But I shall insist despite everything that I finish the course and be sent home to Yugoslavia."

Pachany went to Palestine ahead of us. There he saw a specialist for treatment, but his foot would not heal in time. He was not accepted for paratrooper training. Wishing me the best of luck like the true brother officer he was, he returned to Cairo. He would await the next available training cycle to attend the school.

We left it simply like that. Soldiers cannot dwell on life's uncertainties in wartime. Pachany and I had always understood and accepted that.

The school began immediately. After a physical examination, we were assigned to the well-known Camp Ramat David. Its commander welcomed us with the reminder that exhausting work and effort lay ahead, which he was quick to point out we had chosen to undergo of our own free will.

Captain Micovich did not disappoint me. Whatever story he actually concocted, he informed us that the examining physician thought the course too dangerous for a man of his weight and physical condition. His release was recommended.

I was really not sorry about his leaving, though I granted the weight factor could be a justifiable excuse. When I later discovered that a British sergeant in our company weighed a good twenty pounds more than Micovich, any lingering doubts about my assessment of the man evaporated.

In addition to Luka and myself, our training group at Ramat David consisted of three Greeks, two Czechs, and two Brits. I christened us the "Foreign Legion," which seemed more and more appropriate as we sweated and drilled without interruption under the fierce July sun.

I liked Luka more and more. With the "spare tire" of a man in his forties, he was subjected to a lot of friendly banter. Yet he had an iron will and endured the strenuous training that taxed even the most fit of the younger men.

The daily two-mile run at noon, the hottest time of the day, was the worst. "Everything but the running," Luka would breathlessly declare as he finished the course dead last again. "It's getting on my nerves." I wished I could help him.

"But let them drive me as hard as they want to. I can take it," he would amend. "Nothing will stop me."

"More power to you, Luka!" I'd say. "Jumping from a plane will surely be easier than this."

By the end of our training program, I wasn't so sure it was true. To my dismay, Luka hurt himself in a practice session drill. For three days, he was confined to his cot in our group tent. I feared he would miss the vital first jump and be forced to repeat the training regimen or be cut from the school.

The morning before the jump, we were up long before dawn getting ready to arrive at the airport by 5:00 A.M. At the last moment, Luka said he felt better and gave notice that he was going with us. Relieved, I ran to inform our instructor and to obtain his permission. Hesitantly, he gave his okay.

Our group was the last scheduled, so we had to wait about an hour before our turn came. Although I wanted to get it over with as soon as I could, I must admit that when the moment to board the plane arrived, I felt a little queasy. I don't think I was the only one, either. There were a lot of forced smiles.

After a last careful inspection, the order came to don parachutes. The instructor reviewed procedures, then announced the jumping order. I would be the first to go.

Taking our places in the plane, the door was shut and we were on our way. Everyone was silent, faces pale, as we gained altitude. The instructor gamely tried to humor us. When the plane leveled off, he opened the door and ordered me to take my position.

"Do not look down," he said, "it won't help."

Somehow I couldn't hear him well, yet I knew he was just behind me. I held on to the door frame, balancing my body in the opening. A moment later there was a loud yell. With the sound, I realized I was already out.

At first, I descended very rapidly with my feet together and my hands close to my body. As my parachute opened, my fall slowed. It was a beautiful, bright early morning without wind.

Down on the field below, I saw the officers of the jump evaluation committee and a Red Cross ambulance. Before I could think what to do next, I reacted as I had been trained and found myself safely on the ground seconds later. Somebody nearby said distinctly, "Very well. Very well."

I smiled and wiped the perspiration off my face. Nothing to it. Luka came in right after me without a problem. "This is a joke," he told me happily. "Compared to running, this I will do every day gladly."

Thereafter, we did jump almost every day. A final night jump marked our official graduation, and school was over. Luka and I had made it.

We were paratroopers and had our official R.A.F. certificates to prove it. The camp bar, which we had been under orders to forgo many times before practice jumps, did some real business that night.

On my return to Cairo, I actually felt glad to see its noisy and crowded streets. My friends greeted me with much kidding about my new military specialty. They were eager to know when I would leave, but I hadn't a clue.

The war situation in Europe was steadily changing in favor of the Allies, especially after the landings in Sicily. I intently followed the latest developments. When, on September 8, Italy surrendered, everyone was euphoric. Mussolini's regime had fallen. Germany would have to fight on alone. I was half-afraid the war was going to be over before I had another chance to get involved.

From that day on, I constantly annoyed Colonel Putkin with appeals for a departure date. He was not pleased with me, but he did understand and tried everything in his power to help. His repeated official requests to the British Supreme Command got the same reply: "There are others, too, who ought to be sent. We are very limited with our planes. Wait, your turn will come."

I vented some of my frustration through a daily conference with Colonel Radovich. We reviewed guerrilla warfare actions, debated small-scale military tactics, and parried with each other over the political state of affairs.

One day, he had a surprise for me. When I was already at lunch, he entered with two American officers, a captain and a major. As soon as Colonel Radovich and his guests were seated, I was invited to join them.

Mystified, I sat down next to the major. Enjoying himself, Colonel Radovich explained that the officers were part of the new American mission to General Mihailovich. At this, I was most happy to meet them.

To my embarrassment, the colonel had apparently given the Americans an inflated appraisal of my qualifications. This did not bother him in the least. Imaginatively, he wove me into his presentation, making it the reality. He did not hesitate to criticize and condemn the present work of the British mission to the Chetniks, or to berate the failure to provide assistance.

Major Seitz and the other officer seemed to agree with him. They wanted to travel to Yugoslavia forthwith so they could judge for themselves and report to their superiors. That is exactly what Colonel Radovich encouraged them to do.

When we had finished lunch and the Americans had left, Colonel Radovich took me back to his office. I had never seen him more serious. "Your first duty, Captain, if you make if back to the homeland alive, must be to assist these two American friends with everything they need and desire to know. Do not forget that this is new to them and far from understandable. Just as it would be for us with some tribe in South America.

"You must always tell them the truth and only the truth, no matter what. This is the only way we will exonerate ourselves from the lies spread about us. America does not have imperialistic economic or political pretensions in the Balkans. Her only interest is to protect the small nations like ours that follow the same principles of democracy.

"Now, let us begin . . ."

An hour later, Colonel Radovich dismissed me, but it would hardly be our last discussion on the subject. There were so many unstable elements to analyze. The government-in-exile had been reshuffled twice. On June 17, Prime Minister Jovanovich resigned and Misha Trifunovich, another Serbian politician, assumed the post. He lasted only until August, when Dr. Purich, a career diplomat, took over.

There were rumors the government might be transferred to Cairo. Colonel Radovich seemed to have pinned his hopes for our country on the Americans. I waited, while the summer of 1943 wore itself out in the blazing heat of Egypt.

In September, new orders came down from Yugoslav Command. Luka and I were going at last. We were to report with our equipment to a designated location for dispatch to the Cairo airport and a flight to an undisclosed air base. From somewhere in Libya, we would be sent on to the Chetniks.

When we arrived at the large house in Zamalek, it was clear we were not the only men in transit that day. There were several British officers gathering there as well. The Brits said not a word about their own assignments, but judging by the desert gear they carried, I had my logical suspicions. We were probably headed in at least the same general direction. Their reticence was perfectly understandable. Conversation and mixing with strangers should always be curtailed for security reasons. Someone can always talk too much.

In my growing excitement, I couldn't eat the ample English-style breakfast that had been prepared for us. I was impatient for the moment of our departure, to be that much nearer home. The British officers ate leisurely. I could see they had no reason to hurry or feel excited. Their country was far off, and they would not soon be returning.

When we got to the airport, it was thronged with officers and soldiers wearing paratrooper insignia and loaded down with full battle equipment. In the crowd, to my great elation and happiness, I spotted Major Seitz, one of the American officers I had met through Colonel Radovich.

With a hurried explanation to Luka, I immediately approached the American. He was in the midst of a lively conversation with a British brigadier general, and as I waited to flag his attention, I glanced at the stenciling on his baggage. He'd evidently won a promotion, as it read: Lieutenant Colonel A. B. Seitz. Just then, he half-turned and saw me. His eyes lit up in recognition and he greeted me very warmly.

Seitz introduced me to Brigadier Armstrong, then said we were taking the same plane, since, after all, we were on the same mission. He left it at that, but as we chatted on about meaningless matters, I thought about the things Colonel Radovich and I had discussed with regard to the Americans. Coming upon Seitz so easily at the airport, I had the feeling luck was with me at the start.

Our flight was announced. We walked out on the runway and climbed aboard the cargo plane through its huge doors. Luka sat next to me, and I deliberately sat beside Lieutenant Colonel Seitz.

Our conversation was lively, despite the fact that Luka spoke little English. Somehow we managed in a strange mixture of Seitz's poor French, which Luka and I spoke well, and my awkward English. I'm not sure anyone understood anybody else, but there was a lot of laughter and camaraderie.

While we prepared for takeoff, Seitz confirmed, as I knew, that there already was an American, Lieutenant W. R. Mansfield, attached to General Mihailovich's staff. He had parachuted into Serbia in the middle of August, joining the Brits already there.

The initial reports Mansfield had wired to Cairo were quite favorable to the general and his organization, Seitz alluded. That was welcome news to me.

Seitz was actually enthusiastic about the prospects of life in the Yugoslav mountains. He'd been in the Canadian Mounted Police after World War I and was accustomed to camping under arduous and snowy conditions. Given that we'd first met in Cairo, I said that I hadn't suspected he was an experienced alpinist.

Privately, I wondered about Seitz's claims, but when I had a chance to examine in detail the equipment he'd brought along, I concluded he had to be knowledgeable. He was unusually well prepared. Lieutenant Mansfield had reported that the mountain nights were getting very cold and had asked for some warm woolen blankets. I had a good idea how cold it was, and it pleased me to see that Seitz took the junior officer's request seriously enough to handle the supply duty himself. He was also personally bringing the lieutenant official notification of his promotion to captain—and mail from America.

By some means, Luka had discovered the organizational status of the British officers on the plane. They were on the staff of Brigadier General Armstrong, the highest ranking officer ever sent to head up the Allied Mission to General Mihailovich. I took this as another encouraging sign. Surely the British now meant to evenly appraise both resistance forces in the country. I had no doubt that aid would follow in much larger quantities, if a British general could see the Chetniks for himself. The facts would speak louder than Partisan propaganda.

Almost without notice, the four hours of our flight passed very quickly until the last thirty minutes. Then the aircraft pitched about strongly from thermal updrafts, a reminder that we were flying over a vast desert.

We landed uneventfully at an American airfield, El Benina,

and after an hour's delay, a truck took us to Tokra, a nearby British camp. Newly constructed just east of Benghazi, my first impression of it was anything but favorable.

Tents sprawled everywhere over the red sand. What water there was came always warm and had an unpleasant taste. Food, to no one's surprise, consisted almost entirely of canned goods. The most serious deficiency, however, was the officers' drinking facility. Its sign proclaimed "Bar," and that, as we discovered after dropping off our gear and rushing over for drinks, was about all it had to offer. It certainly was not up to the standards of the desert "watering holes" everybody had known previously.

There were few permanent officers in the camp. It was built for transients, and every night men would depart from the R.A.F. airstrip to Libya on their way to many destinations around the Mediterranean. A day or so at most, and we would be flying out, too.

Sitting in the library, Luka and I would watch with envy as the latest group gathered their belongings, took a last cup of tea, and bid farewell to those of us who remained behind. Some of Brigadier General Armstrong's staff officers had been the first to go.

No one told us to prepare, so Luka and I waited expectantly. After several more days, we began to be seriously disturbed, for we had to make our jump by moonlight. The full moon was waning.

Luka decided to write a letter to Colonel Putnik in Cairo, pleading with him for quick intervention on our behalf. Most of the staff officers had now gone. Besides us, only Lieutenant Colonel Seitz and the brigadier himself were left.

They had been unlucky on four attempts: once the jump target eluded them, strong winds turned them back another time, and then engine failure twice aborted their mission. The brigadier was angry and issued daily protests, complaining about everything and everybody. The various flight crews were beginning to consider him a jinx, and while quite willing to see him on his way, no one was anxious to have him on their plane.

Our own situation seemed hopeless. "If we do not depart within the next two days," Luka said to me with a worried look, "we will find ourselves here for another month. And who could live another twenty days in this terrible suspense?" It was already September 23.

I couldn't have agreed more. "Brigadier Armstrong returned again last night. Until he departs successfully, there is no salvation for us." Luka was expressionless. "Yes," I continued, "even though I cannot understand why we must wait for him, when the other officers of his staff are already in the country."

Luka wasn't any happier, but we finally agreed not to ask anybody when we would be flown out. We would wait patiently and use will power to strive to maintain our outward calm. No sooner had we made this vow than it seemed the camp commander sought us out. He was smiling.

Instantly, I knew what he would say. "Captain Todorovich, Colonel Baletich, tonight be prepared," he said cheerfully. "Immediately, go along to requisition your parachutes and other necessary equipment."

We both jumped around like excited children. The day was finally here, I kept thinking. Only hours more on this red sand, and by tomorrow I'd be on top of our beautiful mountains, surrounded by forests and high meadows.

Luka and I completed all our tasks mechanically, our thoughts far away, thinking of our brothers in arms across the sea. Around nine in the evening, the camp commander issued the final orders. Tonight, it was we who said good-bye to the others left behind, we who happily climbed into the truck to be taken to the airstrip.

In the dark, we boarded a four-motor Halifax bomber crewed by men who seemed, by our standards, much too young for the job. Accompanying us was a paratroop instructor. He tried to encourage us, going over jump procedures yet again as we silently took our places. It hardly seemed necessary. I listened instead to the wonderful roar of the motors starting up.

The bomber flew at twelve thousand feet. Icy cold penetrated the plane. An hour passed.

Luka dozed, and I began to talk with the instructor. He told me about his village in Scotland, the wife and child he'd left behind and hadn't seen for over a year. He was tired of the war. It was dragging on too long. Worse, after scores of jumps, he was starting to think of the danger. That was the ruin of a good parachutist, to distractedly think of possible disaster when he must focus only on reacting. Many times already, he had survived the worst, attack by an enemy aircraft or ground fire.

He was a likable, sincere chap and not that night full of the normal paratrooper bravado. I responded with stories of my own. In the dark, he listened to me as the miles went as intently as I had been listening to him. In war, which does with men as the wind blows leaves, hard-bitten soldiers can find amusement at unwittingly impressing each other.

We had been flying for nearly two hours. I was pretty tired, so I stretched out on a cabin bench, but managed only some fitful sleep. It was 0300 hours, three in the morning.

"The fires! The fires!" I heard all of a sudden. The excited instructor shook me awake and pointed to a small window. I scrambled up to look. Far below, six small fiery dots marked out a perfect landing zone. My heart began to pound.

The plane dropped rapidly, then the usual purr of the motors resumed. The instructor opened the outer door. Across from me, I noticed Luka was pale and serious. I tried to joke with him, but he said nothing.

I was the first to go. The darkness was complete, for the moon had been clouded over. I sailed through space, the silk mushroom of my parachute billowing out over my head. I fell slowly, but rocked and swayed about dangerously in the wind.

When I looked for the landing zone, I saw nothing, absolutely nothing, below. Where were the fires? Did the pilot make a mistake? Was the altitude wrong? I should have reached the ground by now. A dozen thoughts flashed through my mind at once.

Where was I? I began to weaken, to expect a crash. I tensed my muscles in anticipation of sudden death. Then I hit the ground with a light thud.

Soft Yugoslav earth saved my legs from paying the price of my standing descent. Speedily, I disengaged myself from the chute harness, looking around me. I was at the bottom of a river canyon.

It seemed I was completely alone, and not knowing what else to do, I began to gather up my parachute. The drone of the plane finishing its supply drops reached my ears faintly.

"Hey you! Parachutist!" Far above me, I saw some faint lights. "Hey brother, where are you?"

I felt a spasm of fear and confusion, then my head cleared and I answered the call. The lights came down faster. In moments, I was surrounded by long-haired men in ragged peasant costumes, guns in hand and grenades at their waists.

They were smiling. I lowered my own submachine gun and stepped forward. One of them came to me. "Captain, I welcome you," he said. We embraced, and I hardly noticed that I was crying with joy.

Many had failed, but I had not. I had returned.

15

Mission and Dissension

IT WAS LIKE being born again. The autumn night was so beautiful, full of the fragrance of pine trees. Everything within me was singing.

The small Chetnik patrol escorted me to headquarters, which was "nearby." I was in such a state of happiness that I hardly noticed we'd been walking for forty-five minutes before we reached our destination.

Actually, there were several camps at the headquarters site. In the very early hours of the morning, the first one I got to was for the Allied Mission. (It was some two miles from the Chetnik General Staff encampment.) Here makeshift tents sheltered the British and American liaison officers.

To my amazement, everyone was awake. I was immersed in greetings, introductions, and welcoming embraces. A huge kettle of "Shumadija tea" was boiling over a fire, and rounds of that hot toddy of plum brandy and sugar were drunk to my health. I was, as I had hoped, only the latest of the safe arrivals, following Lieutenant Colonel Seitz, Brigadier Armstrong, and the members of their staffs. It would take me a while to sort everybody out, but it was great to see a lot of already familiar faces.

In my euphoria, I still had one persistent concern in the back of my mind. Had Luka made it? When I saw him lying by the fire, I felt a rush of relief.

My elation was short-lived. When I went over to him, I saw

that he was conscious, yet not coherent. He must have been badly hurt, for when I asked him simple questions, he could not answer correctly.

There was nothing else I could do for him. Leaving him in capable hands, I was shown to a tent constructed from a used parachute. Inside, I threw myself down on a thick pile of straw and was asleep instantly.

Shortly after dawn, I awoke with a start. Outside my tent, I could see in the growing light a forest of huge pine trees that hid us from prying eyes. The headquarters group had been here since September 8, having outwitted the Germans in the latest episode of the cat-and-mouse game we played with the enemy.

The closest town was Priboj, held by Italian occupiers, and there were German forces about three hours away on foot. We were deep in the heart of Serbia—45 miles from Kraljevo to the northeast and some 150 miles to the south of Belgrade, but only as the crow flies. The terrain was mountainous and as difficult to travel through as any guerrilla could wish for.

Some comrades from the patrol that found me, I noticed, were drinking tea by the fire. As I joined them, they offered to give me a tour of the immediate area. I accepted.

The rays of the September sun were breaking over the mountains of Zlatibor as we approached a group of cabins in the woods. Here lived General Mihailovich, I was told, the great man who was directing the entire Chetnik resistance and the destiny of our people.

In front of our cabin, bearded men were listening to a radio. "May God be with us!" we greeted them, and they gave us the customary response: "May God help you!"

Room was made on the bench and I sat down, just as if I had arrived from a local village and not from completely across the Mediterranean. I expected that I would be flooded with questions as soon as the broadcast finished, but I was mistaken. Except for being asked if I had been hurt in the jump and how I felt that morning, they seemed barely interested in me. Perhaps they wouldn't have addressed me at all were I not wearing my tropical-weight uniform.

Hoping to improve matters, I mentioned that besides my dinner in Benghazi the night before, I had spent some time in Africa. So had a number of these Chetniks, it turned out, and a livelier conversation started. They did indeed want to know what was happening in the outside world.

Our talking was interrupted by a colonel in the company of another heavily bearded officer. I rose from the bench. The colonel proceeded to introduce me: "General, this is Captain Todorovich, who arrived last night from Africa." I was stunned.

I saluted the man before me, although I would never have recognized him from the pictures I'd seen in England and Cairo, or even based on my memory of him as a military professor in Belgrade. In turn, General Mihailovich welcomed me with a cordial handshake. "You will tell me all about everything shortly," he said, "but now join us in our morning tasks."

With that simple meeting, beyond the Uvac River in the free mountains of occupied Yugoslavia, my life with the Chetnik resistance began.

The next day, I attended my first working session of the General Staff of the Chetnik Army. It was held in a rough cabin. Yanko, a bowlegged orderly, helpfully pointed it out to me. As I entered, those present turned toward the door and answered my greeting, then continued with their work.

I couldn't see much at first. The bright morning sunshine had left my eyes a bit dazzled, and there were only two small windows on opposite sides of the cabin to relieve the semidarkness. Then, as my eyes adjusted, I realized the room was filled with a pungent, hospitable mix of burning wood and tobacco smoke. I stayed beside the door, not wishing to disturb anybody's concentration, and looked around.

Never before had I been assigned to a General Staff headquarters. I had read much about the work of various World War I commanding generals and headquarters staffs, but what I saw at that moment was unlike anything in the history books. The miserable conditions hardly reflected the usual well-supplied nerve center of a national army.

The fire was burning in an open hearth that lacked a chimney. Some personal belongings, a duffel bag, and a pair of boots were stacked in a corner. At the room's other end were two crudely made peasant beds filled with straw and covered with old quilts. Next to them was a small table, probably hewn by the shepherds who spent their summers in cabins like these. It was covered with military maps. A pair of three-legged stools and some sawed-off stumps served for chairs. That was all the furniture there was.

Little better than a field bivouac in the woods, this headquarters couldn't hold a candle to any of the official Yugoslav offices I'd seen since my escape from Germany nearly seventeen months ago. But it didn't matter. For on a bed was the supreme commander of our forces, General Draza Mihailovich, and there wasn't the likes of him anywhere in Marseille, London, or Cairo. He made all the difference.

The general sat with his head propped in his weather-beaten hands, studying some papers before him on the table. Grouped around were the men of the High Command's operational section, attending to the duties of the day. I recognized most of them, despite their beards and woolen peasant costumes.

Two were unknown to me. I had never seen their faces before, but I was sure they were not officers. Both were older men, over fifty. The taller one was rangy with a saintly appearance, his intelligent face mildly lined and framed with gray hair. He was sitting beside the general, leaning on his cane and staring at its handle as a report was read.

Next to him, perched on a stump, was the other man, also gray-haired. He was slightly stooped and appeared as if he belonged far more behind an author's desk than here in the woods with a band of Chetnik guerrillas. As I was puzzling over their identities, one of the general's aides, Captain Acim, collected me from the cabin doorway.

Chicha, he said, had invited me to sit down.

He meant the general. It was what all the Chetniks called him among themselves, partly for simplicity and greatly out of love. Chicha—familiarly, "old man," but of a kindly nature. Today, it also identified the man who represented our hopes for freedom and democracy in Yugoslavia after the war.

In a whisper, I inquired about the two men I hadn't recognized. They were Dr. Moljevich and his secretary, I was told. The name I knew. Dr. Steven Moljevich was a Serbian political leader, a member of the Central National Committee set up in 1941 as a civilian wing of the Chetnik armed resistance.

The General Staff was in the midst of dealing with a wide range of problems. These included not only the struggle against the enemy forces of occupation, but also protecting the civilian population from reprisals, dealing with refugees, supplying food to ravaged and devastated districts, and most dismayingly, conducting a burgeoning civil war versus the Partisans. For this relatively small staff, the demands were overwhelming, requiring work that in other warring nations occupied the entire machinery of government.

Nonetheless, the work progressed easily and naturally. I had never thought that such a measure of democratic spirit prevailed among these military men of the forest. Before my arrival, I'd imagined that they had become rough and crude, only able to maintain discipline through the most severe treatment.

Chicha was reading reports received during the night from leaders of the various guerrilla corps. As their situations were updated, notes and markings were made on the maps. Code names such as "Rampini," "Tva-Tva," "Old Man Branko," and "Old Man Peter" as yet had no meaning for me.

Since I couldn't contribute anything to the active discussion, my attention naturally fell on Chicha. I observed him with care. Even his heavy beard could not completely conceal an expressive face. His hazel eyes, although somewhat hidden behind horn-rimmed glasses, reflected firmness and the strength of his character. Chicha looked strong and healthy. The poor diet and more than three years of life in the mountains did not seem to have weakened his physical constitution.

He was dressed as the other Chetniks, very modestly in a peasant costume of crude material. His headgear was a round, fur cap, and he wore ordinary military shoes. I was impressed with the way he tersely dictated orders for his commanders in the field. When he finished, evidently the morning's work was drawing to a close. I reluctantly shifted my attention from Chicha to Lieutenant Colonel Lalatovich, chief of operations, who made a few summary remarks.

The orderly Yanko brought in Yugo-Sandzak "coffee" for everyone. Made from nothing but barley, it was a poor parody of the famous Yugo-Brazil blend. The arrival of the coffee signaled that the staff meeting was over and we would take a break for lunch.

Stepping outside the cabin, I enjoyed a breath of the clean mountain air. Many new thoughts of Chicha were in my mind, and I decided I would very much like to know him better. In time, I did.

I would discover that he never asked any special favors or comforts for himself. He ate the same food everybody else did, often only a few baked potatoes a day. He smoked almost continuously while working. On occasion, after a hard day's work, he drank a little *raki ja*, the common plum brandy of Yugoslavia.

His love of music found an outlet in listening to Drashko, a simple Chetnik soldier, play the accordion. He also greatly enjoyed discussing economics and sociology. It would become a special pleasure for me to listen to him comment on such subjects with Dr. Moljevich, who was regarded as an authority.

Coupled with his Spartan personal habits, Chicha's sense of organization, his personal bravery, and a gift for direct contact and cooperation with the people had made him our national leader. Yet there were few outside his circle of intimates who knew him well. Some admired his sincerity in revealing the truth of the military and political disasters that had befallen the country. Some were inspired by his calls for social justice in a new society built upon a solid foundation of democratic principles. And then there were those who thought he was but insurance for their own futures in a Yugoslavia ruled by a king.

General Mihailovich had to struggle against men and the ideas of men who failed to understand his higher aims, or who sought to destroy everything he stood for.

I really didn't feel hungry, but skipping meals when battle might break out at any time was hardly a good soldier's habit. As I hesitated, Dr. Moljevich unexpectedly walked up to me. He was interested in hearing my first impressions. I really had no ready comments, though I was flattered by his attention.

Since he seemed in the mood to talk, I encouraged him and suggested he show me where lunch was being served. As we walked along together, Dr. Moljevich spoke earnestly: "You saw this morning under what conditions we work. But it is a far cry from our early beginnings, believe me.

"I am glad you came to us. We need young hands, as there is much work before us. Do not falter because of the difficulties and lack of understanding you are bound to encounter. You will often be witness to such lies that your blood will boil with rage. But we must control ourselves and continue to fight against the forces of occupation.

"Do not forget that one of your most important duties is to suppress the idea of revenge. Judge for yourself. Back in August of 1941, I first heard about Chicha. I did everything I could to find him and to offer my services, traveling far from my home in Banja Luka."

I realized then that Moljevich, a Serb, had lived in Croatia before the war. He had somehow escaped the horrible atrocities of the Ustashi and the German occupiers. Many people he knew must now be part of those dry statistics in the official reports.

He continued: "Countless thousands of Serbs had already been sent to Ustashi concentration camps when somehow they heard I was alive. They prepared a terrible deed, to send my wife to the camp at Yasenovats and my two daughters into a whorehouse. One of my friends got wind of these plans, with only a day to spare, and my family fled.

"Yet we must show, by our personal example, that we will seek out and punish only the guilty. It is our sacred task. We are preparing a list of all war criminals. . . ."

We were headed toward a huge shade tree that stood alone in front of Chicha's cabin. Beneath it was a table, and there sat nearly all the members of the General Staff. They had just had lunch and were happily laughing.

Excusing myself from Dr. Moljevich, I sat down at the table. Yanko brought me a dish of meat and rice with a large hunk of black bread. The meal was so unexpectedly good that I suddenly found I could eat with the greatest appetite.

They did not, I confirmed, eat as well every day. The excellent dinner had resulted from a raid on an Italian warehouse by units of the Zlatibor Corps. The chief quartermaster, the famous "Uncle Taras," was very proud that he could prepare such a fine meal. It was the subject of many jokes from everybody at the table.

Uncle Taras had been an officer with Chicha from the first day of the resistance and was seldom far from him. Short and husky, he looked comical with his huge beard. Sitting there with his usual heavy frown, he grumbled at the jokes and comments directed at him from all sides.

Someone ventured a remark to the effect that Uncle Taras had been scared out of his wits long ago in Ravna Gora, the area where the Chetnik movement commenced. The quartermaster immediately reacted. "So would you be scared, brother, if you found yourself all alone facing an entire Partisan battalion!"

"Tell us! Tell us!" the good-natured cry went up.

"Very well. Early in December of 1941," Uncle Taras began, "relations between us and the Partisans were already bad. Some skirmishes had taken place. Then we had to evacuate Ravna Gora in face of the German punitive expedition and head toward the high mountains of Sandzak. I was delegated with two aides to bury all the archives and join our retreating column afterwards.

"It was very cold and a heavy fog fell. We had trouble digging a hole deep enough and then camouflaging it. To warm up, I went into this cabin, and also to have something to eat."

There was taunting laughter from the audience, but Uncle Taras just grumbled in his beard and ignored them.

He resumed his story: "Suddenly, I heard a commotion around the cabin and the voices of many men. Some broke in. I grew pale when I saw five-pointed red stars on their caps.

"These young Partisans ordered me to go with them for questioning. I had no choice, so they dragged me before their leader. He was a Montenegrin, a former student, and already a commander of a battalion. I thought to myself, 'Imagine the nerve of this punk. I spent twenty years in the army before I became a captain and here he is—overnight no less—the head of a battalion!'

"He asked me where I was from and I said the nearby village. It seemed to be going over, when this kid in the escort spoke up. 'The old man's lying, Comrade Commander, that's Major Uzelac from the personal guard of Draza Mihailovich.'

"I thought my heart had stopped beating. I knew what to expect, but I still protested loudly that I was from the village. The commander ordered me placed under guard while he checked out the facts.

"They stuck me back in the cabin. It was very cold, but I was perspiring. Every little while, I asked the guards to let me out . . . for a few moments of 'necessity.' They laughed and said, 'Tonight you'll have no more necessity for going out so often.' But they still let me go, watching me closely.

"I was thinking of escape. The fog was getting thicker, and my frequent exits had relaxed these youthful guards. I looked around, they were turned away, and next thing I ran down the hill.

" 'Halt! halt!' the guards shouted, and they let off a few echoing shots. I cannot imagine, as fat I am, how I could have run so fast and so long. My breath stopped in my throat, but I kept on running. I finally hid in a ravine and waited for darkness to come. Then I would go and find the column.

"And right there, I solemnly swore that I would never separate myself from our Chicha again. Look what nearly happened to me when I was alone!"

At that, everybody broke down in laughter.

Later that afternoon, my new orderly, Mita, helped me to set up and arrange my tent. With unusual curiosity, he observed everything I pulled from my duffel bag, not forgetting to mention how he had nothing himself. Mita seemed to admire every item that I possessed. I laughed to myself at his crude tactics. Giving him some of the "little things" he really needed, I enjoyed his surprise even more.

Mita had news for me of Lieutenant Colonel Baletich. My friend Luka, who never gave up, was recovering. Yet when he did, our duties in different staff sections would not allow time for the friendly companionship and long chats we'd once enjoyed. Luka had come home, as we all had, to the hard realities of a war.

My work was cut short by a friendly call from Captain Acim. He asked me to join the group assembling with Chicha under the large shade tree. The new head of the Allied Mission, Brigadier C. D. Armstrong, was arriving soon to present his credentials. He'd then be officially attached by the Allied High Command to the general's staff.

I sensed the excitement of the other officers. The appointment of an Allied general seemed to indicate that the Chetniks' importance had finally been recognized. After a three-year struggle, they felt they were being counted on in the Allied strategic plans and as a major factor in the Balkans. Naturally, everyone was interested in meeting this British general, and some had brought cameras to snap a record of the important scene.

Across the hillside, fifteen or so military men came striding toward us. Brigadier General Armstrong was accompanied by his staff officers: Major Jacks (Operations), Major Green (Supply), Major Flood (Intelligence), and Lieutenant Colonel Howard (Chief of Staff). The group included the "old British hands," Colonel Bailey and Major Duane "Marko" Hudson, and the Americans, Lieutenant Colonel A. B. Seitz and the now-promoted Captain Walter Mansfield.

I recognized nearly all of them, and they knew who I was. With that knowledge, I felt more like an observer than a participant as a round of introductions began under the tree. Carefully, I watched the Yugoslav officers. Joy was evident in their faces and they could not restrain their happiness. It was as if these Allied visitors indicated that our struggle for liberty had already succeeded.

Chicha spoke first, greeting Brigadier Armstrong. He expressed his delight that an Allied general was among us and would be a true witness of our situation. We had nothing to hide, he declared. The brigadier could go wherever he wished and see whatever interested him. We were proud of everything: the bravery of our fighters, the loyalty of our people, even the poor arms and matériel we had mostly taken from the occupiers. The brigadier would see and be convinced.

Brigadier Armstrong, who heard all this through his interpreter, Colonel Bailey, responded in like manner. Yanko produced glasses of raki ja and we toasted one another before breaking into smaller groups to talk and exchange impressions.

Darkness gradually enveloped the Zlatibor Mountains and the evening breeze brought the fragrance of the pine forest. The mountains were sinking into dreams. Everything was quiet, except for a few men still talking under the tree before Chicha's cabin.

I was tired and had heard enough of great hopes and the fine future ahead of us. Mita was waiting for me in front of my tent. With a soft rag, he fondly rubbed the Tommy gun that I had earlier bestowed on him. "Good night, Captain," he said. "Tomorrow we shall be one step closer to liberty."

Crawling into the tent, I lay down on the straw without

undressing. I heard the faint sounds of music. Drashko was playing his accordion and singing:

> Oh mountain, mother of love!
> Oh mountain, my beautiful flower!
> In thee live their lives,
> The sons of our freedom.

As September gave way to October of 1943, I became all too familiar with the markings on Chicha's military maps. They showed developing changes in the situations in Bosnia, Sandzak, and some parts of Montenegro. The Germans were ever-present, but Tito's forces appeared to be on the move.

Undoubtedly, it was clear to the Partisan leaders that only he who holds Serbia can be master of Yugoslavia. With the Italian surrender to the Allies in early September, their forces of occupation in Yugoslavia were finished fighting. From them, the Partisans gained significantly in arms and in men, as many Italian soldiers thought to join the Allied side via an approved resistance group. (Hitler moved quickly to hold most of Italy with German troops.)

The Partisans' intention was to reorganize all forces in the Sandzak region and eastern Bosnia, and then cross into Serbia. In earlier years, they had lacked the military strength for such an effort. Always they faced no welcoming support from the vast majority of the Serbian people. Yet with the Chetniks unable to solve the dilemma of Allied military support, they saw their opportunity.

Meanwhile, Chetnik operations under the command of Lieutenant Colonel Ostojich, whose nom de guerre was Uncle Branko, were being extended westward into Bosnia. Some smaller towns had been seized, including Vishegrad and Rogatica, as the main force moved forward toward Sarajevo. To take that important city (where World War I had been ignited), the poorly armed Chetnik forces would surely be strained to the limit.

Yet, as planned, Sokolac had fallen after a few days battle, and the first ranks of Major Rachich's corps were already at Pale, near Sarajevo. Reports reaching headquarters said there was great excitement in the city and that its evacuation had in fact begun. Secretly, the Croatian Home Guard unit sent a representative, Major Predoyevich, to parley with Lieutenant Colonel Ostojich.

He offered cooperation against the Germans, with certain conditions. If our attack went well, the Home Guard garrison would not attack us; but if we failed, then all bets were off. This major also requested that nothing be said of his offer, since he did not want his comrades to fall under German suspicion. As for himself, he did not wish to return to his post and was being escorted to our headquarters.

The fall of Sarajevo was expected any day, and the General Staff grew optimistic. Hardly any attention was paid to the movements of small Partisan units. The news that they had taken Rogatica, now in the rear area of our operations, came as a complete surprise.

Rogatica had been left with a policing force of only some forty Chetniks, since every available man was needed in the battle for Sarajevo. It was hardly difficult for a small band of well-armed guerrillas to enter and defeat these few defenders who lacked any automatic weapons. Upon gaining the town, the Partisans' purpose was clear.

They took revenge on all those who had previously aided us, concentrating their forces immediately. They were poised to deal a death blow against any Chetnik operations in Bosnia that might appear potentially successful. As if by seeming agreement, the same day the Partisans entered Rogatica, the German-Ustashi garrison in Sarajevo made a strong counterattack on us.

Now our units found themselves, after two days of hard battle, facing enemies on both sides. Given such an untenable position, Lieutenant Colonel Ostojich had no choice. He ordered a strategic retreat back toward Rogatica and Vishegrad.

To our consternation, the B.B.C. proceeded to glorify "successful battles" of the Partisans. They had, according to London radio, fought strong German-Ustashi forces in eastern Bosnia. Thousands of the enemy were dead or wounded, at least in the reports filed by the Partisan General Staff.

After these events unfolded, I spoke to the officers of the Allied Mission. I wanted to know their reaction. They only shook their heads. "Even we cannot understand the position taken by the B.B.C.," Major Green told me in the presence of several of his fellow officers. "If I could just go to London, I'd tell them once and forever who is fighting the enemy."

"Brigadier Armstrong has sent several protests," enjoined Colonel Bailey. "He has received no answer to them."

I had nothing to say to that. Brigadier Armstrong and Lieutenant Colonel Seitz had both sent many messages, but had gotten few replies.

"Captain, you should know that our politicians and military take different stands," said Major Jacks. "That is how it is now. The goal of politics is not to abandon the Serbian people, but the military aids everyone willing to fight the Germans."

"Why don't you help us then, if that is true?" I asked. "Aren't you witnesses to our struggle? You've seen our units operate against the enemy. In the past month, you've witnessed battles yourselves, yet all this means nothing."

"How do you know the Partisans are not fighting the enemy?" Major Hudson interjected.

"I don't know if they are or not," I answered, "but you know very well what they did two days ago. They took Rogatica and hit Lieutenant Colonel Ostojich's forces from the rear while he was under attack from the Germans. What do you call that, Major?"

"Probably they were just taking up better positions for later operations against the Germans," he offered. "They were accommodating themselves to the situation."

"Call it what you wish," I said, "but it is clear to me that such actions only aid the enemy. Yet I am sure for this 'heroic' occupation of a defenseless rear position, Radio Free Yugoslavia and the B.B.C. will glorify the Partisans again. Military supplies will be sent to them, while requests made by Major Green on behalf of our General Staff will go begging.

"We Chetniks are told," I added, "that weapons cannot be sent because there is fear we will use them against the Partisans. Does the same standard apply to them also? Judging by their recent acts, it does not appear so. Why, may I ask? Can you give me an answer to this question?"

My heated remarks produced an awkward silence. Had I gone too far? I asked myself.

I looked at their faces and felt they were really in agreement with me. These Allied officers had submitted accurate reports, there was no doubt. Yet, as well I knew, they also had to obey their superiors. In that, as honorable men, they had no choice.

Despite my impression that British policy had condemned our whole national movement, as Colonel Radovich had foreseen in Cairo, my own options were logically unchanged. I had to maintain the best relationship I could with the Allied Mission, especially with the Americans.

"This Brigadier would like to climb Varda Mountain today," Colonel Bailey informed me one morning, shortly thereafter. "Would you ask Chicha if there are any objections?"

"I shall be glad to," I answered.

When I entered the staff cabin for the morning meeting, Chicha saw that I was preoccupied. "What is it? What 'request' are you bringing now?" he asked. The others there laughed. They understood correctly the brigadier's haughty nature.

I explained.

"Let him climb wherever he will," Chicha agreed humorously. "It would be well were you to remind him of the aid that still does not come, in spite of assurances." As though to himself, he continued seriously. "Today, all the commandants are coming for a meeting. I know that every one of them will ask for arms and munitions. I'll have to make promises, for that is all I can give them now.

"I command them to fight and demand action in order to aid our allies. They carry my orders out, they fight, and many die. And what do I give them? Promises of Allied help. I am certainly the only chief commander in the world who can give his troops only orders and nothing else."

There was silence in the room.

Then Chicha resumed: "Ostojich took back Rogatica this morning. They didn't even wait for him. The Partisans ran away as soon as our forces appeared, their real mission already accomplished. Yet not one of our allies wants to see that.

"Not one."

16

American Liaison

THE DAY AFTER Brigadier Armstrong made his ascent of Mount Varda, I received an unexpected order. Signed by Lieutenant Colonel Novakovich, it was brought by a staff orderly during our lunch and called for immediate preparations to move. I informed the brigadier at once.

He broke off the meal and I left for the General Staff quarters. As I walked, a German Me-110 flew up. Usually I'd pay no attention to such a common occurrence, but this was different. I could tell by its sound that the plane was dropping lower. The fighter disappeared for a moment, then came back very low with machine guns chattering. I watched transfixed as its strafing run went right over the Allied Mission camp.

What should I do? Return, or go on to the General Staff? In an instant, I decided that information was the priority. If anyone had been hurt at the Mission, Sergeant Gardashevich was there to help, but my first duty as a liaison was to know what was happening.

The plane climbed rapidly into the sky and was gone. The deep woods around headquarters were still. I decided it was an isolated incident, a chance opportunity for some straying plane, and not the forewarning of an enemy who really knew our location. It would, however, have been nice to be back on Mount Varda, where I had been some twenty-four hours ago. From that superb vantage point, you could view the entire area.

As the brigadier had requested, he and Colonel Bailey and I had set out yesterday on horseback to tackle the peak. It was a very nice mid-October day. I rode in the lead, and though our horses faced a difficult advance up the steep slopes, we'd reached the top in about half an hour. There a simple marker read: 1,398 meters (4,500 feet).

Beside it was a lookout post of the Chetnik Zlatibor Corps, equipped with a German binocular telescope, a type usually used to direct artillery fire. The sentinels stood guard while the brigadier, aided by Colonel Bailey, scanned the surrounding terrain and the approaches to our encampment. The colonel's comments showed how well he knew the geography, and I had to admire him for that.

The air was extremely clear, especially to the southwest. One could see not only to the mountains of Bosnia-Herzegovina and Montenegro, but almost to the high peaks of the Albanian border. Far below, and closer to hand, lay the town of Rudo, its main bridge in ruins. From there, the road twisted and turned like a white string as it followed the Lim River valley south.

To the north, past Priboj, more mountains loomed. The Drina River ran there, joined by the waters of the Lim below the town of Vishegrad about twenty miles to our northwest. Together, the two rivers marked out a rough boundary between Serbia and the western part of Yugoslavia.

Turning to the east, the brigadier spotted much smoke on the slopes around Mokra Gora, and explosive echoes reached our ears. The only ready explanation was that the enemy was again avenging himself on a defenseless Serbian village. My musings were interrupted by one of the Chetniks. "A column on the road, Captain. It's moving from Priboj down toward Budimlia. There are plenty of trucks."

The telescope revealed things more clearly. Judging by appearances, there were the troops of the former Italian occupation garrison at Priboj, a village now under our control, on their way to either Dobruna or Vishegrad. The column stopped at the Budimlia crossroads.

From a strictly military point of view, their situation wasn't enviable. Their division had gone over to the Partisans, but this unit was caught between us, the Partisans, and the Germans, who constantly insisted they join them for the salvation of Italy. In the middle of our country, without hope of reaching their native land, these Italian soldiers seemed to be a disarmed group straying without purpose. However, I couldn't feel sorry for them, not after all they had done. Yet as they were now officially on our side (since the recent Italian surrender to the Allies), but no longer wished to fight, they would probably end up in some German concentration camp.

"Does Chica know anything about this movement?" Colonel Bailey asked me.

"He probably does, but I'll send a fast messenger with a report," I answered.

That had been the conclusion of our day of mountain climbing. Today, far below that lofty height, I would soon learn that the defeated Italians had not been the only soldiers on the march.

When I reached the General Staff cabins after the fighter attack, I saw wagons being loaded with the equipment of "Uncle Taras," the quartermaster. All the officers of the operations section—Lieutenant Colonels Novakovich and Luka Baletich, Majors Gogich and Terzich, and Captain Slepchevich—were ready to move. But there was little definite information.

A column of unidentified soldiers had been reported crossing the Lim River, less than four miles from our present site, and was advancing in our direction. Chicha himself had ordered the quick relocation of headquarters and, as always, had personally gone to observe from our threatened forward positions. He hadn't yet returned.

Leaving my orderly behind in case of further instructions, I slowly walked back to the Mission camp. No one had been hurt by the machine-gun fire. Everything was packed, and the horses stood by, ready for our departure. We waited only for the order.

The sun was sinking in the west. Lieutenant Colonel Seitz and Captain Mansfield approached, and laughingly I called to them: "What about our apple pie, eh? Fate did not wish us to enjoy it this evening."

I was referring to the apple pie planned as the pièce de résistance of a dinner scheduled for that very night. I had been invited by Captain Pevets Joze, an old schoolmate of mine from the Military Academy, to bring along the two American officers to enjoy a homemade dessert.

Captain Pevets alone could have produced such a miracle. He was head of the General Staff's Information Center, but unofficially he had a knack for obtaining what no one else could. With his aides, Lieutenant Aleksa and Second Lieutenant Jesha, the captain was always able to secure not only the best lodgings, but also the best food and drink, including top-notch raki ja. More than a few officers took to dropping by his quarters whenever they could claim "urgent business" in his vicinity.

That morning, when I'd informed Seitz and Mansfield of the invitation, they'd both gladly accepted. The three of us could hardly wait for the dinner hour. But it was not to be.

"That's all right," Colonel Seitz told me. "At our new location, we'll find Pevets again. Do you know when we leave, or where we're going?"

"Not at present. We're waiting for Chicha to return. We may leave any minute."

"Our third radio set isn't ready to move," Colonel Bailey interjected as he joined us. "If we're to move immediately, I'll have it hidden. We can send a man back for it in a few days."

"I think that's best," I agreed, "and we should start loading the horses before it gets really dark." I turned to a group of soldiers waiting nearby. "Load up!"

Suddenly, shots went off. Firing broke out along the edge of a field about two to three hundred yards from the Mission. A second section erupted, then it came from all sides. Over at the General Staff area, I caught a glimpse of twenty to thirty men running toward the sound of the attack, weapons at the ready. I felt all eyes turn to me. Nobody panicked, yet I had received no communications, no orders.

Clearly, to remain where we were risked the loss of the Allied officers into enemy hands. My responsibility for them was a heavy burden. I would much rather have gone to the field where the battle raged. On my own authority, I ordered everyone to start moving in the direction of the Zlatibor Corps a few miles away.

My aim was to get us into the woods about a hundred yards ahead, where we could at least take cover. I told Colonel Bailey I would ride ahead as point man and asked him to lead the rest after me. If I ran into gunfire, he should then turn south and try to escape.

Bullets were flying around us. I mounted my horse and plunged into the woods, submachine gun in hand. Of course, I knew it wasn't of much use when I could be ambushed from any tree. Hopefully, the other Allied officers and men were coming after me.

When I got to the Zlatibor Corps command post, it was empty. The battle was drawing nearer. I spotted Chicha! He was with a small force, but they couldn't hold out much longer.

Like an answered prayer, a column of General Staff troops burst out before me. They swept up to reinforce our positions, several of the officers dropping back to ask me what was going on. Chicha had been in the first line of defense, we realized, offering stubborn resistance to the attackers.

And just who had attacked? A Partisan battalion, I was told.

The full blackness of the night enveloped us. Some of the Allied officers had caught up to me. We hugged the ground while listening to rifle and machine-gun fire from the front line about two hundred yards away. At intervals, a grenade exploded. Given the timing, I judged they only had a single launcher. Still, their arms were superior to ours.

I wanted to wait for Chicha there, but a messenger arrived with an order to fall back immediately. We slowly moved out, descending down the hillside in the dark. I urged the men leading the horses to hurry. Evidently the Partisans were trying to seize higher ground in order to cut us off.

At each step, somebody halted, loads fell off the horses, the column broke apart. I could hardly see the man in front of me. "Form up, form up," I heard the soldiers calling softly. By the time we reached the location of a temporary command post at a lumber mill, half the column had gotten lost.

Out in the mill yard, a captain was shaping up an ad hoc defensive group. Without regard to their original units, soldiers, orderlies, and messengers were falling in. They would try to delay the Partisans' pursuit. As I led my men in, I heard some good news.

Though the last to leave the position, Chicha had arrived before us. Inside the mill, the headquarters staff had set up a large, clean room for him and the staff officers. There was even some electric light, for the mill had its own power plant.

I was called to enter alone. When I did, I found Chicha in the midst of issuing orders: "One, bring up in trucks a part of the Tser Corps now located in Rogatica, the objective being to disrupt the enemy at the town of Lower Ravanica.

"Two, empty the magazines in Priboj during the night.

"Three, send reinforcements to our garrison at Vishegrad." He paused and saw me. "Have all your men arrived?"

"Not yet, General. About half are with the brigadier and Colonel Bailey, and they're not here. I've sent patrols out in all directions to find them."

"Ask the officers with you to come in and have some supper," Chicha ordered. "We can't stay here long."

In a few minutes, Colonel Seitz, Captain Mansfield, and Majors Jacks and Green had joined us. While they ate, Chicha explained about the Partisans' surprise attack. They had not only hit the Chetnik General Staff encampment, but also several towns and villages. As he was talking, a messenger arrived.

The Partisans had taken Rudo and killed Lieutenant Bodiroga, the leader of the defenders. Chicha was distressed. The young lieutenant had been one of the most courageous Chetniks. When the resistance began, he and his men had reputedly managed to shoot down two German bombers using only light machine guns. On his wrist, Chicha still wore one of the compasses taken from the downed aircraft.

"Now you can see, gentlemen," Chicha continued quietly, "who attacks whom. Once more, you see who is aiding the enemy. They weren't satisfied to stop our offensive at Sarajevo, but probably wanted to capture me as well. That wish won't take place for a long time yet.

"It will not be hard to liquidate their forces. In an hour, Major Rachich will arrive with enough force to take back Lower Ravanica. Tomorrow, Rudo will be in our hands again, but that will not bring back to life Lieutenant Bodiroga or the other defenders. This weakens us constantly, while the Germans rub their hands in satisfaction. There is no choice. If we do not defend ourselves, we will be exterminated without mercy."

I went out to scrounge up some food for the missing Allied officers I hoped were all right. In the yard, wounded Chetniks were being readied for transport to Vishegrad on trucks taken from the Italians. If only we had more of them . . .

As soon as the wounded were evacuated, Chicha ordered us on the move. It was hard to get organized in the dark, with everyone massing around the lumber mill. While we were gathering the horses on the road, the lost members of the Mission finally turned up.

I was glad they had made it. Immediately, I gave them food, knowing they hadn't eaten. Brigadier Armstrong detailed their adventures in the woods as we all fell in with the departing column.

We were headed to Dobruna, a village between Priboj and Vishegrad. This was considerably easier than our last cross-country hike, since we went along the road. Trucks rumbled by us from the other direction, their lights blinding. They were carrying Major Rachich's troops back from Rogatica.

I thought of the surprise in store for our enemies who expected anything but a counterattack. We passed another column of troops marching to take up our vacated positions. These men were in perfect order, quiet, and unarmed. They would be equipped with the weapons of the former Priboj garrison.

Unexpectedly, Lieutenant Aleksa appeared out of the dark. He recognized me and joined up with our column.

"What about our apple pie?" I asked sorrowfully.

"When I got the order to move," he said, "the pie was just baked. I had hardly taken it from the oven when the gunfire started. I just had time to wrap it up in a towel and place it in my bag. Captain, I searched all night for you, but how could anyone be found in this mess?"

I had no answer to that.

"Anyway, you are lucky to have seen me. Half is still in my bag. I intended to have it for breakfast tomorrow, but I see that its end has come." With that, Lieutenant Aleksa brought forth the remaining pie.

I didn't wait to be invited twice. Taking a share, I offered the rest to Colonel Seitz and Captain Mansfield. They were as happy as kids, for we had all dreamed so fondly of eating Captain Pevets's special treat. And I must admit, for a long time afterward, nothing tasted better than that apple pie did.

The village of Dobruna had a small railroad station. It amounted to nothing more than a building, a siding to allow trains to pass, and the narrow-gauge track switches. Here Chicha ordered the column to halt at about one in the morning.

The entire General Staff and attached units somehow crowded along this fifty-foot stretch. The horses were tied to the station fence and their packs removed, but they were kept in harness. We found hay to put between the tracks and lay down under the clear night sky.

It was quite cold, but we slept. At the first light of day, we moved on. By 1100 hours we had climbed high into the mountains to better survey the chaotic military situation before considering the options. When the column took a rest, I and Major Flood, the brigadier's intelligence officer, were delegated to find out what Chicha was up to. We joined him on the highest ground, looking out toward the terrain around Vishegrad.

From that direction, the sounds of a great battle reached us. Information received during the night indicated the Partisans were concentrating all their forces in the Lim River valley. They'd been strengthened with most of the Italian units and their arms; we were weakened from twenty days of battle with the Germans.

Our army's territorial organization also favored their strategy. It was difficult for us to quickly gather dispersed forces to stop these attacks. Vishegrad was the key. It was defended by our small garrison. But if taken, then the present position of General Staff headquarters was imperiled. Even as Chicha made this analysis, we noticed a column crossing the river and taking to the fields. The firing at Vishegrad slowly ebbed, but we couldn't discern any final result.

The major and I had to return to our group. The Mission officers didn't have the luck to finish lunch this day, either. As we were about to eat, orders were given for a hurried march. German troops were on a sweep. In less than fifteen minutes we were ready, and the climb continued.

The mountain was very steep and the horses progressed with difficulty. But we went forward. In the vanguard was General Trifunovich and Uncle Taras, the rest of the column trailing behind. I rode beside Trifunovich for a while. He told me we were going into Serbia where the General Staff could operate safely.

How strange this is, I thought to myself. We are now retreating from the Germans and under attack by the Partisans, instead of all Yugoslavs acting against the occupiers. This civil war between guerrillas was terrible. The Partisans used the same methods we did and knew the mountain passes just as well. But why? For whose benefit? Not the people's. Of that I had been more than convinced.

It was nightfall before we started to descend again, toward Priboj. We stopped around midnight at an abandoned mine. Its shacks were a welcome stable for our horses. The animals needed food and sheltered rest. The tired soldiers, after unpacking the horses, fell beside them in exhaustion.

I found some space for the Mission officers in the upper story of a mine building, though it hardly mattered. The march was to continue before sunrise. We only had three hours.

By nine in the morning, we had reached our objective. This was a large grazing ground called Dikava, high in the mountains between Vishegrad and Dobruna. The local peasants brought their stock here in the summer.

There were some scattered log cabins about, now empty, and two occupied houses. At one of them, I secured lodging for the Allied Mission. It was nothing like the peasant homes we were used to. The main room had a dirt floor with a fireplace in the center that belched acrid smoke. Another smaller room was too crammed with herding gear to be used, so a nearby cabin would have to serve as our work space. But the Mission had the choice quarters.

Chicha always gave them the best. In this instance, he had set up his own people in tents, despite the severe cold. The General Staff camp was pitched along the eastern edge of the great forest, while the horses were actually stabled under the trees.

In addition, the food situation was critical. Even though the peasant whose house we lived in did all he could to help, food was scarce. Had we not brought reserve supplies with us, we would have gone hungry from day one.

I found myself totally occupied with running back and forth between the Mission and the General Staff. The brigadier asked constantly for news, while Chicha was absorbed with restoring the communications with his commandants that had been broken by our hasty movements. The staff officers were mapping out future strategy.

The sounds of battle were sometimes far away, sometimes nearer, but they were never absent. Everyone was on edge. A alert—to march or to fight—was constantly maintained. I knew we could not remain long at Dikava, a week or two at most.

One evening, on returning to the cabin, I found Colonel Seitz and Captain Mansfield in the midst of preparing reports for the Allied commands in Cairo. After saluting them, I sat down in a corner. I couldn't get into my work, but instead thought about the Americans. Their position had its difficulties. After the recent Chetnik experiences with the English, all eyes had turned to the American officers, even Chicha's. They alone seemed to offer the possibility of help.

Everyone showed them great affection. When Mansfield, the first American assigned, had parachuted in two months ago, Chicha himself was at the landing zone. He liked the young American so much that he nicknamed him Boshko. It was the name of a great Serbian hero of the Middle Ages, Boshko Yugovich.

The American officers endeavored to show their appreciation of this special esteem, I felt. However, they couldn't do much officially, for they were not an independent unit. The agreement between the British High Command and its American counterpart specified that American officers would go into Yugoslavia only as part of British missions, or under the direct command of British officers. Their reports were subject to review prior to transmittal, if requested by the British officer in charge.

In short, it was strictly a British show. True, Lieutenant Colonel Seitz was present at almost all meetings between Brigadier Armstrong and General Mihailovich, but he wasn't allowed to express his opinion, valuable as it would be. In spite of this, these conferences did allow the colonel to see the trend of British politics and demands. I felt that he did not approve of them.

The limitations likewise did not prevent Captain Mansfield from sending accurate, factual reports that often put British policy and its support of the Partisans in an unfavorable light. As a result, I heard British officers declare that the Americans lacked knowledge of Yugoslav affairs. I failed to see what, if anything, they lacked. They had well observed who was fighting the forces of occupation in Yugoslavia, and under what conditions.

When Seitz and Mansfield took a break from their work, I resolved to speak more openly about these things on my mind. "Chicha is very grateful for the pistol," I said to Colonel Seitz, who had given him this gift. "But he's worried about the Allied stand toward him. His only hope lies with you two."

"I can't stand it much longer," Seitz answered determinedly. "With telegrams, no matter how detailed, we avail nothing. Our superiors in Cairo refer every little matter to the British. We need to go there in person, explain everything, and show undeniable proof. Or go to Washington."

"That is an excellent idea," I agreed wholeheartedly.

"But before that," Captain Mansfield cautioned, "we should consider making a tour of Chetnik-held areas to examine your troops and acquaint ourselves with their organization and armament. We need to know their morale and fighting methods."

Mansfield's own enthusiasm was definitely kindled. "I could bring my camera for photo documentation, to get the kind of hard evidence we want. And we'll have to learn the opinion of the people. Does General Mihailovich have their support? In America, that's very important."

I waited as the two Americans mulled over a feasible plan. "We must have the general's consent first," Mansfield suggested. "Then a detailed report must be prepared and sent to headquarters in Cairo, with observations to date and future intentions."

"All done in secrecy," Seitz remarked carefully. "Not one of the English officers must know." He thought a moment, then continued. "We cannot hide our inspection tour from the brigadier, but he should know nothing of our plans to leave the country. No one must know that except Chicha. This is the only way we'll succeed. Otherwise, I'm sure the brigadier will disrupt our plans and may order us to stay here. Like it or not, as officers we'd have to obey."

Mansfield was all for pushing ahead. "We could show Chicha

a list of questions we want answered, Colonel. I'll get on it right away."

As the two officers conferred, I happily considered the new plan. If successful, it might spark a reversal in the Allies' stand toward us. I hoped so. But how indeed would the brigadier receive Seitz's proposal? The thought worried me.

"I'll inform Chicha in the morning," I declared. "I'm sure he'll do everything he can to make your plan work." Someone would have to conduct the Americans on this tour, I pondered silently. Someone who could help them see everything. Could I win that chance?

The next day, I asked Chicha for a private talk. He agreed and took me outside. We walked from his tent toward the cabin of Lieutenant Colonel Ostojich and his staff. After I outlined Seitz's plan, he was in complete accord.

"Tell Seitz," Chicha said, "that my only wish is to have the truth in all its strength made public."

The general had to attend to other business. I left him and started back across the ditch that separated the staff area from the field where the Mission's house was.

A strange column was coming toward me. Peasant women on foot were leading pack horses carrying men wrapped in blankets. Other men hobbled alongside. I stopped and waited.

When the column halted, I suddenly realized that these were evacuees from a Chetnik field hospital. The wounded men looked very badly off. Their pale cheeks were sunken and most were clad only in underwear. They had no socks and shook from the cold. Some fifty of them were seriously wounded, yet there appeared to be only one doctor and three nurses.

The doctor approached me. He was an old man, fatigue and exhaustion written on his face. From him, I discovered that the peasant women were mothers unable to bear separation from their wounded sons.

As we talked, I watched the women. One offered milk from a bottle to her stricken boy. Another took the shawl from her own shoulders to use as a wrap. "We are the field hospital of the Vishegrad brigade," the doctor was telling me. "We are going to Serbia where we can shelter these men and give them at least some nursing."

My God, I thought, then our garrison at Vishegrad has fallen. So General Trifunovich was right. The General Staff will have to retreat deeper into Serbia. Fighting spirit alone had not, and could not, overcome the superior matériel of our enemies.

Even our hospital units had no supplies. The doctor spoke plainly. "We have nothing, not even the most necessary medicines, not to speak of anesthetics. Just look at these barefooted wounded! How can they get well when every one of them will get an infection? I feel terrible. I should be more than a moral support to them and their mothers."

I asked him to stay put until I returned in a few minutes. He nodded wearily. Hurrying to the Mission's work cabin, I was lucky to find all the officers there. When I asked the brigadier if he would view a hospital unit in retreat, he assented at once.

Everybody went with us. I watched the expression on the officers' faces at the sight of the column of wretched and wounded men. They were all deeply affected. Here were no political or military concerns, only their feelings of common humanity.

My next request was simple. Their answer, British and American alike, was to collect all the clothing they could spare. With over twenty suits, underwear, and many pairs of socks, I returned to the hospital unit.

The doctor was grateful, almost beyond comprehending this gift. But the wounded received these things without a show of feeling. Ghostlike, they were incapable of responding.

The column had to move on. At the doctor's signal, they all lumbered forward, a picture of suffering that impressed itself in my mind forever. Slowly, they disappeared up the mountain path.

The last day of October, Lieutenant Colonel Seitz informed Brigadier Armstrong that he intended to inspect certain of the Chetnik units throughout Serbia. Promptly, another conference meeting was held with the brigadier, Chicha, and Seitz in attendance to thrash out the matter. I impatiently waited to learn what happened.

That evening, Seitz filled me in. The brigadier, as senior officer of the Allied Mission, of course had to grant his approval. To my surprise, he had done so forthwith. The American officers could visit many of the brigades: Tser, Kolubara, Valjevo, Rudnik, Guards, I Shumadia, II Shumadia, I Ravnagora, II Ravnagora, and Javor.

However, the brigadier then requested that the English officer "Marko" Hudson accompany them. In response, Seitz insisted to Chicha that I be assigned to his inspection party, but the brigadier demurred. He needed me for interpreting duties, he said.

Chicha suggested a compromise to Colonel Seitz—take along Major Terzich from the operations staff. But Seitz would not consent. All around, it seemed a bit of a standoff.

In our discussion afterward, Seitz repeated that he wouldn't go without me. He knew me well and trusted me. Besides, I had helped him plan the whole thing. And I knew Colonel Seitz. His mind was made up, and that was that. Thanking him warmly, I said I would make our mutual resolve known to Chicha in the morning.

It was the regular time for the nightly news on the radio. As was the Mission's custom, we all gathered around to listen. That evening, everybody was surprised to hear the B.B.C. announcer intone that the partisans had taken the very position we now occupied and had annihilated strong enemy forces. The number of dead, wounded, and captured Germans was given, as well as the quantities of military spoils.

I started to laugh aloud. Turning to Colonel Bailey, I quipped, "We shall not be surprised, Colonel, if the B.B.C. announces tomorrow that Partisan units of Josip Broz have landed in England. Since *this* report was possible, we may expect anything in the future."

The colonel was ill at ease. He said he didn't understand this one-sided propaganda for Tito, and broke away for some rapid conversation with the brigadier that I wasn't able to follow. The result, I learned the next day, was another strong protest to Cairo—the eighth. Without effect.

The sound of firing awakened me. It was early in the morning, 4:20 A.M. by my watch. Everyone but the sentries was asleep. I listened harder. Judging by the sound, the battle was getting closer, coming from the direction of Dobruna. That put it beyond the first fields near the General Staff bivouac.

No messenger arrived with orders, but somehow I knew this was not another brief enemy sortie. I got up and had the sentries wake up the Mission's detachment of soldiers. The horses were harnessed. As these tasks were being done, an orderly arrived.

We were to prepare for immediate departure. While the Allied officers crawled from their beds, I hurried toward the tents. I had to talk directly with Chicha.

On the way, I ran into Captain Slepchevich and Uncle Taras forming up the front ranks of the march. They informed me that the general and his officers were in the field northeast of the cabins. I caught up with them as the first rays of the morning sun were lighting up Dikava.

"What do you want here?" Chicha asked when he spotted me. "Your place is with the Mission."

I explained we were ready, but I wanted to know what was happening. Chicha said nothing. I saw that Chetnik soldiers from various units were gathering on the field. The battle was over for the moment, but we had gained only time to move again. The II Racha brigade was expected to arrive shortly and would provide cover for the retreat.

Then, when Chicha was momentarily alone, I had my chance to discuss my real reason. I told him what Seitz had said to me.

There was no time to lose. Plans had to be made before the opportunity was lost.

"All right. I agree," Chicha abruptly declared. "You may go with them."

He looked at me searchingly. "You know English and you've seen much. As you pass through the land, you will see more. We shall arrange the details later, but you should go with them to the very end . . . even if they leave for America. I shall send you as my personal delegate."

17

The Forgotten Army

THE FIRST DAY of the General Staff withdrawal into Serbia took us as far as the village of Rudo. Its inhabitants, on seeing our column, deserted their homes, not knowing who was coming. When they were sure we were Chetniks, they gradually returned and welcomed us.

I had been up since before sunrise and was quite tired, but even knowing our march would resume that night, I couldn't sleep. When Chicha called me to his temporary room in the evening, I was still wide awake. Yanko, his trusted orderly, was preparing cornmeal for supper.

"Do the English know anything of your intentions?" he asked me.

"The brigadier knows, from your previous consent, that the American officers will be accompanied by his man, Major Hudson. He knows nothing more, except that today I asked his permission to go, too, at your wish. He agreed. But only if I take up my duties again as soon as we return. He said they'd become accustomed to me and would not like to look for another liaison officer."

Chicha pondered this. "You have a few days yet before you start," he said. "When the column reaches the territory of Major Rachich, you will leave us. I have issued orders to that effect. Also, I shall give you papers requesting the brigade commanders to place themselves at your disposal.

"Be careful that the Americans see everything they wish. Try to provide the greatest comfort for them and furnish explanations for things that may seem strange. On their tour, the people of Serbia will rush to see them, so be careful that the enemy does not learn of your movements. If they do, all is finished."

The nature of my responsibility was self-evident. I had made a commitment to General Mihailovich and would see the tour through to whatever its end, here or abroad. As I thought this, Chicha concluded: "Let's get some rest before we start out again, Captain."

It is very difficult to begin a march at midnight. Men and animals are sleepy, loads are hard to pack, and your column stumbles along in the dark. Yet somehow we moved forward.

I marched with Colonel Seitz and Captain Mansfield, who were as happy as I was at the news of my assignment to their tour. To my amusement, they imagined themselves already back in America at their respective homes in Virginia and Boston. They would take me there, they declared.

What did I know of either place? Just a little from my geography studies. What really interested me was our journey into Serbian lands that I knew so well. I could hardly imagine the world across the ocean.

By narrow peasant trails, the column headed northeast toward the Drina River valley. Early in the morning, we reached Mitrovac on Tara Mountain. The sun at the beginning of November was still quite warm on the heights, and it made our weariness even greater after a sleepless night.

After the Mission's camp was set up, I washed myself, then managed to sleep for about four hours. A soldier I'd sent to look for food returned with a fine big ram and promised it would be ready for supper. After the tasteless boiled oats we had eaten earlier, it was a godsend.

That afternoon, I arranged a meeting with Chicha on behalf of Colonel Seitz. Nearing twilight, the Americans and I slipped away as unobtrusively as we could from the Mission's camp and joined the general. As we sat around a fire at the onset of the evening chill, Yanko brought us glasses of brandy. Chicha was in good spirits and talkative.

"Do you see this place?" he asked us. "Here I fought my first battle in this war. This is the place where guerrilla action commenced in occupied Yugoslavia.

"I refused to recognize the order of capitulation and started with a handful of men toward Serbia. On May 10 of 1941, I arrived here at Mitrovac. Right over there," he pointed to some buildings in ruins, "was a gendarme station. We stopped to rest and I spoke to everyone who'd come this far. I told them exactly the terrible difficulties we faced. There were about two hundred of us. Afterward, eighty men took the oath of allegiance to my cause. I was satisfied, for I knew these eighty would never leave me.

"We were preparing to move on when a group of quisling gendarmes showed up who had accepted the German order to return to their posts. We tried to get them to join us. Some refused and opened fire, but we easily overpowered them without any losses. When the Germans heard of this, they sent troops, but we were already far into Serbia. In their anger, they burned the gendarme station so we 'bandits' could not use it again."

After a short pause, Chicha went on. "Here I began my work. From this same place, I am now sending you to inform great America of the truth in Yugoslavia. You are perfectly free to act as you wish, to go wherever you please, to demand to see anything. I want you to understand that my eyes and those of my fighters are turned only to America, that great protector of democracy."

We were all deeply moved. Colonel Seitz especially so. "I consider it my great good fortune to be on this mission," he told the general. "My greatest reward will be to help you succeed and to place my country's interests on the right path."

The retreat had become one long march punctuated with brief stops during the day. With nightfall, we pulled out of Mitrovac and went down Mount Tara toward the town of Baina Bashta, its lights glittering in the distance. We had been marching for three consecutive nights, and everybody was tired.

Around midnight, having lost thirty minutes in seeking the road, we reached the Racha monastery. It had been destroyed by Bulgarian occupation troops who suspected the monks of aiding the Chetniks. Nothing was respected in this war, not religion nor historic churches.

By 4:00 A.M., we were in the Serbian village of Solutosh. About eleven, the threat of a Bulgarian attack prompted an alert, but it was a false alarm. At dusk we were gone.

The most dangerous part of the retreat was ahead, for we had to use the main road running from Baina Bashta to Uzice for almost a mile. German motorized units could appear at any moment. Yet as we made our way steadily uphill, our spirits were high. When we forded a small stream, Yanko missed his footing and fell into the cold water up to his waist. The joking was merciless, and Chicha's orderly swore like a mule driver.

Again, it was five in the morning when we reached the next village. Hastily we sought quarters after taking care of the horses. I wound up sleeping in a garden under the clear sky, but I didn't care. We were to leave before noon and pass into the territory under Major Rachich's command. And that meant Seitz's inspection tour could start the day after.

At least Chicha had a decent place to stay. He was in the home of a highly decorated veteran of World War I. After a few hours sleep, I reported there for my daily briefing. The owner was shining with happiness because he had such distinguished guests. He drank toasts to Chicha. "Voyvoda Draza," he called him, the savior and leader of the Serbian people.

"We will all go with you," the old man said, "to the last man, even if we lose everything. I am not sorry. Two of my sons are with you, and if you want me, just say so."

With kind words, Chicha had to decline the heartfelt offer. Then we talked privately. He had a special code for me, to use if I wanted to send information to him in the strictest confidence.

"I have no money to give you," he added gravely.

"I have a little with me," I answered, "but I don't need much anyway." I realized that soon I would have my last words with Chicha for a very long time to come.

After our conversation, I was preparing for the early departure when Colonel Bailey unexpectedly drew me aside. "I know Chicha has lost confidence in me," he said quietly, "even if it is not my fault. The men around him do not comprehend my role. Before, we used to be inseparable."

I didn't know quite how to respond.

"Armstrong is a typical troop commander," Colonel Bailey continued, "who cannot forget his barracks or understand about guerrilla warfare. I've lived in your country for sixteen years. I see things better. The cables we send can be interpreted several ways, but my direct verbal report would open eyes. I'd sincerely like to help." He looked straight at me. "Tell Chicha to arrange my leaving the country. I can do what is necessary for him and for your cause. I would like, Captain, to have you accompany me on that trip."

"I'll be glad to convey your proposal, Colonel." My brain raced to weigh Bailey's intentions. Did he know of Colonel Seitz's plans to leave the country? Was this a trap to flush me out and prevent our departure at the last possible moment?

"Not a word of this to anyone," he called after me as I returned to my packing. My impression was that Colonel Bailey had made a sincere proposal. Yet who could be sure? He was serving his country. No, another voice said in my mind, there have been misunderstandings, but Bailey is honest. True, but . . . The debate in my mind went back and forth.

After the column had formed and moved out slowly, I slipped my horse ahead to join Chicha. Drawing him away, I explained Colonel Bailey's offer. "Everything in order!" Chicha said. "Then we shall let him go. In any case, conditions cannot be any worse. But does he know?"

"I'm afraid he has learned something. But that won't change the minds of our Americans."

Chicha was relieved. "Don't tell Bailey a word of Colonel Seitz's plans," he ordered. "By tomorrow, your secret will be out of everyone's reach." This was it, then. *Until we meet once more, General.*

The inspection tour left on the morning of November 7, 1943. The party consisted of Lieutenant Colonel Albert Seitz and Captain Walter Mansfield, accompanied by myself, the British officer Major "Marko" Hudson (who spoke fluent Serbo-Croatian), and four Chetnik soldiers. Major Rachich, the local commander, was also with us. He would guide the tour through his area first.

Over the next five weeks, the impoverished Chetnik troops we saw repeatedly awakened our admiration and astonishment—admiration for their fighting spirit and astonishment at how well they performed with scarcely any equipment or supplies. These men were determined to fight on, even if forgotten by the Allies, even if ignored in favor of the Partisans.

Our own mission was straightforward. The American officers wanted to inspect as many brigades as possible, gather relevant military data, and personally bring the information safely out of the country. To do this, we planned to travel deeper into Serbia—north almost as far as Valjevo, circling eastward through the Shumadia region, and swinging back past Chachak. We would end up near Raska in Major Cvetic's command area, not far from our starting point.

From there, it was some 125 miles west to the Adriatic coast. Somehow, we'd have to get through hostile territory that was in the hands of Germans, bandit groups, and Partisans. After that, if we could beg, borrow, or steal a small boat, we'd try to cross over to Allied-held Italy. Our tactics were to travel fast and light and hope we never ran head-on into enemy forces.

Beginning with Major Rachich's area, we soon discovered that each subordinate commander tried to present his unit as best-equipped as he could. It was obvious that many items were borrowed and due to be returned when we left. With regard to clothing and shoes, the situation had to be worse than detected.

Typically, the Chetniks wore sandals they made themselves. Yet even these were not sufficiently available, so it was not unusual to see men going barefoot.

Everywhere the local people welcomed us with warm hospitality, and devotion to the king and to General Mihailovich was evident. In the villages and towns only their names were heard. Together, they were the symbols of the present struggle and a guarantee of future freedom.

The peasants had made up songs, truly songs of the people themselves. "Draza will succeed. He will bring back the King," I heard a number of times from humble peasants. "It is our good fortune that we have Draza to lead us." Timidly listening to our conversation with their menfolk, the women would sigh, "God grant that all this will end well."

By November 25, we had pushed on as far as the town of Konjusha in the command area of Major Smiljanich. Learning it was America's Thanksgiving Day, the Major and I decided there ought to be a celebration. When I informed the town's mayor of this, he willingly grasped my intention. He immediately asked the local schoolteacher to help, and plans were set in motion.

Everybody in the nearby villages wanted to come. I told Colonel Seitz that in honor of the Americans, the local peasants wished to observe their special day. I then asked him for his advice so that the celebration might resemble the one in his homeland. All afternoon, his suggestions were quickly carried out.

Fortuitously, Colonel J. Simich arrived the same day to see the American officers and welcome them. Since he served on the commanding staff in northern Serbia, Mansfield was able to obtain from him vital information on units we'd be unable to assess. Also joining us was Major Vuckovich, the commander of the brigade next scheduled for inspection. He brought with him another American liaison officer, Lieutenant George Musulin, who had parachuted into the country just a month ago.

When night descended, the celebration commenced with a

fiery spectacle. The hills were ablaze with large bonfires, a salute in the traditional Serbian manner. The flames mounted into the sky, uncontrollable and vigorous, twisting toward those ethereal heights where freedom is eternal. I watched in somber appreciation. Until now, I thought, we have surmounted all powers who have threatened to suppress us. But how long will it be thus?

The call of our hosts shook me from my pessimistic meditations. We entered a large room where everyone was expecting us. After grace, we fell to and ate a merry feast complete with turkeys. The speeches that followed grew more frank as the wine went to our heads and everyone revealed what was uppermost in his mind. There were many questions.

What were the British up to? Why were we Chetniks being abandoned? Poor Major Hudson, their sole representative, became very uneasy. If he knew something definite, he rightfully estimated that it was not the moment to speak.

The inspections with Major Rachich and Major Smiljanich had gone well. The nice weather held until the last week in November. Then the ill-famed cold rains began and did not stop—the preliminary to the long Serbian winter. The village roads were seas of mud.

The day after our American Thanksgiving, when we inspected the Second Takovska Brigade, they stood to attention in a cold sleet. Of the 350 soldiers, thirty were without shoes.

"Don't they even have socks?" Colonel Seitz asked quietly.

"Sir, stockings would not help much in this mud," Major Vuckovich, their commander, responded. "A sturdy army shoe would be the only thing."

"I wonder how they can hold out at all," Seitz said to me. "It's a wonder they don't freeze. Believe me, I shivered all morning even wearing two pairs of woolen hose and excellent mountaineering shoes."

" 'When it must be done, it isn't even difficult.' That is an old Serbian proverb," I answered, proud of our men.

When the troop review was finished, Seitz asked me to segregate all the shoeless men. After having his picture taken with them, he asked me and Major Vuckovich if there were some way shoes could be obtained. I thought that shoes might be bought on the black market by a courier who had access to the larger towns, but the price would be great. The colonel promptly took our $250 from his pocket and handed it over to Vuckovich.

The major took the money. "Two days ago, they were fighting at my side barefooted," he said simply. "Believe me, I do not notice it anymore, for I am accustomed to even worse."

If Major Vuckovich was intensely concerned for the welfare of his men, the affection was mutual. "Our commandant is a wonderful man," a young escort told me as we walked along together. "Always first everywhere, on the march and in battle."

We were circling southward in the general direction of Pranjani, still in Vuckovich's command area.

"Everything he has he gives to us," the young Chetnik continued. "He does not know his own worth. Since August, he is either on the march or fighting almost every day. How long do you think he can keep that up, sir?"

I had no answer.

"When our struggle began in 1941," he said, "I thought it would end in a few months. Then came the winter. We consoled ourselves—after the winter will come freedom. But here we are in a third winter and there is no trace of freedom."

Major Vuckovich himself then joined me. "You walk very rapidly. I scarcely caught up with you." The major was famed for his fast gait that left other men behind.

Grinning, I replied, "At one time I enjoyed hiking."

We walked on in silence. We were approaching Gornji Milanovats, and the surrounding mountains held many memories for me of my school days. Many times I had climbed along these slopes with geodetic instruments in hand, going freely about and ending the day with a happy crowd in the café Knez Mihailo or Beograd.

"Do you see Gornji Milanovats?" Major Vuckovich's voice startled me.

"Yes, yes," I answered. "It looks the same as when I last saw it."

"You cannot see the ruins and ashes from here." He paused a moment. "When I recaptured it in August of 1941, it was still untouched. At the time, I cooperated with the Partisans, and together we liberated the whole section. There were no Germans anywhere.

"The Partisan authorities immediately established political commissars in any town they entered. They demanded that our officers also have their documents and arrested anyone without them. There was constant friction.

"As Chicha said, 'We fought in blood, and they carry out social reforms.' Chicha had nothing against that, but now was not the time. We had to unite the command."

I knew that was why Tito and Chicha had met in the early days of the resistance. But they had been unable to reach any durable agreement.

"Nothing has changed," Vuckovich added. "Was it only some two years ago that I was happily returning to Gornji Milanovats, convinced that the Partisans might deal honorably with us? A few days later, a German punitive force arrived and we all had to disperse. The town was pillaged and burned. Its people were massacred."

The major's story was depressing. The German occupiers had taken full advantage of our internal strife. It had happened many times.

The inspection tour had settled into a relentless routine. Day after day, we passed through villages, inspected troops, and gathered whatever other information we could.

In the village of Savinats, I was overjoyed to run into my old school friend Mika Djordjevich. He was helping to operate the clandestine radio station "Gedza." Since August, they had been able to make direct radio contact with America.

"The station is a three-hour walk from here, so inaccessible that only a mountain goat could reach it," Mika explained. "Our chief engineer would like to construct a larger and stronger transmitter, to counter the Nazi broadcasts from Belgrade and the Partisan's Radio Free Yugoslavia."

I was glad to introduce Mika to Colonel Seitz, who was excited about the project and promised help if he could. He took down technical data on needed supplies and regretted there was no time to see the station. We had to continue immediately, as the First Takovska Brigade awaited us in Pranjani.

From Savinats to Pranjani, we marched mostly on the open road. Major Vuckovich was afraid of a surprise attack by the enemy and continually went on ahead to scout. We arranged for patrols ahead and behind us with orders to fire warning shots should anything develop.

After a full day's march, we finally arrived at Pranjani. We had covered about thirty miles and were fairly tired. I had a horse, but I'd walked all the way, despite Mansfield's insistence that I should ride. I told him it was good training for what lay ahead.

The rest of Major Vuckovich's staff was waiting for us in the town. They were preparing for the inspection. The next day, a bright sun brought a large crowd out from the neighboring villages, eager to see the American officers. On a large field, a battalion of young men were assembled. They had just completed their military training.

Even without arms, the unit made an excellent military impression. Their noncommissioned officer, a sergeant from the Infantry Reserve, held himself irreproachably. He was obviously proud of his men, and though without shoes himself, he stepped smartly through the frost as he formally reported to Colonel Seitz. They exchanged salutes.

Colonel Seitz, obviously satisfied with the review, asked him at parting, "What would you like America to send you?"

"A Tommy gun and enough ammunition, sir," the sergeant answered unhesitatingly.

"But don't you want shoes?"

"No, sir. Send me the Tommy gun and I will get my own shoes. From the enemy."

Seitz couldn't get over the man's reply. "Now I begin to understand the strength of the Serbian people," he exclaimed to me later.

We left Pranjani the morning of November 30. Most of our escort had to leave us and return to fighting duty, as German units strengthened with collaborationist troops had been reported on our trail. As we headed toward Kotrazh, we would pass through many small villages: Kamenica, Gojna Gora, Jelen Do, Krstac, Gucha.

A brigade of Captain Markovich's Pozhega Corps learned we were in the vicinity. They quickly sent over a battalion to meet us around Kamenica. Another unit had just returned from fierce fighting. So great was their desire to see the American officers that even the wounded men of the rank and file stood for the inspection.

In Gojna Gora, we received a report that the Bulgarian occupation garrison in Jelen Do had fled at the sight of some Chetnik men. We decided our inspection party could advance immediately during daylight. While we were carefully descending into the town's valley, the weather changed. A cold rain began, and our horses started to slip. To spare them, we did not ride. It also made us a less visible target from below.

Our advance patrol soon reached the Jelen Do railroad station. We were recklessly following after them. Almost into the village, I saw Major Vuckovich, who had gone ahead with Major Hudson, come running toward us.

"Back, back!" he cried. After one paralyzed moment, I quickly pulled Seitz and Mansfield behind a small wall. The Chetnik Major jumped in with us.

"What's happened?" I asked in alarm.

"A train with German troops is about to reach the station. As usual, they'll scatter about looking for something to steal. You'd better hide."

"Okay," I answered, "you look after Hudson. I'll guard Seitz and Mansfield." Thank goodness we'd left the horses with one of our escorts while we checked out the town. They couldn't have been hidden.

Vuckovich took off. I explained what was going on to the Americans, then suggested we drop back to another wall forty feet behind. From there we could watch the train station as well.

The new hiding place was the best we could do. With my binoculars, I saw the German soldiers get off the train and wander around the station as Vuckovich had predicted. Several seemed like they were straying in our direction. The minutes dragged on to eternity.

At last, the soldiers were called back and the train left. But I only breathed easily when we were on the other side of the river from Jelen Do. The Germans had been too close for comfort.

In the evening twilight, we slowly climbed toward the village of Krstac. The rain had not let up. Then the following day, we continued toward Kotrazh. That was where the Dragachevo brigades of Captain Simovich, who was part of Major Vuckovich's command, were to assemble.

Snow began to fall heavily before noon. Soon the muddy landscape was covered with a white cloak, and we had to pause occasionally to wipe our eyes. Fortunately, this stretch was very familiar to me. Here I had begun my own "career in the woods" after the Yugoslav army capitulated.

Around Gucha, we proceeded warily, for there was another enemy garrison. Through the snowstorm, we could just make out the church tower. The snow was really sticking to our shoes, making every step treacherous, but we dared not stop.

At five in the afternoon, we somehow made it into Kotrazh. Our rendezvous point was a roadside café. When we entered, the proprietor rushed to seat us near a large stove, then shut the outer door and pulled the wooden shutters over the windows. To a passer-by, the café looked closed for the night.

It was nice to sit beside a warm stove after walking all day in heavy snow. As our wet clothing dried, the smell of perspiration filled the room, but that was soon overcome by something much nicer—the pleasant odor of hot whiskey. Later, during dinner, Captain Dacha Simovich arrived.

His appearance reminded me of pictures of Serbian rulers in the Middle Ages, or of the saints on the altar screen in the nave of a village church. He wore very long hair and a full beard and was almost ascetically thin. In his face, his large brown eyes shone feverishly, and though he seemed a very calm person, his voice was most firm and determined.

After introductions, Captain Simovich informed me that his brigades had not yet arrived. He expected one to be in Kotrazh the following day, while another would reach the village of Vuchkovitsa. He spoke of his own recent battles with the Germans and Partisans around Nova Varosh. Once again it was the "third participant," striking at both attacking and defending forces, who was the evil spirit of every operation.

The meal was nearly over when someone mentioned that King Peter was going to speak over the radio at 8:00 P.M. Father Mika, a Serbian Orthodox priest and one of our dinner companions, proposed we adjourn to listen. We only then realized it was December 1, Unity Day.

Since 1918, Unity Day had marked the formation of the free and united Kingdom of Yugoslavia. Seated in a warm, humble room exactly twenty-five years later, I wondered why none of the earlier Serbian leaders did not foresee that federation, not an enforced centralization, was the best way to national unity. The Yugoslav ideal could not be planted in the hearts of the poeple by orders and decrees. No national groups can become overnight something they do not understand, or never have been.

The past quarter century of our history had been a bitter lesson. The new Yugoslavia, for whose freedom we fought, must have nothing in common with what Unity Day commemorated. Finally, the broadcast started.

I watched the faces of those around the radio. Their reactions could clearly be read. The king spoke as someone addressing a third party, and not his own people. He sounded forced, as if he could scarcely wait to finish an unpleasant obligation. Factually, he spoke of the resistance, but did not mention by name those who carried the burden of the struggle. Only the general term "patriot" (used now frequently by the B.B.C. for several months) figured in his appeal to his "dear Serbs, Croats, and Slovenes."

When the speech ended, we in the inspection party evaded any comment. However, Father Mika could not refrain from saying something: "That young man should come here as did his grandfather and father, and not make speeches from London. That is no way to preserve the love and confidence he now possesses. I know what questions will await me tomorrow. I assure you my answer will be the same, I tell you. The people have begun to doubt. The time for forgiveness is past when it concerns the betrayal of the whole nation."

The others in the room were silent. It was obvious they agreed with Father Mika. With a speech like this one, the King was doing an injustice to the people who were his main support. What he hoped to attain by that, I didn't know.

The next morning in Kotrazh, we reviewed the First Dragach-evo Brigade in the deep snow. Then Major Vuckovich and Mansfield worked together all the rest of the day. The major answered every question put to him, while I translated.

The captain's notes had grown by leaps and bounds as he recorded information on every aspect of the brigades. He also had added personal observations and took photographs whenever he could. Everything would contribute to his final report.

He wasn't finished when Captain Simovich entered the room with another man I didn't recognize. He wore a civilian coat over military trousers. I thought he could be anybody from an ordinary citizen to someone on the staff.

"This is Franya, the well-known Franya," Simovich said to me as they took seats. "You probably heard about him from Chicha. He's now with me as a demolitions instructor."

"Yes, I did." I turned to the man who sat quietly beside Simovich. "I understand you were serving in the navy in 1941. Correct?"

Franya needed no further encouragement to tell his story. "It happened like this, Captain. Perhaps you know something of the fate of our navy when Yugoslavia got invaded by the Germans and Italians? I was a mechanics petty officer on the battleship *Velebit*, anchored in the Bay of Kotor.

"Days went by without orders to sail, while Italian bombers hit us daily. After ten days of waiting, the men thought all was lost. Then we got orders—everybody could leave the ship. The Italians were closing in. Nobody was fighting. I and a couple of Serbs took off through Herzegovina toward Bosnia. On the road, we met officers and soldiers lead by this Colonel Mihailovich. We joined him, and that was that."

Evidently, Franya had been with Chicha in his first camp at Ravna Gora.

"Captain, a lot of times they tease me that I am the only Croat in the movement, but I laugh at such jesting. True, I am a Croat. That I do not hide. But I am so closely tied to Chicha's cause that no other aim in life exists for me.

"At Ravna Gora, they looked for an expert in radio telegraphy. At one time I had taken a course, so I offered my services. The radio set we had could never reach London, but I hoped for local reception.

"Finally, on September 14, a response came to our daily signal. Malta answered. There was no end to our excitement when we succeeded in sending the first message."

Franya took from his pocket a small notebook. Written down were copies of all the initial messages he had handled for the General Staff. "This was the first," he said, and began to read:

Free military station of unoccupied Serbia. We kindly ask the British military station to send this information to the Yugoslav government in London:

To Zivan Knezevich, Lieutenant Colonel, London. Speak personally over Radio London G.S.C. or G.S.P. I hear you everyday. It is urgent. Your Drago, 50 Class.

We operate daily at 0400 Central European time on the same

wavelength and await answer and confirmation of this information in the daily news broadcasts in Serbian from the London station. We listen to the news daily. We will wait for your answer at 0600 time.

When the reception was confirmed, Franya went on, they had jumped with joy and kissed one another. They immediately informed Chicha. Soon everyone at headquarters knew. There was indescribable enthusiasm.

I sensed the other Chetnik officers had Franya's story practically memorized. Yet I wanted to hear him out for myself. "And then what happened, Franya? Back in 1941."

"We hoped that we would no longer be alone and that help would soon follow . . ."

1944

FROM THE VILLAGE of Kotrazh, Boris and his party went on to complete the inspection trip as planned. They had only one more command area to inspect on their itinerary, that of Major Cvetic, located around Rudno and Golija Mountain. Geographically, they had closed the circle of their journey and were back in the Sandzak region, near where they started.

Reaching Rudno by December 5, the Americans finished their work during the next week. Further communications were anticipated from the General Staff but hadn't yet arrived, and Cvetic's radio was at first inoperative. The decision was made to wait for this important material and then dash for the Adriatic coast.

While Lieutenant Colonel Seitz, Captain Mansfield, Boris, and the English Major Hudson hid out in small villages, conditions in Yugoslavia continued to deteriorate. The civil war between the Chetniks and Partisans had escalated. To cross out of Serbia and go through Montenegro to the coast meant that the inspection team would basically be in Partisan-held territory.

The Partisans might well help an Allied soldier, but they were sure to shoot any Royal Army officer like Boris unlucky enough to fall into their hands. The German occupation troops were still a formidable menace, and some of the self-proclaimed guerrillas in the hills were little better than armed brigands. The dangers the small inspection party faced were considerable, and the longer their departure was delayed, the more difficulties they could expect.

On December 23, a note was delivered by courier from a Captain John Wade, another of the English liaison officers operating in Yugoslavia. He was about three hours away from them. Captain Wade and his group had received orders from Cairo to cross over to the Partisans in order to leave the country. He had been advised that a safe passage to Italy was being guaranteed.

This news presented an excellent opportunity. They could join Captain Wade's evacuation. Colonel Seitz felt that if the team waited much longer, the information they'd so painstakingly collected would grow stale. After further discussion, however, it was decided that only Seitz and Hudson would join the Wade group. Captain Mansfield and Boris would stay behind in hope that the balance of the promised material would be forthcoming.

The next day, December 24, the inspection team split up. Colonel Seitz took Mansfield's penciled notes and statistical data with him when he went. On Christmas Day, a cheering message from General Mihailovich reached Boris and Mansfield. He was sending everything with Major Lukachevich, who would provide them escort to the coast.

A week later, as the new year of 1944 began, there was still no sign of the major. Boris and Captain Mansfield realized their position was becoming more tenuous. Given the increased Partisan infiltration into the Sandzak, they could not hide out indefinitely. They started to head west, reconnoitering for Major Lukachevich or other Allied liaison operatives.

The hundred miles to the Adriatic turned into a deadly game of hide-and-seek. Boris and Mansfield had no choice but to make roundabout marches to avoid hostile forces. They discovered that Major Lukachevich was in Nova Varosh, separated from them by Partisan and German troops, but when they tried on the night of January 13 to sneak through the lines, their two guides were captured by Partisans and they barely escaped.

Heavy snows had fallen recently, hampering movement, but Boris and Mansfield managed to rendezvous with Lieutenant Colonel Ostojich near the town of Priboj. He told them that

Major Lukachevich and a party of sixteen officers had already left for the coast. They could follow after and probably catch up.

Before they left, Lieutenant Colonel Ostojich gave them letters from General Mihailovich addressed to President Roosevelt, William Donovan, head of the American O.S.S. (the Office of Strategic Services, forerunner of today's C.I.A.), and General Eisenhower. Mansfield sewed them inside his jacket. Then he and Boris took up the pursuit of Lukachevich.

Depending on how many men a local Chetnik commander could assign, they traveled with an armed escort of five to sixty men. It was a grueling trek. They made several forced marches, once for twenty-two hours without pause, and often at night to duck the Partisans.

Finally, by the end of January, they caught up with Major Lukachevich. With him was Colonel Bailey. He, too, was seeking to exit Yugoslavia.

Providentially, Colonel Bailey had brought a radio to contact Cairo and arrange a "pinpoint." This was a standard military procedure. A location, time, and signal code were set, and if both sides showed up, a pickup or drop was made. Thanks to the pinpoint, Boris and Captain Mansfield would not have to buy, beg, or steal a boat, after all.

The combined escort party now numbered about 180 men. Pushing through to a spot near Lubinje, they found themselves blocked by several hundred Germans faced off against a Partisan brigade. Trying to thread the needle and slip between the two opposed groups, a column led by Captain Mansfield bumped into a German patrol.

He was only saved by Major Lukachevich's fast thinking. The major intervened and pretended to be looking for the German commandant. The ruse worked, and after some added double talk about vital intelligence and the Partisans, everybody was granted open passage.

Around February 1, the Allied officers, Boris, and the Chetnik escort at last neared the coast. They met up with the local Chetnik commander in the vicinity of Dubrovnik and quickly agreed to a pinpoint site that a young Yugoslav Navy lieutenant had recommended, about four miles south of nearby Cavtat.

The following two weeks then turned into a period of unnerving frustration and bad luck. First, Colonel Bailey's radio batteries had to be charged. That accomplished, not without some doing, Cairo was contacted. A day or so later, the pinpoint was confirmed for a three-hour time slot on three successive nights.

The weather, which had been excellent, now blew up into a big storm. The first night of the pinpoint, the sea was too rough for any small craft, but nonetheless the embarking men were at the site, signaling with a flashlight for three hours. The second night was similar, and on the third a boat failed to show.

Discouraged, the Allied officers were forced to begin the procedure from scratch again. The radio batteries had to be recharged while Chetnik sympathizers kept the men hidden in their homes. There would be yet another hazardous climb down to the rocky cove at Cavtat. And worse, a Chetnik spy had sent word that the Gestapo knew they were in the area and was diligently searching for them.

The day after a heavy snowstorm, the nine men who were leaving by sea took a different, more difficult route down to the cove for security reasons. On the shore, they had been flashing the pinpoint signal—the Morse code letters R-N—for only twenty minutes when they heard the low hum of a motor. Out of the night seas, a shadowy British gunboat appeared, bristling with machine guns. It slung a dinghy overboard.

Ten hours later, Captain Mansfield, Captain Todorovich, Colonel Bailey, and the six other men with them arrived in Bari, Italy. It was the morning of February 15, 1944. The officers of the American inspection party had successfully completed their mission.

As Boris described it: "We had crossed practically the whole of Serbia, the Sandzak region, and eastern and central Bosnia-Herzegovina. We had had several encounters with occupation forces, and had marched more than seven hundred miles across the mountains. We had seen the entire Chetnik organization and participated in their fighting. We saw their life and the life of the people."

Germany's defeat was becoming inevitable. In June of 1944, the Allies were to land at Normandy. Rome was then almost simultaneously liberated by American troops. After D-Day, the Anglo-American armies from the west and the Russian armies from the east were to drive steadily forward. Both would reach the borders of the German heartland before the year was out.

In Yugoslavia, too, the Germans were withdrawing. The civil war was practically won by the Partisans, and the Chetniks found themselves increasingly isolated. Meanwhile, the three major powers of the Allies were pursuing subtly divergent policies.

The British had never abandoned their sense of primacy in the region. Their decision to support the Partisans and to stop aiding the Chetniks was, however, given a purely military justification. Namely, it was declared that the Partisans fought the Germans while the Chetniks did not. Geopolitical considerations had supposedly nothing to do with this.

Only the naive could take at face value Churchill's declaration that fighting the Germans was *his* sole test for support. The courting of Marshall Tito was neither idle whim nor military necessity. It was a deliberate attempt to build up British influence, to seek postwar leverage, and in a larger sense, to maintain Britain's standing as a Great Power by doing the sorts of things Great Powers do.

Certainly the Prime Minister, in 1944, astutely focused on the political aspects of reaching Central Europe ahead of the Red Army. Yet he accepted a Communist Yugoslavia as inevitable and had adjusted British thinking accordingly. There is no doubt about this. For in a meeting with Stalin in October, of which the Americans were not accurately informed, spheres of influence in the Balkans had been agreed to: Rumania, 90 to 10 percent, favoring the Russians; Yugoslavia, 50 to 50 percent; and Greece, 90 to 10 percent, favoring the British.

Stalin put his tick mark on the written memorandum, and

then Churchill said: "Might it not be thought rather cynical if it seemed we had disposed of these issues, so fateful to millions of people, in such an offhand manner? Let us burn the paper."

"No, you keep it," Stalin replied.

The Americans were actually hewing closer to the declared "terms" for military assistance than were its British promulgators. If Tito was fighting, the Americans agreed he should get aid, but only for military and strategic reasons. It did not mean that Allied political support of Mihailovich and the government-in-exile was to be lessened, or that any endorsement of a Tito postwar regime was acceptable to the president or the State Department. It was not.

The Russians still considered Yugoslavia a sideshow of no essential importance to them. Even though the Partisans were fellow Communists, they had been sent no arms in 1943. And it was not until February of 1944 that the Russians would post a military mission to Tito. The Soviets still maintained correct relations with the Yugoslav Government-in-Exile (despite Partisan pressure), had avoided any open show of solidarity with Tito, and wished to do nothing that might jeopardize their grand design to keep Western troops out of Eastern Europe.

Thus, with a nice touch of historical irony, a strongly pro-Soviet Communist leader was winning his workers' revolution with fighters who were predominantly peasants and non-Communists, greatly aided by British backing, using American matériel, and mostly in spite of the Russians.

Boris was only in Bari a short while before he flew on to Cairo. He was no doubt anxious to take word of Mihailovich to the outside world, particularly America. Also, King Peter and the government-in-exile had relocated to Cairo in September, 1943, partly because the British could well do without their presence in London, and partly in hope of an eventual return to the country. That, as well as Boris's previous connections, made Cairo a useful stop for him.

He must have been distressed at the signs of Allied support for

Tito in Bari. There were many Partisans and their sympathizers there, working with the Americans and British. The Chetniks were forgotten. In fact, an O.S.S. operation masterminded by two maverick agents had already sent 6,000 tons of supplies by ship across the Adriatic and into Partisan hands. This compares with a mere 125 tons dropped by air in the same period.

Additionally, the ships had evacuated thousands of wounded and sick Partisans. Boris had not been wrong when he thought more Allied assistance could be provided, but it was not the Chetniks who were receiving it. The O.S.S. itself would later estimate that the total amount of supplies ferried over had made possible the activation of thirty thousand guerrillas.

Lieutenant Colonel Seitz happened on Boris at the Cairo airport in late March. He had only been in the city a day and a half, but he'd felt the strong undercurrent of sentiment for the Partisans. Despite an earlier start, he had not gotten out of Yugoslavia until March 15, when he flew from Berane to Bari. So Captain Mansfield, who had gone to Cairo on February 20, was almost a month ahead of him, despite a later start. The captain would also be the first to get information on the Chetniks back to Washington.

Apparently Boris's reception in Cairo had been none too hospitable. When Seitz saw him, he looked thinner than usual and showed the strain of several weeks of questioning by the British. Since the American officer was rumored to be killed, Boris might also have been a bit surprised to see a "ghost."

Nor had Boris found Pachany in Cairo.

His friend did eventually take and pass the parachutist course in Palestine. But Pachany was unable to follow after Boris. The door had closed—the British refused to drop any more Royal Yugoslav officers to Mihailovich.

Stranded in Cairo and anxious to somehow get into the real war, Pachany had resolved on a different course. He had joined the French Foreign Legion after passing the officer's examination, and was duly shipped out. In his new uniform and under the French flag, he was to serve with distinction.

From Cairo, Boris flew to London and then on to Washington, D.C. Lieutenant Colonel Zivan Knezevich, his former superior in London and an equally devoted supporter of Mihailovich, was already in the U.S. He was the military and air attaché at the Royal Yugoslav Embassy, and Boris was promptly named the assistant military attaché.

From their base at the embassy, the two men worked long hours trying to rally support for the Chetniks. The ambassador, Constantin Fotich, had been unwavering in his own advocacy of Mihailovich, and he welcomed his subordinates' efforts. But it was an uphill battle.

Much of the Western press, caught up in the glow of East-West harmony and not uninfluenced by Communist propaganda, had anointed Tito and the dashing Partisans. Official American circles were cautiously fretful, but saw no reason to risk irritating the other Allies. Besides, as the British were the self-proclaimed experts here, it was tacitly assumed they knew what they were doing.

Yet within a small circle of loyal American friends, the cause of Mihailovich was kept alive and influence was sought on his behalf. Ruth Mitchell, the sister of General Billy Mitchell (the "father of American air power"), did everything to help at her own expense. A journalist in her own right, she had traveled widely in the Balkans, had been imprisoned by the Gestapo, and was passionately pro-Serb and pro-Mihailovich.

Her soirées drew high-ranking officers of the army, marine corps, army intelligence, and such officials as Attorney General Francis Biddle and Assistant Secretary of State Adolf Berle. All to no avail. Policy was obviously being determined at the highest level.

In Yugoslavia, the Partisans had begun the final drive to power. It would put them in Belgrade within a year (though not without help from the Red Army) and make Marshall Tito the master of the country. By the time the Allies would get around to discussing the political future of Eastern Europe, Tito would present them with a fait accompli. He had always planned to secure his rule immediately, irrespective of British, American, or even Russian timetables for the postwar reconstruction of the Balkan nations.

The political moves made by Mihailovich and his civilian allies were long delayed. In 1944, a Chetnik congress held at Ba, which affirmed democratic principles and values, could do little to counter the Partisan's A.N.V.O.J. organization (Anti-Fascist Council for the National Liberation of Yugoslavia). With two years of steady political activity behind it, and especially after its meeting of November 29, 1943, A.N.V.O.J. had all but appropriated the status of a provisional government. Tito had the apparatus of an authoritarian regime in place.

Nor could letters from General Mihailovich compare with Tito's private correspondence with Churchill or compete with the broad range of his successes: his audiences with top Allied military men and diplomats, his skillful handling of the press, his welcoming of Major Randolph Churchill as a British liaison officer. His importance had been obviously confirmed to the world by the haste with which the Allies rescued him from the Germans. He had been fêted in Bari and granted complete freedom of movement in Allied-controlled territory.

As for Mihailovich and the Chetniks, time was running out. They had very few cards left to play. Isolated and ignored by the Allies, they clung to their Serbian honor and a sense of nobility in defeat.

There was barely any pause as 1944 seemed to blend almost seamlessly into a new year. The world at war was preparing for the long-sought finale. In Yugoslavia, a final chapter was being written in the modern quest for freedom and democracy.

There was not going to be a triumphant conclusion like the one the Allies would celebrate amidst the rubble of Berlin. In retrospect, there was no inevitable necessity for what soon happened in the Balkans, no ultimate reason beyond the capricious and unlucky roll of those historical dice that grant favor to one man over another.

1945

Boris never saw General Mihailovich again.

At this late hour in the civil war, the Chetniks could only delay and harass their enemies and inflict some retaliatory damage. Undaunted, General Mihailovich led his loyal forces on, but they battled against overwhelming odds. With no outside help, they could not halt the Partisans' final campaign to consolidate their hold on the entire country.

The British had withdrawn the last of their liaison officers to Mihailovich by the beginning of June 1944. There was no longer an Allied Mission at his headquarters. Yet, though he had been abandoned, Mihailovich performed one final service for the Allies. He had continued to search out and rescue Allied airmen forced to bail out over Serbia.

The level of Allied bombing raids had sharply escalated the previous spring. Many targets were hit in the eastern war zone, especially the Ploesti oil fields in Rumania, by bombers based in the Middle East. The shortest routes meant flights over Yugoslavia.

Inevitably, aircraft were disabled and the pilots forced to bail out. By early July, more than one hundred of these airmen had come down in Chetnik-held areas. Despite British objections, an American Air Crew Rescue Unit was sent to Mihailovich to get the fliers out.

Strictly ordered to conduct only evacuations and not act in any way as a Mission, the unit set up operations on an airstrip at Pranjani in Serbia. Between August 9 and December 27, 1944, with Mihailovich's help, 432 Americans and more than a hundred other Allied personnel were flown out.

The British had meanwhile completed the realignment of their political posture. Tito had their confidence, and they recommended to King Peter and the Yugoslav Government-in-Exile that they, too, see the light. Or the handwriting on the wall. Reluctantly, the young king had to comply.

A new prime minister was appointed in June, Ivan Shubashich. He had been governor of Croatia when the Germans invaded and then a refugee in the U.S. His basic mandate was simple: to disavow Mihailovich and to seek accommodation with Marshall Tito. A month later, after Shubashich had reached an agreement that no elements hostile to the Partisans would be included, he formed a new government.

Though General Mihailovich had been minister of war for two and a half years, he was of course now totally excluded.

Among others deemed no longer acceptable was Ambassador Fotich. On July 8, he resigned, refusing to recognize the Shubashich Government. He was not alone. The military attaché and assistant military attaché also refused—and so Knezevich and Boris were designated as unattached Yugoslav Army officers.

The Americans contemplated these developments without enthusiasm. General William "Wild Bill" Donovan, head of the O.S.S., tried to implement plans to get independent American operatives into Yugoslavia and to reestablish contact with Mihailovich. He was blocked after strong British objections were personally made known by Prime Minister Churchill to F.D.R.

There was one more calculated act to unfold. On September 12, King Peter in a broadcast from London called on all loyal Serbs, Croats, and Slovenes to unite and join the National Liberation Army led by Marshall Tito. Succumbing to the steady British pressure, even the king had resolved to consign his former champion to oblivion.

In this darkest hour of the Chetniks, few outside the country stood by them. Boris and Lieutenant Colonel Knezevich felt they had to return to Yugoslavia and General Mihailovich. With the consent of British General Wilson, the supreme allied commander of the Mediterranean theater, they flew to Bari, Italy.

They had left Washington with the apparent blessings of the U.S. State and War Departments and with orders signed by U.S. Chief of Staff General George Marshall. But in Bari, it seems that Wilson's headquarters had second thoughts. The resident British political advisor opposed sending two such "subversives with long histories" on to Mihailovich. The king and Tito, it was asserted, would be suspicious of Allied motives.

In short order, Boris and Knezevich found themselves under virtual internment in a British rest camp at Salerno. In a letter dated November 3, 1944, Lieutenant Colonel Knezevich wrote to U.S. Ambassador Alexander Kirk in Caserta requesting "that General Wilson . . . immediately give us our freedom or . . . bring us before a military court in order that we too may learn of the crimes . . . for which we have already for two months been in custody."

The Americans intervened when they realized that Boris and Knezevich might be turned over to Tito by the British. After their release, the two officers petitioned to enlist in the U.S. Army. Permission was not granted.

Yugoslavia had already effectively fallen to the Communists. By October of 1944, the Red Army was in Yugoslavia under a carefully worked out agreement between Tito and Stalin that precluded their staying around indefinitely. With this military force backing him up, Tito and the Partisans seized Belgrade on October 20 and made a triumphant entrance. The apathetic population showed little enthusiasm.

Installed in the capital, Tito went ahead with his own plans. After much political maneuvering, he assumed the leadership of a combined A.N.V.O.J.-Exile Government on March 7, 1945. In Belgrade, ambassadors from Britain, the Soviet Union, and the United States arrived to take up residence. With this de facto international recognition secured, Prime Minister Tito set about organizing his country along strictly party lines.

Exiled from their homeland, Boris and Knezevich were returned to the United States. There Boris was promoted to the permanent rank of major before the Tito regime declared the Royal Yugoslav Army dissolved. The Yugoslav dream of postwar freedom and democracy was over.

In Europe in 1945, the Allies swept on to victory. Hitler's last, desperate gamble, a counteroffensive in the west that he had launched at the end of December, had utterly failed by the end of February. The Nazis had drained away Germany's manpower and exhausted its resources. There was little left to resist the great Red Army offensive that began in January.

The rule of the Axis powers in Europe, of the Thousand Year Reich and Fascist glory, was finished. Like a storm that rages for hours and then seems to subside in a few minutes, the paramount leaders who had contrived and orchestrated the madness of war for years were themselves gone in days. Mussolini was killed on April 28. Hitler committed suicide on April 30. On May 7, 1945, Germany surrendered.

Only Japan remained to be dealt with. Their aggression ended with two brief glimpses into the future the world has lived with since. That August, atomic bombs were dropped on Hiroshima and Nagasaki. The Japanese shortly thereafter unconditionally surrendered. World War II was over.

Within Yugoslavia, Tito and the Partisans concentrated on completing the defeat of the Chetniks. The Germans had already withdrawn to the northwest, mostly Croatia, and were no longer an offensive threat. By the time the United States was celebrating its ultimate victory over Japan, the Partisans have accepted the local German surrender, eliminated internal military opposition, and firmly brought Yugoslavia to heel.

Those who had tried striking bargains with Marshall Tito began to learn the worth of his promises. Perhaps King Peter had some inkling of what was in store. He'd had one last spasm of self-assertion, dismissing Subashich in January 1945, though within a week he was persuaded to reappoint him. Tito has solemnly agreed that the question of the monarchy would be a decision of the people after the war. When the Federal People's Republic of Yugoslavia was proclaimed on November 29, 1945, Peter II was exiled in Britain as an ex-king.

But even after Tito had seized the reigns of power, General Mihailovich continued resistance. He had lost many men after King Peter's broadcast, and he lost more to frost and starvation and a typhus epidemic in January of 1945. Yet, despite Allied offers, he refused to quit the country. Ruthless battles with well-equipped Partisans in early May decimated what was left of the Chetnik ranks. The general was forced to go into hiding.

The Partisans and the Yugoslav secret police hunted relentlessly for their arch foe. He slipped through their fingers for almost ten months and then was captured only by an elaborate ruse—the circumstances have never been clarified, but a trusted lieutenant may have betrayed him. Whatever the case, the general was in the custody of Tito's men on March 13, 1946.

Branded a war criminal, Mihailovich was brought to trial in June. Most of his General Staff officers—Ostojich, Novakovich, Lalatovich, Baletich, Lukachevich—were already dead, but twenty-three other military and civilian associates were tried with him, some of them in absentia.

As the stenographic record in English translation reveals, it was a "show trial" without even a Stalinesque flair for theatrics. As it dragged on to its foregone conclusion, General Mihailovich often seemed dazed and disoriented, possibly from drugs or other mistreatment. Endless pages of trial testimony essentially prove one thing: he fought against the Partisans. His defense counsel repeatedly made the point that to fight a civil war opponent is not quite the same thing as a crime against humanity. The court, an instrument of Communist party vengeance, could see not the slightest merit in this argument.

Many American airmen who had been rescued by the Chetniks offered to testify on behalf of Mihailovich, but without success. Colonel Seitz was denied permission to even enter Belgrade. A group of distinguished Americans formed a "Committee for a Fair Trial" and took extensive testimony in the U.S. Captain Mansfield appeared before them and made a resolute statement.

In Belgrade, none of this evidence was admitted by the court. But then the outcome was certainly never in doubt. As expected, all the defendants were found guilty.

Despite worldwide appeals, General Draza Mihailovich was executed by firing squad on July 26, 1946.

On March 29, 1948, President Truman awarded General Mihailovich a posthumous Legion of Merit, the highest U.S. honor that can be granted a foreign national. The citation reads:

> General Dragoljub Mihailovich distinguished himself in an outstanding manner as Commander-in-Chief of the Yugoslavian Army forces and later as Minister of War by organizing and leading important resistance forces against the enemy which occupied Yugoslavia from December 1941 to December 1944. Through the undaunted efforts of his troops, many United States airmen were rescued and returned safely to friendly control. General Mihailovich and his forces, although lacking adequate supplies, and fighting under extreme hardships, contributed materially to the Allied cause, and were instrumental in obtaining a final Allied Victory.

But it was ultimately Winston Churchill who was the more forthright. He acknowledged privately that his handling of Tito was his biggest mistake of the war. When he declared in 1946 that an "Iron Curtain" had fallen across Europe, stifling any but Communist voices, he did not exempt Yugoslavia.

By then, Mihailovich could be heard no more. And many Yugoslavs who had dared cry with him *Sloboda ili Smrt* ("Liberty or Death") were captives of a Communist dictatorship that offered only one of those options.

Epilogue: After the War

WHEN WORLD WAR II ended, Boris was thirty-two. He was a professional soldier without an army, a former diplomat of a government without recognition, a man without a homeland. Yet the energy and drive that had brought him so far from his native land was still his to command. Unlike some refugees, he did not sink into despair, or live only on dreams of returning one day to the old country.

Typical of Boris, he faced facts. He was in a new country. And he liked it. He was quick to grasp the future possibilities, and certainly his knowledge of English and his service in Washington, D.C., aided the transition.

So he was here to stay, as surely as he knew he would be imprisoned—or likely shot—should Tito's Communists ever lay hands on him.

In the immediate postwar years, Boris was often torn between his own personal situation and the cause he could not relinquish. It was a matter of principle for him. Yet he was also determined to accept the challenge of America and test his abilities in the business world.

Though forced to consider his options as a civilian for the first time in his life, he devoted considerable energy to the fading hopes of the remnants of Mihailovich's supporters, both in the U.S. and abroad. He wrote many articles on Yugoslav affairs and edited both the *American Serbobran* and the *Voice of Canadian Serbs*. There was one further complication as well, a young woman he had met in Washington.

By 1947, he had wed his American sweetheart, Ljubica Todorovich. They moved to Detroit, where Boris was briefly in the import-export business.

During 1948, Boris began his association with the Provident Mutual Life Insurance Company. The manager of its Detroit agency at the time, Roland Benscoter, had met Boris and recognized his great potential. He strongly encouraged him to pursue life insurance underwriting as a career.

That offer was premature. Within six months, Boris had accepted a position with the Voice of America at the request of the U.S. State Department. He served there as an editor and broadcaster in the Yugoslav section of the international radio station.

If Boris had hoped to have some influence on the U.S. atittude toward Communist Yugoslavia, it was not to be. Tito's break with Stalin in 1948 (a rift that had not healed) was held to be vitally important to Western interests. There would be no effort whatsoever to "rock the boat" as long as Tito turned his back on the Soviet bear and sought U.S. assurances.

In 1953, Boris felt his broadcasting efforts in the name of Yugoslav freedom were blocked. Always a realist, whether in politics or business, he saw no use in continuing to plead to deaf bureaucratic ears. He would never abandon his convictions, but he refused to glorify futility.

Resigning from the V.O.A., Boris resumed his career with Provident Mutual Life.

Working in New York City, he soon started to set unprecedented performance records. Within ten years, Boris had joined the ranks of those men who had returned from World War II and created great American success stories. In his case, he had done it with a force of character and integrity that left a lifelong impression on many people.

His records peaks for itself. Boris was the company leader of the year more than a dozen times and was an inductee of the Senior Agent Hall of Fame. He is one of the founding members of the Provident Mutual Leaders Association and earned "Top 50" designation twenty-one times.

A recipient of the National Sales Achievement Award sixteen times and the National Quality Award twenty-two times, Boris was a member of the New York Estate Planning Council, the American Society of Chartered Life Underwriters, the Association for Advanced Life Underwriting, and the American Society of Pension Actuaries. He was a Lifetime Qualifying Member of the Million Dollar Round Table.

In New York City, Boris founded and operated BJT Consultants, Inc. His company engaged in estate and business planning, particularly in the areas of executive compensation and employee benefits. Besides being president of his own concern, he also found time to be an author, lecturer, and educator.

As an author, Boris was a contributing editor to J. K. Lasser's *Estate Tax Techniques* and *Keeping Current*, a quarterly publication of the American Society of Chartered Life Underwriters. He wrote numerous professional articles and was a staunch advocate of higher professional standards in the insurance industry and related fields.

He lectured professionally at the Practicing Law Institute, the American Law Institute of the A.B.A., and the American Society of Chartered Life Underwriters (C.L.U.) Institute. He was a guest speaker at the Columbia University Law School, and also spoke to numerous civic groups on recent events in Yugoslavia.

But it was teaching that most appealed to him. As a Chartered Life Underwriter, he wanted to see others in his profession educate themselves to better serve the public. He became the driving force behind a graduate-level professional education program at the Graduate School of Financial Sciences of the N.Y. Center for Financial Studies. In short order, Boris was appointed dean.

He devised and guided the C.L.U.'s advanced classes from the very first certificate courses in the late 1960s. Personally selecting the instructors from experts in accounting, pensions, law, and finance, many were subjected to his enthusiasm. They felt his encouragement as Boris inspired, nagged, and even practically coerced them into working at the Center when other demands on their time threatened to draw them away. Yet they saw he demanded no less of himself.

Aside from his many business interests, Boris lived for many years in Irvington-on-Hudson, New York, with his wife and three children. Eventually he was able to reestablish contact with his family and relatives still living in Yugoslavia, and his concern for that distant land never waned.

But he never again set foot on Yugoslav soil.

American airmen and other supporters are still trying to erect a statue in honor of General Mihailovich in Washington, D.C.

For years, the U.S. State Department politely opposed this effort on the grounds that it might upset relations with the Tito regime.

Even today, more than seven years after Tito's death, U.S. foreign policy has not shaken off the legacy of his adroit maneuvers. By pitting the West against the Russians for his favor, Tito assured Yugoslavia a continuing role in the worldwide calculations of the two superpowers. It remains to be seen if the truth of the nation's recent history will forever be sacrificed to the demands of the Communist credo or international politicking.

Of Boris's two great friends from the war, only one is still alive. Pachany settled with his wife in southern France after a long career in the French Foreign Legion. Now retired, his tours of duty included service in both Indochina and Algeria.

Walter Mansfield became a distinguished jurist in New York City. The military intelligence report he wrote in 1944 after the inspection trip through Yugoslavia was eventually declassified, and he published it in pamphlet form in 1974, with an appreciative foreword by Boris. He was still active on the bench at the time of his death in 1987.

As for Boris himself, he died on August 11, 1984, after a valiant battle against recurring cancer. To his delight, and some consternation from his doctors, he outlived a terminal prognosis more than once. True to his soldier's credo, he did not surrender to the enemy until all choice was gone.

IN MEMORIUM

An annual professional achievement award given in the name of Boris J. Todorovich has been established by Provident Mutual Life Insurance Company to permanently recognize his contributions to the company.

The Dean Boris J. Todorovich Memorial Fund, established by the Board of Trustees of the New York Center for Financial Studies, provides educational opportunities for members of the New York C.L.U. (Chartered Life Underwriters) Chapter.

Editors' Note

OVER MANY YEARS, the author labored to finish this book himself. Unable to devote full time away from his active New York business and professional life, he intermittently resumed work on various parts of the manuscript. One expansive version runs in excess of five hundred pages.

The earliest account was typewritten in Serbo-Croatian after the war ended. This was translated into English, and the years 1941–42 were substantially rewritten later. There were additional fragmentary pieces, as well as other materials in his personal papers.

Despite the effort Boris put into the manuscript, he was never satisfied. As his fifth or sixth language, he was fluent in English, but not a stylist. Of that he was perfectly aware, although it continued to annoy him. He went on rewriting.

As his editors, our key goal was to enhance the reading qualities of the book. A more intelligible structure was needed, we thought, and a polished draft was overdue. We have attempted both without grossly changing the original organization of the work or jeopardizing the direct, distinctive forcefulness of the author's voice.

Secondly, in keeping with his stated wish that the book be accessible to a younger generation of Serbian-Americans and their interested friends, we have assumed that the reader may know very little about World War II history, the military, or occupied Yugoslavia. Rather than append voluminous footnotes, we have concisely explained in text or provided supplementary information elsewhere. (See the following Background Informa-

311

tion for relevant facts about Yugoslavia, chronology, and the resistance forces.)

In editing, we compared and combined the available drafts into one manuscript. Redundant and inessential sections were cut to reduce the length. Throughout, we have not altered the author's expressed opinions, nor have we injected any of our own. (Within limits of reasonable inference, his comments have on occasion been amplified for the sake of clarity.)

Our material has been sparingly added, but *not* to the main text. Specifically, besides the introduction, the lead-in chapters ("1941," "1942," "1943") and the brief concluding ones ("1944," "1945") plus the epilogue were written by us. These largely cover orientation points and information, or summarize Boris's views.

Otherwise, limited changes were made. The following were converted to standard American usage: most military times; metric measurements; and Roman numerals (e.g., in German P.O.W. camp names).

We have corrected numerous transcription mistakes and other minor errors. Barring these lapses—and as we anticipated—the original manuscript proved decidedly reliable in detail when checked against reference sources. Still, every effort has been taken, insofar as possible, to confirm names, dates, locations, and the events cited.

The editors both conferred with Boris about his book several years ago, and one of us, J. Stryder, has known the family longer than a decade. Clearly, from inception the book's purpose varied little. Boris wanted the record of his wartime experiences to be a straightforward testament, and perhaps an admonition.

What he had done, and what he had been unable to do, was past. He was far more concerned that today's Americans, especially those of Serbian decent, should know something of how freedom was lost in Yugoslavia. In editing his book, we have striven to abide by his aim.

THE TRANSLITERATION PROBLEM

Minor variations of dialect aside, the language spoken by Serbs and Croats is the same. It is a member of the Slavic family of languages (and thus a relative of Russian and Polish) though often described as more melodious than its confreres.

However, the spoken language is currently written in two alphabets. The Serbs use the Cyrillic alphabet, while the Croats use the familiar Roman. To compound the problem of transliterating Yugoslav names and places, the sounds of some Croatian Roman letters diverge from English expectations not to mention the diacritcal markings borrowed from Czech.

Particularly confounding to an English reader's eye is *j* (pronounced as we would a *y*). For example, the Croato-Serbian word "Jugoslavija" is of course Yugoslavia, but was frequently transliterated in the past as *Jugoslavia*. Inconsistent renderings into English abound, outside of academic circles. Phonetic or partially phonetic, with and without accent marks—given the various plausible ways to proceed, all seem to have been tried.

Again, readability was our chief concern. In retaining basic accuracy, readers could well be spared a close encounter with Serbo-Croatian orthography. Guided by Boris's manuscript spellings, we chose a practical approach.

Most Yugoslav (or foreign) words have been translated or transliterated into simple and consistent English equivalents. The common *ić* ending is always *ich*. Accent marks are eliminated, and these substitutions made: č = ch, š = sh.

The notable exceptions are historical figures whose names were corroborated from other works, and place names readily found on modern maps. These have been as spelled elsewhere for easier reference.

Lastly, special acknowledgement must be made of Mrs. Ljubica Todorovich. Without her energy and enthusiasm, this book would have remained in unfinished form. She has been attentive to its editors, patient when they labored with textual problems, quick to offer her assistance, and diligent in reading every edited page along the way to the final result.

The Editors:

J. Stryder
Andrew Karp

Background Information

About Yugoslavia

- Present-day Yugoslavia (about the size of Wyoming) comprises six socialist republics (Slovenia, Croatia, Serbia, Macedonia, Montenegro, and Bosnia-Herzegovina). These are roughly the traditional "countries" of the region, established from the seventh century A.D. onward; all were under foreign domination for extended periods.
- Yugoslavia is bordered by Austria and Hungary to the north, Rumania and Bulgaria to the east, Greece and Albania to the south, and to the west, the Adriatic Sea and a bit of northern Italy.
- The five largest Yugoslav national groups are: Serbian, Croatian, Slovenian, Macedonian, and Bosnian Muslims. As before the war, today there are nearly twice the number of Serbs as Croats, while combined the two groups account for 65 percent of the population. The seventeen minority groups include Montenegrins, Albanians, Turks, Italians, Hungarians, Slovaks, Czechs, and Germans.
- Serbo-Croatian is the chief language and lingua franca, but Slovene and Macedonian are also official. All are related members of the South Slavic language group.

Selected Chronology

1878 Serbian independence internationally recognized in Treaty of Berlin, ending five hundred years as vassal state of Turkey (Ottoman Empire)

1912 First Balkan War; Turkey finally expelled from European possessions, except Istanbul

1913 Second Balkan War; Serbia successfully seizes larger part of
Macedonia from Bulgaria

1914 Archduke Ferdinand, heir-apparent to the Austro-Hungarian
Hapsburg empire, assassinated in Sarajevo by Serbian nationalist

Beginning of World War I (1914–1918)

1918 Kingdom of the Serbs, Croats, and Slovenes established under
Peter I

1920 National Elections (November 28)

1921 Alexander I succeeds; Yugoslav Communist Party banned

1929 Dictatorship declared; country renamed Yugoslavia

1934 Alexander I assassinated by Croatian terrorist in Marseille, France

Regency of Prince Paul; parliamentary government revived; political instability

1939 Italy invades Albania (April 7)

Germany invades Poland (September 1); beginning of World War
II (see also; "World War II" below)

1940 Germany defeats France (June)

Italy invades Greece from Albania, but its forces are driven back
by Greeks (October)

British troops arrive in Greece to support allies in Balkans

1941 Prince Paul's government signs Tripartite Pact with Nazi Germany (March 25)

Coup d'état of March 27 installs Peter II (Alexander's son) as
king; pact nullified

Germans invade and defeat Yugoslavia and Greece (April 6)

British forces withdraw from Greece; Germans take Crete, control
all of Balkans

Germany invades Russia (June 22)

Pearl Harbor attacked (December 7); U.S.A. enters war

1942 King Peter II visits U.S. (June 22)

German attack on Stalingrad fails (October 20)

U.S. forces land in North Africa (November 8)

Germans send army into Vichy France (November 12)

British Mission led by Colonel Bailey arrives at Chetnik headquarters (December 25)

1943 British policy on Yugoslavia changes (June), Partisans now preferred

British and American Allies land in Sicily, Italy (July–September)

Italy surrenders (September 8), but Germans occupy country and take Rome (September 10)

Partisans, Chetniks, and Germans all move to grab former Italian-occupied territory in Yugoslavia (September 9)

First American liaison officers arrive at both Partisan and Chetnik headquarters (August)

Red Army liberates Kiev (November 6); slow Russian rollback of German forces continues

1944 U.S. troops enter Rome (June 4)

D-Day (June 6); Allied invasion of Normandy

Paris liberated (August 25)

Red Army enters Rumania (August)

Red Army enters Yugoslavia (October 1)

British Allies enter Greece (October), help prevent Communist partisan takeover as occupiers withdraw

1945 Allied forces drive toward Germany from east and west

Tito signs treaty with U.S.S.R. (April 11)

President Roosevelt dies (April 12)

U.S. and Russian troops meet in Europe (April 25)

Germany surrenders (May 7)

Tito proclaims People's Republic; King Peter II deposed

1946 Communist rule consolidated

Mihailovich captured; show trial (June) and execution (July 17)

1948 Tito breaks with Cominform and Stalin
1980 Tito dies

World War II (1939–1945)

Chief Axis Powers & Leaders:

Germany: Adolph Hitler
Italy: Benito Mussolini
Japan: Hideki Tojo

Chief Allied Powers & Leaders:

Great Britain: Winston Churchill
U.S.A.: Franklin D. Roosevelt
U.S.S.R.: Joseph Stalin

The Map of Europe (1942):

Austria is absorbed in the Third Reich

Pro-Axis: Bulgaria, Rumania, Hungary, Finland

France: German occupied zone in north; "Free France" (Vichy) in south

Occupied: Poland, Czechoslovakia, Norway, Denmark, Netherlands, Belgium, Luxembourg, Albania, Greece, Yugoslavia

Neutral Nations: Switzerland, Spain, Portugal, Sweden

The Two Resistance Groups in Occupied Yugoslavia

Chetniks (Ravna Gora Movement)

Led by: General Draza (Dragoljub) Mihailovich, *aka* "Chicha"

Supported by: F.D.R.
Churchill (1941–1943)
Government-in-Exile (1941–1943)
Yugoslav Embassy, Washington, D.C. (Ambassador Constantin Fotich)

National base: Serbia

Nominal authority: Royal Yugoslav Government-in-Exile (London)

Chief backers: British (before 1943)

Radio Voice: B.B.C. Overseas Service (from London, 1941–1943)

Partisans

Led by: "Marshall" Tito (Josip Broz)

Supported by: Churchill (1943–1945)
                Stalin (1942–1948)
                Government-in-Exile (1944–1945)

National base: Croatia

Nominal authority: Yugoslav Communist Party, Comintern/ U.S.S.R.

Chief backers: British (after 1943)
              U.S.S.R.
              U.S.A. O.S.S. faction in Mediterranean theater

Radio Voice: Radio Free Yugoslavia (from U.S.S.R.)

If you have enjoyed this book and would like to receive details of other Walker Adventure titles, please write to:

Adventure Editor
Walker and Company
720 Fifth Avenue
New York, NY 10019